AIR PUBLICATION
4215

WAR OFFICE CODE No.
9514

26/G.S. Trg. Pubns./2177
14th January, 1960

MILITARY PARACHUTISTS MANUAL

Prepared by direction of the Minister of Aviation

Promulgated by Command
of the Army Council

WAR OFFICE

Promulgated by Command
of the Air Council

AIR MINISTRY

RESTRICTED

Published by

The Naval & Military Press Ltd
Unit 5 Riverside, Brambleside
Bellbrook Industrial Estate
Uckfield, East Sussex
TN22 1QQ England

Tel: +44 (0)1825 749494

www.naval-military-press.com
www.nmarchive.com

This a facsimile copy of an original 1960 (Air Publication 4215) laced binding working copy that was amended with additions and extractions until December 1962.

In reprinting in facsimile from the original, any imperfections are inevitably reproduced and the quality may fall short of modern type and cartographic standards.

A.P. 4215

AMENDMENT RECORD SHEET

To record the incorporation of an Amendment List in this publication, sign against the appropriate A.L. No. and insert the date of incorporation.

A.L. No.	AMENDED BY	DATE	A.L. No.	AMENDED BY	DATE
1	*signature*	23/10/61	34		
2			35		
3	*signature*	23-2-61	36		
4	*signature*	23-2-61	37		
5			38		
6	*signature*	23/2/61	39		
7	*signature*	23/2/61	40		
8	*signature*	29/10/61	41		
9	*signature*	30/10/61	42		
10	E. Fall	2-12-62	43		
11			44		
12	*signature*	23/2/61	45		
13	E. Fall	2-12-62	46		
14	E. Fall	2-12-62	47		
15	E. Fall	2-12-62	48		
16			49		
17			50		
18			51		
19			52		
20	E. Fall	2-12-62	53		
21	E. Fall	2-12-62	54		
22	E. Fall	2-12-62	55		
23			56		
24			57		
25			58		
26			59		
27			60		
28			61		
29			62		
30			63		
31			64		
32			65		
33			66		

(Continued overleaf)

RESTRICTED

A.L. No.	AMENDED BY	DATE	A.L. No.	AMENDED BY	DATE
67			104		
68			105		
69			106		
70			107		
71			108		
72			109		
73			110		
74			111		
75			112		
76			113		
77			114		
78			115		
79			116		
80			117		
81			118		
82			119		
83			120		
84			121		
85			122		
86			123		
87			124		
88			125		
89			126		
90			127		
91			128		
92			129		
93			130		
94			131		
95			132		
96			133		
97			134		
98			135		
99			136		
100			137		
101			138		
102			139		
103			140		

RESTRICTED

A.P.4215

NOTE TO READERS

The subject matter of this publication may be affected by Army Council Instructions, or Air Ministry Orders, or by "General Orders and Modifications" leaflets in the associated publications listed below, or even in some others. If possible, Amendment Lists are issued to correct this publication accordingly, but it is not always practicable to do so. When an Order, Instruction, or leaflet contradicts any portion of this publication, the Order, Instruction, or leaflet is to be taken as the overriding authority.

The inclusion of references to items of equipment does not constitute authority for demanding the items.

Each leaf, except the original issue of preliminaries, bears the date of issue and the number of the Amendment list with which it was issued. When this Manual is amended by the insertion of new or replacement leaves in an existing chapter, the new or amended technical information will be indicated by triangles, positioned in the text thus: ◄ — — — — ▶ to show the extent of amended text, and thus: ▶◄ to show where text has been deleted. When a Section, or Chapter is issued in a completely revised form, the triangles will not appear.

* * *

LIST OF ASSOCIATED PUBLICATIONS

	A.P.
Parachutes and parachute harness	1182 A
Safety harness	1182 B
Dinghies and associated equipment	1182 C
Airborne/Air-transported operations	L/A Warfare pamphlet No. 4/53
Air Publications in the 4200-4250 Series	

RESTRICTED

A.P.4215

PREFACE

1. In modern warfare it may be necessary to move formations of assault troops and equipment quickly to pre-selected battle areas. One method of carrying out such a move, without the limiting factors of securing airfields or ports, is to drop men, equipment, weapons and vehicles by parachute from transport aircraft.

2. To ensure that the effectiveness of parachute troops as fighting units is not impaired, it is essential for them to be given sound fundamental training in parachuting techniques. Without such training, troops dropped by parachute become potential casualties and, therefore, jeopardize the success of any operation for which they are detailed.

3. This manual has been written as a book of reference for trained parachutists and should be used as a guide by instructors employed in the training of parachutists. It describes the organisation of a Parachute Training School, the techniques of ground training, parachute jumping, balloon car and aircraft drills and provides technical data and techniques related to parachuting.

A.P.4215

LIST OF SECTIONS

1. Parachute training — general
2. Parachutes
3. Ground training
4. Practical parachuting
5. Aircraft and balloon car drills
6. Airborne equipment
7. Dropping zones

A.P.4215

SECTION 1

PARACHUTE TRAINING—GENERAL

RESTRICTED

SECTION 1

PARACHUTE TRAINING—GENERAL

List of Chapters

1. A parachute training school
2. Medical aspects of parachuting
3. Meteorological aspects of parachuting
4. Reference and textbook library
5. Forms relating to parachuting at a parachute training school

CHAPTER 4

REFERENCE AND TEXTBOOK LIBRARY

Chapter 4

REFERENCE AND TEXTBOOK LIBRARY

LIST OF CONTENTS

	Para.
Introduction	1
Officer in charge of the library	3
Services provided	4
Use of the library	5

Introduction
1. This chapter is concerned with the reference and textbook library at No. 1 Parachute Training School, but it will also act as a guide to Officers and N.C.O. associated with opening or maintaining of a library elsewhere.

2. The No. 1 Parachute Training School library is approved by the Air Ministry and qualifies for an annual grant to be expended on the purchase of a press-cutting service and the provision of books and periodicals. The purpose of the library is to make available to the school staff, the publications, papers, photographs, statistics and other information necessary to further their knowledge of parachuting. In addition, a section devoted to publications on physical education enables the Parachute Jumping Instructors to keep up-to-date in this field of their work.

Officer in charge of the library
3. The administration and organisation of the library is the responsibility of an officer appointed by the Officer Commanding the Parachute Training School. This officer will maintain an up-to-date catalogue of all the books, papers, photographs, official publications and other documents and records held in the library. He will ensure that all items on loan from the library are properly recorded. In addition, he is responsible to the Officer Commanding the School for all demands and for purchases made under the grant referred to in para. 2.

Services provided
4. The library provides the following services:—

(1) Air Publications and other Official Publications relevant to the work of the Parachute Training School are maintained in the library.

(2) Books presented to the school and books purchased under the reference and textbook library grant.

Note...

These books are classified as either books concerning parachutes and parachuting or books on physical education.

(3) Photographs concerning parachuting that are of historical interest are kept in albums.

(4) Cuttings received from the Air Ministry press-cutting service, which are taken from British and foreign newspapers and are concerned with any aspect of parachuting.

(5) Course reports and individual record cards, and reports and files of historic value are kept in the library.

(6) A comprehensive series of statistics are held in the library. These statistics must not be removed from the library but they are always available for perusal by members of the school staff.

(7) Master sets of Airborne Forces Parachute Training Posters (Air Diagrams) and drawings of ground training apparatus are kept in the library.

Use of the library
5. The library is open at all times during normal working hours; members of the school staff are encouraged to make full use of its facilities. Other personnel may use the library only on the authority of the officer in charge of the library. The services provided in the library are of particular value to instructors under training who should make full use of them to further their background knowledge of parachuting and to become conversant with the history of the school and its work.

6. To ensure a wide circulation, press cuttings, photographs, periodicals and details of any other recent additions to the library are displayed on an information board in the instructors' crew room in the training hangar, prior to being catalogued and held in the library.

RESTRICTED

A.P.4215, Sect. 1, Chap. 5
A.L. 10, Apr. 61

CHAPTER 5

FORMS

Chapter 5

FORMS

LIST OF CONTENTS

	Para.
Introduction	1
Form 1—Arrival form	4
Form 2—Record of abnormalities and emergencies	5
Form 3—Daily flying detail	6
Form 4—Centre signal, daily recording form	7
Form 6—Report on personnel returned to unit (R.T.U.)	8
Form 8—Injury proforma	9
Form 10—Course activities	10
Form 11—Time sheet/analysis of descents	11
Form 12—Syndicate Officer's return	12
Form 13—Record of abnormality	13
Form 14—Attachments	14
Form 17—Pupil's record card	15
Form 18—Air experience manifest	16
Form 19—Parachute descent manifest	17
Form 20—Exit, flight and landing details	18
Form 23—Aircraft inspection schedule for Despatchers (Hastings aircraft)	19
Form 25—Allocation of Instructors	20
Form 26—Dropping Zone reconnaissance report	21
Form 28—Hastings/Beverley aircraft intercommunication drill	22
Form 30—Assessment of Parachute Jumping Instructors (Final examination)	23
Form 32—Parachute training flying record	24
Form 33—Record sheet (Air Despatcher)	25
Form 34a—Inspection sheet for parachuting from Beverley aircraft (upper deck)	26
Form 34b—Inspection sheet for parachuting from Beverley aircraft (lower deck)	27
Form 39—Form of indemnity	28
Form 42—Breakdown of instructional progressions	29
Form 43—Air Quartermasters Course (nominal roll)	30
Form 44—Working synopsis, four weeks Air Despatchers course	31
Form 46—Inspection check list (Twin Pioneer, parachute role)	32

Introduction

1. This chapter contains a list of locally raised standard forms as used at No. 1 Parachute Training School, R.A.F., Abingdon. Additional forms are raised as the necessity arises. The forms are listed by Serial No. and title and each has a short description of its purpose.

2. The details on the forms are not dealt with as each form is self explanatory. Certain forms contain a number of abbreviations in their detail, but as these abbreviations are understood by the personnel concerned they are not dealt with in this chapter.

3. The following form Serial No. have been either declared obsolete or have not been taken up: 5, 7, 9, 15, 16, 21, 22, 24, 27, 29, 31, 35, 36, 37, 38, 40, 41 and 45.

Form 1—Arrival form

4. This form is completed by the Section Instructor on the first day of a course. The nominal rolls of the complete course and syndicates are made up from the details contained on the completed forms. Each Instructor fills in the details of each pupil parachutist allocated to his section.

Form 2—Record of abnormalities and emergencies

5. This form is completed by the No. 1 Despatcher after each sortie. It should record any particular or unusual actions which may occur in the aircraft, e.g., refusals, bad aircraft drill or exits. The No. 1 Despatcher needs the close co-operation of all the other despatchers when he completes this form.

Form 3—Daily flying detail

6. This form is completed by the Parachute Training School Marshaller on the day prior to the flying programme to which it refers.

Form 4—Centre signal, daily recording form

7. This form is completed by the N.C.O. at the centre signal on the Dropping Zone. It should be a record of all abnormalities or unusual incidents as seen from the D.Z.

RESTRICTED

Form 6—Report on personnel returned to unit (R.T.U.)

8. This form is completed by the Officer Commanding No. 1 P.T.S. for the Officer Commanding R.A.F. Abingdon after certain of the details have been completed by the Section Instructor and the Medical Officer. The purpose of this form is to record the details which necessitate the termination of training of personnel taken off a course and returned to their unit for refusing to jump, injuries or for disciplinary reasons. Territorial Army personnel have an additional block on the form which is completed if they are to be permitted to return for further training later.

Form 8—Injury proforma

9. This form is completed by the Syndicate Officer after certain details have been filled in by the Section Instructor and the Medical Officer. The form will record any injury to a pupil parachutist undergoing parachute instruction either during the ground training or aircraft training phases.

(1) If a pupil parachutist reports sick at the normal sick parade, the Medical Officer will raise the form in duplicate; the Syndicate Officer fills in the relevant details. One copy is retained at the Sick Quarters and the other copy is retained by the Syndicate Officer for inclusion in his course report.

(2) If the injury occurs on the D.Z. or otherwise during the parachute training and the injured pupil parachutist has to be seen by the Medical Officer otherwise than quoted in sub-para. (1), then the injury proforma is raised by the Syndicate Officer.

Form 10—Course activities

10. This form is completed by the Syndicate Officer as each course progresses. Additional subjects such as Interest Films, Demonstrations and Visits should be added as necessary.

Form 11—Time sheet/analysis of descents

11. This form is double sided and is completed by the Syndicate Officer. On the time sheet side, the hours when the syndicate is under R.A.F. Command are shown by shading. When parachute descents have taken place the times should be in RED and if any injuries occur the number and class are superimposed. The analysis of descents side shows a numerical analysis of the four descents made by pupil parachutists (*P.T.S. Form 20*). The lower half of the analysis shows the injuries which may occur during any of the four descents.

Form 12—Syndicate Officer's return

12. This form is completed by the Syndicate Officer and forms a major part of the report of the results of each course trained. The completed form is given to the Squadron Commander together with Forms 6, 8, 10 and 11, the nominal roll of the syndicate and each pupil parachutist's own Record Card at the end of each course.

Form 13—Record of abnormality

13. This form is completed by the Syndicate Officer and records any unusual parachute canopy development or damage caused to a parachute assembly during any part of the exit or flight phase of the descent. When completed, this form is forwarded to P.T.S. Headquarters for investigation.

Form 14—Attachments

14. This form is raised by the Syndicate Officer. The details show the previous training and parachute descents made by pupil parachutists who fail to complete the basic course they started training with and have been considered suitable or fit for further training. The non-completion of previous training may have been caused by adverse weather conditions, injury or other causes. Space is provided on the form for a record of the necessary training required and/or achieved to qualify each of the attached pupil parachutists.

Form 17—Pupil's record card

15. This form is a guide to Instructors on how to complete their pupil parachutist's Record Cards.

Form 18—Air experience manifest

16. This form is completed by the Parachute Fitter and contains a record of each aircraft load when pupil parachutists are detailed for an air experience flight, wearing full parachute equipment and in stick order. Each pupil is given an air experience flight before a parachute descent is attempted. Completed forms are submitted, through the Marshaller, to the Officer Commanding the Support Squadron.

Form 19—Parachute descent manifest

17. This form is completed by the Parachute Fitter and contains details of the parachutes to be worn by pupil parachutists about to make a descent and stick details for each parachutist.

Form 20—Exit, flight and landing details

18. This form is completed by an instructor detailed by the N.C.O. in charge of the D.Z. team and records full details of each pupil parachutist's exit from the aircraft, parachute flight and landing technique. This information is used by the Syndicate Officer during his debriefing lectures, so that each pupil parachutist may be made aware of his own particular faults which he must strive to correct before the next parachute descent is made.

Form 23—Aircraft inspection schedule for Despatchers (*Hastings aircraft*)

19. This form is completed by the Parachute Jumping Instructor detailed to inspect and pass an aircraft as serviceable for parachute jumping.

Form 25—Allocation of instructors

20. This form is completed by the Parachute School Warrant Officer and shows the establishment and strength of the School Instructors and their allocation to the various duties of the Parachute Training School.

RESTRICTED

Form 26—Dropping Zone reconnaissance report

21. This form is completed by the Officer detailed to carry out a reconnaissance of a proposed dropping zone.

Form 28—Hastings/Beverley aircraft inter-communication drill

22. This form details the standard inter-com. procedure to be adopted by No. 1 Despatcher and the Captain of the aircraft concerned.

Form 30—Assessment of Parachute Jumping Instructors (*Final examination*)

23. This form is completed by the examiners and details their assessment of the personal appearance, personality, voice delivery, teaching methods and technique of the Parachute Jumping Instructor being examined.

Form 32—Parachute training flying record

24. This form is completed by the Marshaller. Any deviation from the planned times are noted so that they can be investigated later.

Form 33—Record sheet (*Air Despatcher*)

25. This form is completed by the Syndicate Officer and contains a record of all sorties flown by each Air Despatcher under training, together with the ground training on parachute technique. Completed forms are filed as part of the report on each trainee Air Despatcher.

Form 34a—Inspection sheet for parachuting from Beverley aircraft

26. *Sheet 1—upper deck*

All items to be inspected and checked by the No. 1 Despatcher on the upper deck of a Beverley aircraft are listed on this form.

Form 34b—Inspection sheet for parachuting from Beverley aircraft

27. *Sheet 2—lower deck*

All items to be inspected and checked by the No. 1 Despatcher on the lower deck of a Beverley aircraft are listed on this form.

Form 39—Form of indemnity

28. Normally only trained Service parchute personnel and pupil parachutists under training are allowed to travel in a balloon cage. Certain other persons are occasionally granted permission by the Army Council or the Air Ministry to observe from a balloon cage. Such observers must sign this form of indemnity before they may be permitted to enter a balloon cage for the purpose of making an ascent.

Form 42—Breakdown of instructional progressions

29. This form gives details of the work to be covered by instructors during each period detailed in the training syllabus. This form is for information only and is an amplification of the syllabus.

Form 43—Air Quartermaster's Course (*nominal roll*)

30. This form is completed by the Officer in charge of the course and contains details of the sorties completed by trainee Air Quartermasters in Hastings and Beverley aircraft.

Form 44—Working synopsis, four weeks Air Despatchers course

31. This form is completed by the Syndicate Officer and records the complete working programme of the four weeks Air Despatchers course.

Form 46—Inspection check list (*Twin Pioneer parachute role*)

32. This form lists all items that have to be inspected and checked by the Air Despatcher in a Twin Pioneer Aircraft.

RESTRICTED

SECTION 2

PARACHUTES

SECTION 2

PARACHUTES

List of Chapters

1. The military parachute

2. Parachute assembly, Type X, Mk. 4 and Reserve assembly, Mk. 1, X type

3. Parachute performance

4. Foreign parachutes

5. Free fall parachutes

6. Supplies dropping parachutes

CHAPTER 1
THE MILITARY PARACHUTE

Chapter 1

THE MILITARY PARACHUTE

LIST OF CONTENTS

	Para.		Para.
History...	1	Requirements ...	6

History

1. The possibilities of using the parachute for military purposes were first realised by a few imaginative people during the 1914—1918 War, but the idea was never given serious consideration by the responsible authorities. The Russians were the first to have the initiative and courage to carry out practical trials and they were soon doing so on a large scale. By 1927 they were using paratroops on manoeuvres, and by 1935 they were able to stage a large scale demonstration at Kiev, when more than 1000 paratroops were landed simultaneously. Similar demonstrations were staged during military manoeuvres in later years and on an even larger scale, which included the dropping of small tanks and other heavy equipment.

2. The French showed early enthusiasm for training and using paratroops, but their plans were not supported by sufficient conviction. At the outbreak of the 1939-1945 war, no more than two companies of French paratroops had been trained, using manually operated parachutes.

3. The Germans, though they started later than the Russians, applied their minds to the subject of dropping troops by parachute in their usual serious and thorough manner. Moreover they realised the vital importance of, and provided, a suitable transport aircraft. The results of German policy were clearly shown in 1940 and 1941, when this new method of transporting suitably trained troops to strategic battle zones helped in the amazing collapse and conquest of Norway, Holland, Belgium, France, the Balkans and Crete. This novel and unexpected method of attack on an uncovered flank was the basic military strategy resulting in the overrunning of the continent of Europe by the Germans.

4. Force of circumstances resulted in the British and Americans taking up paratroop training in the summer of 1940.

5. The adaptation of the parachute for military purposes was a step of incalculable importance in the history of the parachute. Previously the parachute had been merely a means of saving an occasional life in an emergency. Now it has to act as a safe and common method of transport for men and equipment between an aircraft and the ground. It was indeed a step forward of great magnitude, and the obligation to improve the parachute and make it completely reliable and satisfactory became one of paramount importance.

Requirements

6. The requirements of a military parachute differ from those of an emergency escape parachute such as those that are now in general use in the Air Forces of the world. A military parachute is designed to transport and land men safely and in a condition ready for immediate action. An emergency escape parachute is designed to save a man's life in an emergency which would otherwise be fatal.

7. The military parachutist's jump is premeditated, where as the aircrew emergency escape jump is not. The essential points of design for an emergency escape parachute are compactness, strength and reliability of opening at high speeds and with the wearer in any position. With the military parachute the jump is made under known and prearranged conditions which do not make any great demands on the strength of the equipment.

8. The requirements of the military parachute may be summarised as follows:

   (1) A reliable and smooth opening at a low height.

   (2) As rapid a descent as possible until near the ground so that the paratroops and equipment will not drift apart or present an easy target for an enemy.

   (3) To land paratroops with the minimum risk of injury, *i.e.*, with minimum oscillation and at a low rate of descent near the ground.

   (4) Sufficient strength to withstand the wear and tear of numerous descents and of use in the field.

   (5) Various harness requirements.

9. These requirements have been achieved to some extent in the 'X' type military parachute by making the following alterations from the normal R.A.F. emergency escape type of parachutes:

   (1) Using automatic or static line opening instead of manually-operated rip cord opening.

   (2) Increasing the diameter of the canopy from 24 ft. to 28 ft.

   (3) Employing a more elaborate and comfortable harness.

   (4) Employing canopy last development, which results in less shock on opening.

RESTRICTED

A.P.4215, Sect. 2, Chap. 5
A.L.22, Apr. 62

CHAPTER 5

FREE FALL PARACHUTES

RESTRICTED

Chapter 5

FREE FALL PARACHUTES

LIST OF CONTENTS

	Para.		Para.
Introduction	1	Pack	9
Types of parachutes	2	Rip-cord and housing	10
Type P.B. 1, Mk. 3 assembly—		**Type P.B. 1, Mk. 4 assembly—**	
Description	3	Description	11
Canopy	4	Deployment sequence	12
Canopy deployment sock	5		
Auxiliary parachute	6	**Type P.R. 1, Mk. 2 assembly—**	
Connecting strop	7	Description	15
Harness	8	General	17

LIST OF ILLUSTRATIONS

	Fig.		Fig.
Type P.B. 1, Mk. 3 and 4 assemblies—components	1	Back view—main parachute	5
Front view of harness	2	Type P.R. 1, Mk. 2 reserve parachute assembly	6
Front view—reserve parachute fitted	3	Stowage of stop-watch and altimeter	7
Side view—reserve parachute fitted	4		

RESTRICTED

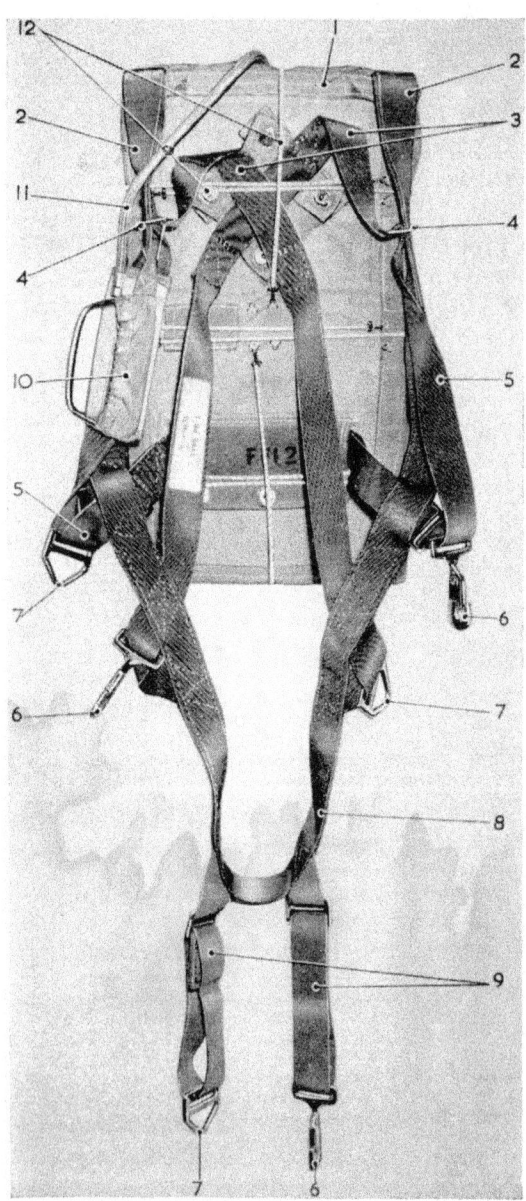

KEY TO FIG. 1 (TYPE P.B. 1, Mk. 3 AND 4 ASSEMBLIES—COMPONENTS)

1. BACK-TYPE PACK
2. LIFT WEB
3. SHOULDER STRAPS
4. SHOULDER BUCKLE
5. CHEST STRAPS
6. SNAP-HOOK
7. D-RING
8. MAIN SLING
9. LEG STRAPS
10. RIP-CORD HANDLE AND POCKET
11. RIP-CORD HOUSING
12. PACK OPENING ELASTICS

Introduction

1. Parachutes used for free fall descents are manually operated by pulling a rip-cord. Later developments of free fall parachutes may embody an automatic delay-opening device which is operated by barometric pressure or other means. All parachutes having automatic operating devices are normally provided with a manual override system so that a parachutist can, if desired, operate his parachute above the pre-set operating height or so that he can operate his parachute in the event of failure of the automatic device.

Types of parachutes

2. The types of main parachutes used for free-fall parachuting are the Types P.B. 1, Mk. 3 and 4; Type P.R. 1, Mk. 2 assemblies are used as reserve parachutes. The Type P.B. 1, Mk. 3 and 4 parachutes are back-type assemblies which are manually operated by means of a three-pin rip-cord. Each parachute of these types is normally issued complete with a reserve assembly, but either the main or the reserve assembly may be changed if one or the other becomes unserviceable. The Type P.R. 1, Mk. 2 reserve parachute is a chest-type assembly, connected by two snap-hooks to the D-ring chest connectors on the harness of either type of main parachute. Operation of this reserve parachute is by pulling a rip-cord on the R.H. side of the pack and is independent of the operation of the main parachute.

TYPE P.B. 1, Mk. 3 ASSEMBLY

Description

3. This assembly (R.A.F. Ref. 15A/1028) consists of the following:—

Sect. 15A/ Ref.	Nomenclature
1104	Canopy, Type I, 28
1097	Sock, canopy deployment
605	Auxiliary parachute, vane type, Mk. 3
1098	Strop, connecting, auxiliary parachute
1095	Harness, Type P.B. Mk. 1
1196	Pack, Type P.B. 1, Mk. 1
83	Elastics, pack opening (set of eight)
1099	Rip-cord, Mk. 14
182	Housing, Mk. 4
1100	Sliding pocket

Canopy

4. The canopy is similar to that used in the standard X-type parachute assembly, i.e. a flat 28 foot canopy (Chap. 2).

Canopy deployment sock

5. The deployment sock is a long tapered bag which completely encloses the folded canopy. It is fitted with rigging line stowages at the mouth end and with air pockets at the apex. A strop is fitted to the apex for the attachment of the auxiliary parachute. During deployment, the sock separates from the remainder of the parachute assembly, but it can usually be recovered after landing.

Auxiliary parachute

6. The vane type auxiliary parachute has eight vanes, roughly triangular in shape, which extend downwards from the canopy. The inner vertical edge of each vane is sewn to a central sleeve which houses a helical spring; the top coil of the spring is square-shaped. The crown of the canopy is reinforced with tape over the areas of contact with the spring. The bottom ends of the eight rigging lines are formed into an eye for the attachment of the connecting strop. In operation the helical spring ensures that the auxiliary parachute springs away from the assembly as soon as the pack is opened, the packed canopy providing a firm kicking base for the helical spring.

Connecting strop

7. The connecting strop is a length of tubular nylon tape with a loop formed at one end for the attachment of the auxiliary parachute; the other end is attached to the apex of the deployment stock.

Harness

8. The nylon webbing harness differs from other parachute harnesses in that it is secured to the wearer by three snap-hooks and triangular D-rings instead of a quick-release box. One fastening is made on each thigh and the third in the centre of the body. In other respects the harness is conventional and consists of a main sling with auxiliary and adjustment straps; the reserve parachute pack is connected to D-rings fitted to the main lift webs at lower chest level and is held firmly to the body of the wearer by straps and quick-release connector fittings on the lower part of the main sling.

Pack

9. The pack is of the long back-type of the three rip-pin variety, and is provided with a three-pin rip-cord and a flexible braided rip-cord housing; the pack cover is made of fabric on a light metal frame. The cover has four 'envelope' flaps which enclose the folded parachute; the longer flaps have additional internal flaps which are folded over the parachute before the outer flaps are closed. A feature of the pack is a flap, inside the back of the pack, which covers the rigging line stowage loops. This flap should always be in position. In the Service application of the pack the rigging lines are stowed on the deployment sock (para. 5). The flaps are secured in the

RESTRICTED

Fig. 2. Front view of harness

Fig. 3. Front view—reserve parachute fitted

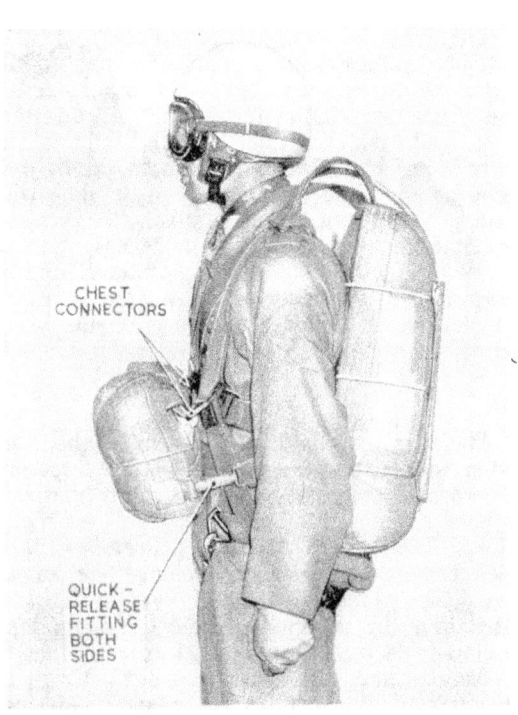

Fig. 4. Side view—reserve parachute fitted

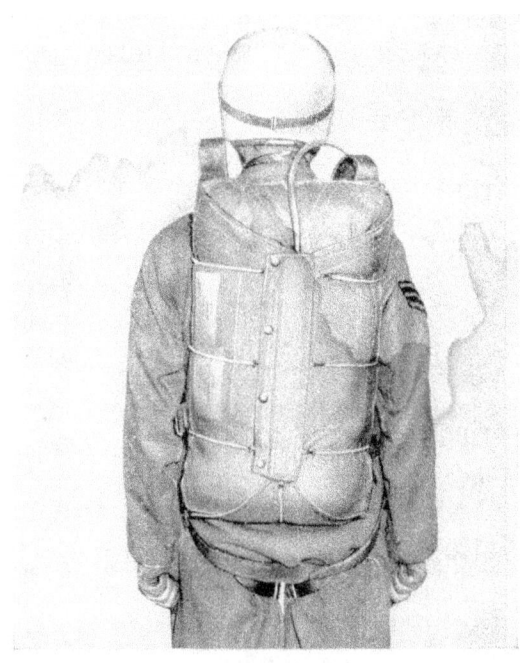

Fig. 5. Back view—main parachute

RESTRICTED

closed position by three conventional eyelets and cone fittings and the three pins of the rip-cord. Scarlet locking thread is used as a safety tie on the rip-cord pins. After insertion, and locking with the scarlet thread, the ripcord pins are covered by a typical external flap which is secured by 'Lift-the-Dot' fasteners. Eight pack opening elastic cords are fitted to ensure the rapid opening of the pack flaps.

Rip-cord and housing

10. As stated, the rip-cord is of the three-pin type and has the handle slightly cranked to facilitate a sure grip. The handle is stowed in a sliding pocket so that its position can be adjusted to suit the requirements of an individual wearer on either side of the harness. The housing is a flexible braided metal tube, reinforced internally with a helical coil of brass wire and externally at each end with ferrules.

TYPE P.B. 1, Mk. 4 ASSEMBLY

Description

11. This assembly (R.A.F. Ref. 15A/1029) is identical with the Mk. 3 assembly with the exception of the canopy and two tabs on the front upper lift webs. The canopy is an open-gore type (R.A.F. Ref. 15A/1106) constructed in the same manner as the I.28 type but has no A or B panel in the No. 1 gore and the C panel is considerably smaller than those in the remaining gores. The peripheral band of the open No. 1 gore is complete and, during packing operations, is stowed in a long pocket which is fitted to the hem of No. 1 gore. The two tabs on the front life webs are used to locate rings which are attached to the end of pull-down cords connected to No. 1 and No. 28 rigging lines. These cords provide a measure of canopy control during descent.

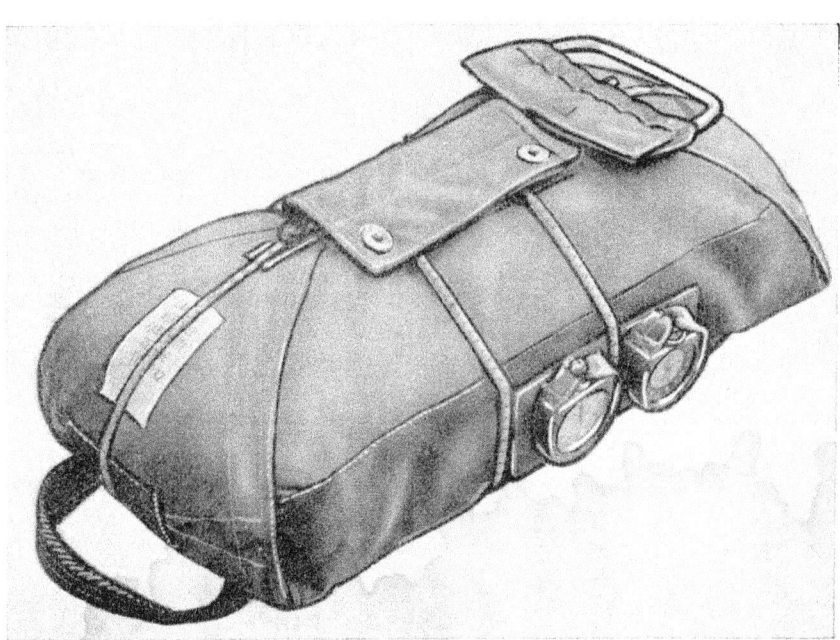

Fig. 6. Type P.R.1, Mk. 2 reserve parachute assembly

Fig. 7. Stowage of stop-watch and altimeter

Deployment sequence

12. The sequence of events in the deployment of the Type P.B. 1, Mk. 3 and 4, manually operated assemblies is as follows:—

(1) The action of pulling the rip-cord from its pocket breaks the scarlet locking thread and pulls the rip-pins from the cone fittings; this allows the pack opening elastics to pull the pack 'envelope' flaps open.

(2) The auxiliary parachute springs off the assembly due to the action of the helical spring against the packed canopy.

(3) The auxiliary parachute extracts the deployment sock and the canopy into a deployed, but not developed, position and the rigging lines deploy from the stowages at the mouth of the sock.

(4) When the rigging lines are fully deployed a mouth lock on the sock is broken, the canopy is extracted from the sock and normal development of the canopy ensues.

13. The 'rigging line first' method of deployment, as compared with the 'canopy first' method, has the following advantages:—

(1) The shock of the opening of the canopy is reduced and consequently the possibility of damage to the canopy and discomfort for the parachutist is similarly reduced.

(2) There is less risk of the parachutist fouling the canopy if he is somersaulting or rolling during the deployment.

14. The possibility of entaglement low in the rigging lines remains, and although it is less serious than in a 'canopy first' deployment, it must still be minimized by a stable 'pulling down' position.

TYPE P.R. 1 Mk. 2 ASSEMBLY

Description

15. This assembly (R.A.F. Ref. 15A/1031) consists of the following items:—

Sect. 15A/ Ref.	Nomenclature
549	Canopy, Type I, 14, Mk. 1
1093	Pack, Type P.R. 1, Mk. 1
1094	Rip-cord, Mk. 13
713	Pack opening elastics (set of six)

16. The Type P.R. 1, Mk. 2 reserve parachute assembly consists of a 24 foot canopy in a pack and, except for the differences which follow, is similar to the reserve parachute used with the X-Type parachute (Chap. 2). The reserve parachute pack is fitted with two snap-hooks for attachment to the D-rings on the main parachute harness. The shorter edges of the back of the pack are fitted with sockets for the quick-release connecting fittings referred to in para. 8. On this type of parachute the rip-cord handle is stowed on, and pulled from, the R.H. side of the pack. Six pack opening elastics are used. Instrument pockets are fitted on the top side of the pack for the stowage of a stop-watch and an altimeter where they can be conveniently seen by a parachutists during his descent. An auxiliary parachute is not fitted to this assembly, otherwise the method of packing and the manner of deployment are similar to those for the reserve parachute used with the X-Type parachute assembly.

General

17. For full details concerning the parachutes and the methods of packing reference is to be made to A.P.1182A, Vol. 1 (2nd Edn.), Sect. 5, Chap. 3.

SECTION 3

GROUND TRAINING

SECTION 3

GROUND TRAINING

List of Chapters

1 Introduction

2 Exit technique

3 Exit training apparatus

4 Parachute flight technique

5 Parachute flight training apparatus

6 Parachute landing technique

7 Parachute landing training apparatus

8 Parachute harness release and dragging

9 Air experience

10 Lectures and films

11 Briefing and discussions

A.P.4215, Sect. 3, Chap. 1
AL.6, Nov. 60

CHAPTER 1

INTRODUCTION

RESTRICTED

Chapter 1
(completely revised)

INTRODUCTION

LIST OF CONTENTS

	Para.		Para
Objective	.. 1	*Training*	.. 7
Training aids	.. 3		

Objective

1. The objectives of parachute ground training are:—
   (1) To teach the technique of military parachuting on the ground, so that all the flying time available can be used for actual parachuting practice.
   (2) To prepare the trainee parachutist mentally for making parachute descents, i.e. to give him confidence in the methods employed, in the equipment he will use, in his instructor and in his own ability to parachute correctly; to instil in him the will and determination to jump.

2. The teaching of the physical skills is achieved by the correct use of synthetic apparatus and by applying the principle of progression in training. The mental condition is achieved by a good pupil/instructor relationship, by building up the pupil's confidence in himself, in the method of training and in the variety of equipment used.

Training aids

3. Various training aids are available which can be classed under the following headings:—
   (1) Parachute training aids
   (2) Films
   (3) Lectures and film strips

4. The various items of synthetic parachute training equipment are described in A.P.2655, Vol. 1, Sect. 5, and the methods of using these items will be dealt with in later chapters of this Section. The following items of training equipment are in current use:—
   (1) Elementary door exit trainer
   (2) Elastic fall trainer
   (3) Elementary flight trainer
   (4) Two tier jumping platforms
   (5) Dummy parachutes
   (6) Reference parachute
   (7) Low ramp
   (8) Spacer-bar attachment
   (9) Training harness
   (10) Progressive landing trainer
   (11) Static flight trainer
   (12) Harness flight trainer
   (13) Balloon car
   (14) Fan descent trainer
   (15) Composite mock fuselage
   (16) High ramp
   (17) Wheel landing trainer
   (18) Slide landing trainer
   (19) Block-and-tackle landing trainer
   (20) Block-and-tackle flight and landing trainer
   (21) Parachute fitting racks
   (22) Double-arm descent training tower
   (23) Eight-cable stick exit trainer
   (24) Beverley wooden mock fuselage
   (25) Hastings dummy fuselage
   (26) Free descent abseil gear

5. The training aids have been designed to reproduce, as closely as possible, physical conditions and sensations similar to those experienced during an actual parachute descent, i.e. exit, parachute flight and landing. The aim is to teach the trainee so that he will react instinctively to make the correct physical movements when making a descent. This should be done in conditions which, physically, are slightly harder than those actually experienced during parachuting; this will help to relieve the added strain imposed by the nervous tension developed by the trainee when actually parachuting.

6. Films are reviewed periodically and brought up-to-date. The details of training films, lecture notes and film strips available will be found in later chapters of this Section. In addition to these aids the training is augmented by air experience flights, briefings and discussions.

Training

7. The period spent on synthetic training is the most strenuous part of the course, much of which

RESTRICTED

is necessarily repetitive instruction and practice. A wide variety of training apparatus is desirable, since the frequent or continuous use of one piece of equipment will prove tedious to both mind and muscle. Each piece of equipment must meet the basic skill requirement it is meant to develop but should differ in construction from others to stimulate and maintain interest. These factors assist an instructor in varying the training programme and in making the training progressive. Excessive use of the apparatus should be avoided, as it may result in injury to, or stiffness in a pupil. Training should be progressive so that the skill of a pupil is built up to the standard required, i.e. the ability, confidence and desire to make a parachute descent. There is nothing to be gained by attempting to train beyond this standard.

8. To step into space is not a natural action, and all reasonable men are afraid initially. It is during this phase of training that pupil and instructor learn to know and respect each other. An instructor must help his pupil to overcome his natural fears by encouragement, by convincing him of the high quality of the teaching staff and the equipment used, and develop in him the desire and determination to parachute.

A.P.4215, Sect. 3, Chap. 2
AL.6, Nov. 60

CHAPTER 2

EXIT TECHNIQUE

RESTRICTED

A.P. 4215, Sect. 3, Chap. 2
A.L. 3, June, 60

Chapter 2

EXIT TECHNIQUE

LIST OF CONTENTS

	Para.		Para.
Introduction	1	Aircraft drill	10
Exit position	4	Hooking up	11
Starboard door exit	6	Standing up	12
		Checking equipment	13
Port door exit	8	Telling off for equipment check	15
Aperture exit	9	Actions stations	16
		Stand in the door	17

LIST OF ILLUSTRATIONS

	Fig.		Fig.
Exit position	1	Snap-hook and locking pin	5
Stand in the door (starboard)	2	Low anchor cable grip	6
Leaving the aircraft	3	High anchor cable grip	7
Stand in the door (port)	4	High anchor cable, strop handle grip	8

Introduction

1. The exit is the first part of a parachute descent, it begins when the parachutist reaches No. 1 position in the aircraft drill and ends when the final tie of the parachute breaks from the static line.

2. The object of developing a correct exit technique is to ensure a clean exit from the aircraft with the body and accoutrements in the best position to ensure an unhindered deployment of the parachute.

3. The method of exit from an aircraft is dependent upon the type of opening through which the parachutist has to pass, it may be an opening in the side or rear of an aircraft or an opening in the floor. An exit can be made from a standing position, a crouch position, a sitting position or it may be made with the assistance of a slide or chute. Experience has shown that exits from a standing position through a side opening are best for military parachutists, but it is still necessary to teach floor aperture exit technique whilst aircraft with floor apertures, such as the Beverley, are in use.

RESTRICTED

Exit position

4. The exit position is the attitude of the body immediately on leaving the aircraft (*fig.* 1) and maintained during the development of the parachute. The details of this attitude are as follows:—

(1) The feet and legs firmly together with the knees bent slightly.

(2) The body curved forward slightly from the hips.

(3) The arms across the top of the reserve parachute pack or holding equipment, if carried.

(4) The head facing forwards and downwards with the chin on the chest.

(5) The whole body must be compact and able to remain so against the buffeting of the slipstream, and the snatch of the opening parachute.

5. To enable the exit position to be obtained quickly and accurately, the take-off or STAND IN THE DOOR position in the aircraft must be accurate and the action of leaving the aircraft must be vigorous yet controlled.

Fig. 2 Stand in the door (starboard)

Starboard door exit

6. A description of the action of leaving an aircraft from a starboard door (*fig.* 2) will explain the basic principles of the STAND IN THE DOOR position and the action that follows. On the command STAND IN THE DOOR, the parachutist at the starboard door should adopt the following position:—

(1) The right leg should be forward with the ball of the foot on the centre of the lip of the doorway and the left leg should be a comfortable pace behind. The weight should be distributed evenly between both feet with the knees bent slightly.

(2) The body should lean forward slightly with the shoulders square to the front, the head up and the eyes looking straight ahead.

(3) The right arm should be extended sideways and the palm of the hand, with fingers and thumb together, should rest on the exterior of the fuselage at hip height.

(4) The left forearm should be resting on the top of the reserve parachute pack, with the fingers gripping the right corner.

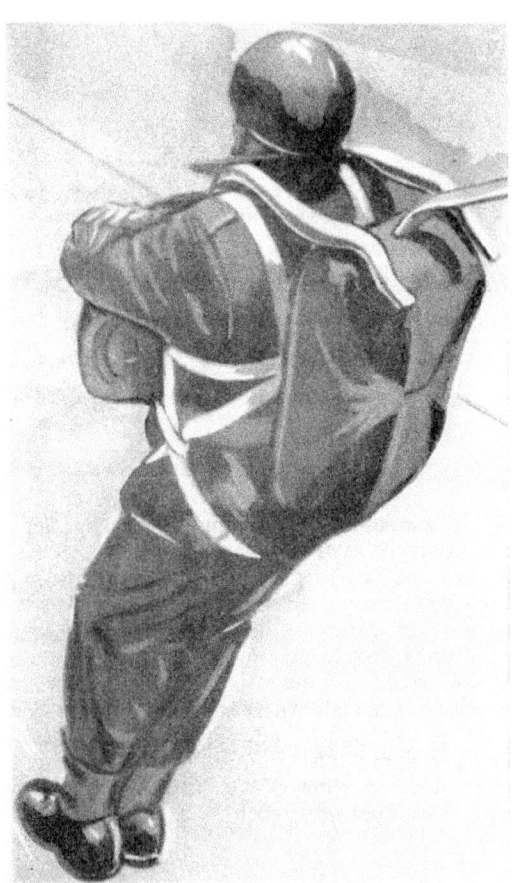

Fig. 1. Exit position

RESTRICTED

A.P. 4215, Sect. 3, Chap. 2
A.L. 3, June, 60

in the STAND IN THE DOOR position both arms should be on the top of the reserve parachute pack or holding equipment. On the command GO, the parachutist should step forward into the centre of the aperture and adopt the exit position immediately.

Aircraft drill

10. To ensure good exits, even sticks and the safety of everyone concerned, it is essential that all movements in the aircraft fuselage are carried out in accordance with an approved drill. This drill may vary for different types of aircraft, but the following basic principles will apply where the parachutist attaches his static line to a strop on a static (*anchor*) cable:—

(1) Hooking up

(2) Standing up

(3) Checking equipment

(4) Telling off for equipment check

(5) Action stations

Fig. 3. Leaving the aircraft

7. On the command GO, the parachutist should make a vigorous, yet controlled, movement forward, with his chest leading (*fig.* 3), avoiding any tendency to jump and he should endeavour to maintain a uniform height during the course of the movement. The left leg and the body weight should move forward together, the right hand acting as a guide and an aid to good balance, the right leg is used to give drive. The instant the parachutist clears the doorway he should adopt the exit position.

Port door exit

8. A similar technique is used for an exit from a port doorway (*fig.* 4), except that the relative positions of the limbs are reversed. Fig. 4 shows equipment being carried by the parachutist, therefore, his right hand is holding the equipment as quoted in para. 4, sub-para (3).

Aperture exit

9. Similar principles of exit technique appertain to an aperture exit through the floor of an aircraft, except that the forward movement is reduced and

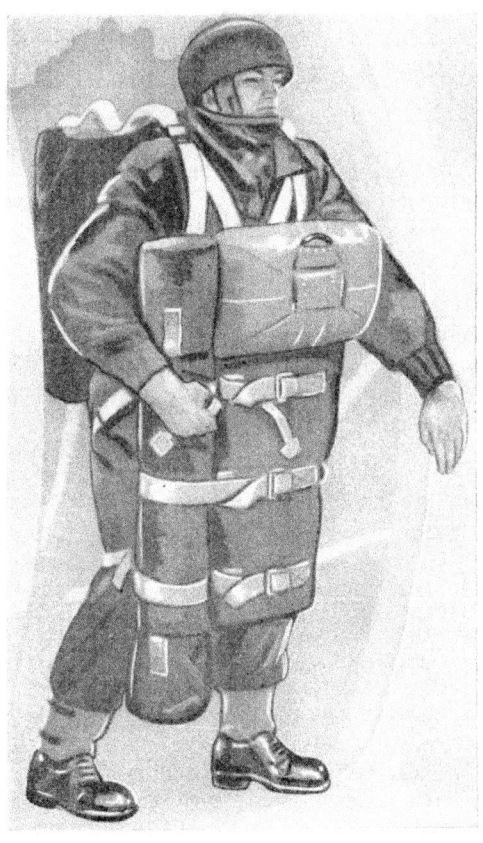

Fig. 4. Stand in the door (port)

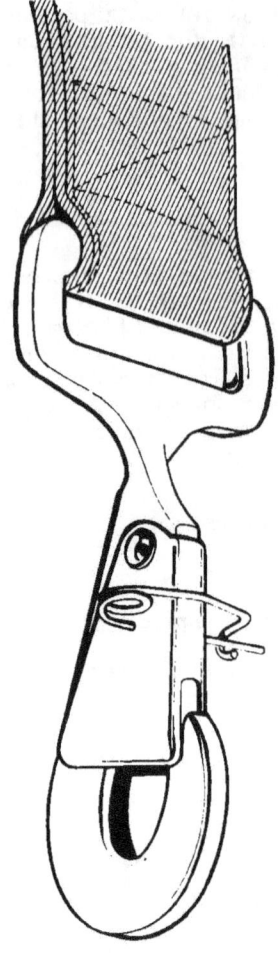

Fig. 5. Snap-hook and locking pin

Fig. 6. Low anchor cable grip

Hooking up

11. A parachutist should check his strop and static line, and connect the two together by placing the D-ring into the snap-hook, taking care that neither strop or static line is twisted. The snap-hook must be locked by a safety pin inserted through the flange and hook as shown in Fig. 5.

Standing up

12. The parachutist is to stand up facing aft and with one movement of the arm nearest the static cable, pass his strop over his shoulder.

Checking equipment

13. To ensure that all the parachutists' equipment is checked efficiently, each parachutist is to check his own front and the back of the parachutist immediately in front of him. The last parachutist in a stick should turn about so that his back can be checked by the last but one parachutist in the stick. The standard checking sequence is as follows:—

(1) The parachutists's own front

(a) The security of the snap-hook, locking pin and D-ring.

(b) The freedom of the strop on the anchor cable

(c) The parachute harness quick-release box for security

(d) The attachment of the reserve parachute pack

(e) The security of the protective helmet

(f) The attachment of any suspended loads or other equipment being carried.

(2) The back of the parachutist immediately in front

(a) The security of the three visible ties of the main parachute

(b) The freedom of the static line and strop, ensuring that it is unobstructed from the pack cover to the anchor cable

Fig. 7. High anchor cable grip

RESTRICTED

A.P. 4215, Sect. 3, Chap. 2
A.L. 3, June, 60

Fig. 8. High anchor cable, strop handle grip

14. In some aircraft each parachutist is responsible for the movement of his own strop as he moves aft towards the exit and in other aircraft he controls the movement of the strop of the parachutist in front of him. This control of strop movement is most important in the case of side door exits where low anchor cables are used, as the strop must be kept clear of the floor. The control of strop movement is done by each parachutist gripping the strop of the parachutist in front at the end of the folds nearest to the snap-hook. The method of gripping the strop is with the palm of the hand downwards, thumb on top of and fingers curled lightly round the strop, as shown in Fig. 6. The last parachutist in a stick grips and controls the movement of his own strop together with that of the parachutist in front of him. Where high anchor cables are used, each parachutist should grip his own strop or strop handle (*fig. 7 and* 8), ensuring that his arm is in front of the strop at all times.

Telling off for equipment check

15. To signify that they are ready to jump, each parachutist in succession from the last parachutist in the stick is to TELL OFF. This is done by each parachutist calling his number and O.K. and at the same time tapping the shoulder of the parachutist in front with his free hand. No. 1 in a stick, in addition to calling No. 1 O.K. will add Port/Starboard stick O.K., as applicable. Should any parachutist not be ready to jump, he is not to TELL OFF, but is to raise his free hand above his head.

Action stations

16. On the command ACTION STATIONS, No. 1 in a stick is to move into a position facing the doorway or aperture, one pace back from the STAND IN THE DOOR position, as described in para. 6, sub-para (1) and para. 9; the remainder of the stick are to close up evenly behind No. 1. To do this in an orderly manner, the parachutists in the stick will move aft in step, left foot forward in the case of port sticks and right foot forward for starboard sticks. As the sticks move progressively aft the rear foot moves up to but never in front of the leading foot.

Standing in the door

17. At this point the aircraft drill ends for No. 1 in a stick and his exit begins. The remainder of the parachutists in the stick still have to complete their aircraft drill until they progressively reach the exit position in the doorway. On the command STAND IN THE DOOR, the whole stick moves forward one position in two foot-movements, rear foot first, i.e., the rear foot takes one pace forward up to the leading foot and then the leading foot takes one pace forward. No. 1 in the stick is now ready to jump. No. 2 takes up the position vacated by No. 1, No. 3 takes up the position vacated by No. 2 and so on throughout the stick. Each parachutist retains his grip on a strop until he reaches the No. 2 position; then the action to be taken by the parachutist may vary according to the aircraft being used, as follows:—

(1) When low anchor cables are installed, each parachutist as he passes through No. 2 position is to cast the strop away with a sideways and downwards movement.

(2) When high anchor cables are installed and a side door exit is being used, each parachutist is to release the strop as he passes through the No. 2 position.

(3) When high anchor cables are installed and a floor aperture is being used each parachutist is to release the strop as he moves into No. 1 position.

18. As a stick moves forward towards the exit, each parachutist is to follow directly behind the parachutist in front of him, keeping as close as possible. This is very important in side door exits, as the curvature of the stick towards the door must be maintained.

RESTRICTED

Look up (*fig.* 1)

5. On completion of the exit, the parachutist will look up to check the development of his parachute.

All round observation (*fig.* 2)

6. The parachutist is to grip the front lift webs and look around him to ascertain his position in the air in relation to other parachutists. To ensure maximum coverage he is to push away with his right hand when turning to the left and with his left hand when turning to the right; he must also look above and below.

Seat strap (*fig.* 3)

7. The seat strap should be eased off the buttocks by parting the legs and pulling it back with both hands sufficient to allow full movement of the hip joints.

Parachuting position (*fig.* 4)

8. The parachuting position is as follows:—

(1) Feet and knees together, legs bent slightly and hanging below the body.

(2) Back rounded, head forward, chin on chest and with the eyes looking at the ground.

(3) Arms fully extended above the head, with the hands grasping the forward lift webs in a comfortable and secure grip. The grip should be ▶◀ with the little finger uppermost and the thumb to the front. ▶◀

(4) The whole body should be relaxed.

Fig. 3. Seat strap

Fig. 4. Parachuting position.

Assessing drift

9. A parachutist is to assess his drift by looking at a stationary object on the ground in front of him. If he is going towards it, he is drifting forwards and if he is moving away from it, he is drifting backwards. Drift to the right or left can be assessed in a similar manner. Care must be taken not to confuse drift with oscillation.

Damping oscillation (fig. 5)

10. Oscillation, which is the pendulum swing of the body below the parachute, is damped out by pulling down on one set of lift webs to distort the parachute canopy either forwards or backwards according to the direction of the drift. The primary object of pulling down on the lift webs is to damp out the oscillation and by selecting the correct lift webs, the drift can be decreased.

(1) When drifting forwards, the parachutist is to pull down on the back lift webs and maintain the pull until the feet are about to touch the ground; he should then let up, keeping the parachute canopy under control and with his body in the accepted landing position.

(2) When drifting backwards, the parachutist is to pull down on the front lift webs. As he approaches the ground, he is to reach back with his legs from the hips to ensure that the soles of his feet make first contact with the ground. He is to maintain the pull down throughout the fall.

(3) When drifting sideways, the parachutist is to pull down on the front lift webs and when he is about 30 ft. from the ground, he is to let up on the side to which he is drifting.

(4) In the condition of no positive drift, the parachutist is to pull down on the front lift webs. If he finds that he has created a forward drift, he is to let up at approximately 30ft. from the ground and adopt the correct landing position.

(5) If the wrong lift webs have been selected, the drift will be increased. When the error is discovered, if sufficient height (200 ft.) remains, the parachutist is to change to the opposite lift webs and pull down, but if he is close to the ground, he is to let up and adopt the correct landing position.

Fig. 5. Pull down on front lift webs

Fig. 6. Reach high on correct lift webs

A.P. 4215, Sect. 3, Chap. 3
A.L. 14, June, 61

CHAPTER 3

EXIT TRAINING APPARATUS

Chapter 3

EXIT TRAINING APPARATUS

LIST OF CONTENTS

	Para.		Para.
Introduction	1	Outdoor exit trainer	12
Mock doors	2	Safety precautions	14
Sequence of instruction	3	Drill procedure	15
Ballon car	4	Composite mock fuselage	16
Fan descent trainer	5	Sequence of instruction	18
Safety precautions	7	Aircraft fuselage	19
Inspection before use	8	Eight-cable stick exit trainer	20
Re-winding the cable	9	Safety precautions	23
Sequence of instruction	10	Drill procedure	24
Recording descents	11	Tell-off for equipment check	25
		Action stations	26

LIST OF ILLUSTRATIONS

	Fig.		Fig.
Mock doors	1	Composite mock fuselage	5
Fan descent trainer-general arrangement	2	Interior of Hastings fuselage	6
Fan descent trainer-air brake	3	Eight-cable stick exit trainer-interior	7
Fan descent trainer-harness	4	Eight cable stick exit trainer-in use	8

Introduction

1. All training apparatus is to be inspected as detailed in Unit Standing Orders. Before use it must be ensured that all working parts of any apparatus are serviceable, any suspension points to be used are secure and that the matted areas have a smooth and continuous surface. Parachute training aids are described in detail in A.P.2655, Vol. 1, (2nd Edn.), Sect. 5. The following apparatus is available for the training of pupils in exit techniques:-

  (1) Mock doors
  (2) Balloon cars
  (3) Fan descent trainer
  (4) Outdoor exit trainer
  (5) Mock fuselage
  (6) Aircraft fuselage
  (7) Eight-cable stick trainer

Mock doors (*fig.* 1)

2. The mock doors represent, in their shapes and dimensions, the parachute exit doorways of different types of aircraft. The mock doors are erected on the edges of platforms, two feet high, with mats provided below them for the pupils to land upon. The purpose of the apparatus is to enable the pupils to adopt the correct STAND IN THE DOOR positions, applicable to different types of aircraft, and to practice making exits singly. It is important that the pupils are taught to understand the effects of the slip-stream when making an exit in the air and, by frequent reminders, are trained to practice with the thought in mind that every exit made from the mock doors is made from an aircraft in flight.

Sequence of instruction

3. The sequence of instruction is as follows:-

  (1) The pupil is to stand one pace back from the door with his left foot forward of his right foot. On the command STAND IN THE DOOR, the pupil is to adopt the attitude described and illustrated in Chap. 2, para. 4 and fig. 2, but is to have his right forearm across his chest as though it was on his reserve parachute.

  (2) The pupil is to practice standing in the door, looking down to ensure that he adopts the correct position.

  (3) The pupil will make his exit on the command GO and will land on the mat in the exit position.

  (4) The importance of adopting the correct attitudes is to be stressed to the pupil and variations from the approved positions are not to be allowed. Practice in the actions which follow the commands STAND IN THE DOOR and GO is essential and is to be repeated as necessary.

  (5) The pupil is to fit his reserve parachute and repeat the practices (1) to (4).

  (6) After the foregoing sequence has been completed satisfactorily the mock doors can be used to teach the ACTION STATIONS positions for the No. 1 man of a stick.

  (7) Floor aperture exits will also be practiced from the mock doors, in the sequences (1) to (5). The position of STAND IN THE DOOR and the action to be taken on the command GO are described in Chap. 2, para 9.

Balloon car

4. The apparatus is a balloon car, as is used for parachute descents from a balloon, in which instruction is given in side door and floor aperture exit techniques. The sequence of instruction is as follows:-

  (1) Instruct as for mock doors.

  (2) Practice balloon car drills as detailed in Sect. 4 and 5.

Fig. 1. Mock doors

Fan descent trainer (*fig.* 2)

5. The apparatus consists of a fan airbrake (*fig.* 3) mounted on the shaft of a cable drum; a cable is wound round the drum and passed over a guide pulley to the take-off platform, where a simple harness is attached to the free end. (*fig.* 4). The assembly is installed in the roof girders of a hangar and is 30 ft. above the floor level, access to the platform being by means of a ladder. Under instruction, a pupil climbs the ladder, fits the harness on himself and jumps from the platform in the approved manner. The cable unwinds from the drum and causes the fan to rotate and so apply a braking effect on the rate of descent of the pupil; the rate of descent is governed by the area of the fan blades and the weight of the pupil (*para.* 7, *sub-para.* (6).

6. The primary purpose of the apparatus is to simulate exit conditions; the height of the platform gives the pupil time in which to maintain a good exit position, and with practice, builds up his confidence in jumping from a height. The secondary purpose is to teach the landing technique, as the pupil must assume the correct attitude before landing on the matted area (*Chap.* 6 *and* 7).

Safety precautions

7. The following precautions must be observed:-

(1) An Officer instructor is to be present when the fan descent trainer is in use. He is to ensure that the platform has been inspected, before use, in accordance with para. 8.

(2) Pupils are to grip the outside of the ladder uprights with both hands when climbing up to the platform.

(3) Pupils on the platform awaiting their turns to jump are to stand well back from the fan and are to come forward only on the command of the instructor.

(4) The ladder and the platform are not to be overloaded, i.e., there are not to be more than 18 men on the platform, and no more than three men on the ladder, at any one time.

(5) Pupils are not to lean on the wire guard which is fitted round the fan blades.

(6) The total weight on the cable is not to exceed 200 lb.

(7) The matted area is to be kept clear of personnel other than those pupils making landings.

(8) Pupils making descents from the platform are to be despatched in the correct manner by a qualified instructor only.

Inspection before use

8. Before a period of training is commenced the apparatus is to be inspected by an instructor who is to :-

(1) Ensure the correct lay-out of the mats on the landing area.

Fig. 2. Fan descent trainer—
general arrangements

Fig. 3. Fan descent trainer—air brake

(8) Re-wind the cable on to the drum, guiding it with finger and thumb into the grooves on the drum (*para.* 9).

Re-winding of cable

9. The cable must be re-wound tightly into the continuous groove on the drum. If there are any spaces or any slack turns the cable must be un-wound and then re-wound correctly. To ensure correct re-winding one hand should be used to guide the cable into the drum groove (*para.* 8, *sub-para.* (8); when re-winding is completed this hand is to be kept on the drum to act as a brake, while the other hand is used to assist the next pupil in fitting his harness. As the pupil makes his exit the instructor will lift his hand from the drum; as the pupil lands the instructor will lower his hand on to the drum to stop it rotating. The instructor must keep his hands and body well clear of the re-winding handle while a descent is being made.

Sequence of instruction

10. The sequence of instruction is as follows:-

(1) The pupil is to stand on the platform as far back as possible and facing the door. He will fit his harness (*like a waistcoat*), putting his arms between the webbing straps on each side and then fasten the waist belt.

(2) The instructor is to check the waist belt, take up any slack in the cable and then order STAND IN THE DOOR. The pupil will adopt the correct position.

(3) The pupil will make a normal exit on the instructor's command GO, adopt the 'tight body' position then immediately relax his lower limbs in preparation for landing.

(4) The pupil will regain his feet quickly after landing and move back from the landing area to unfasten his harness.

(5) The instructor will re-wind the harness ready for the next pupil; both door and aperture exits are to be practiced.

(6) When the pupils have overcome their initial nervousness by making several descents from the platform, exit and landing practices will be continued with the pupils wearing reserve parachutes.

Recording descents

11. The instructor is to record, on the log card provided at each fan, the number of descents made during each training period. If a defect is found during inspection, or arises during training, the

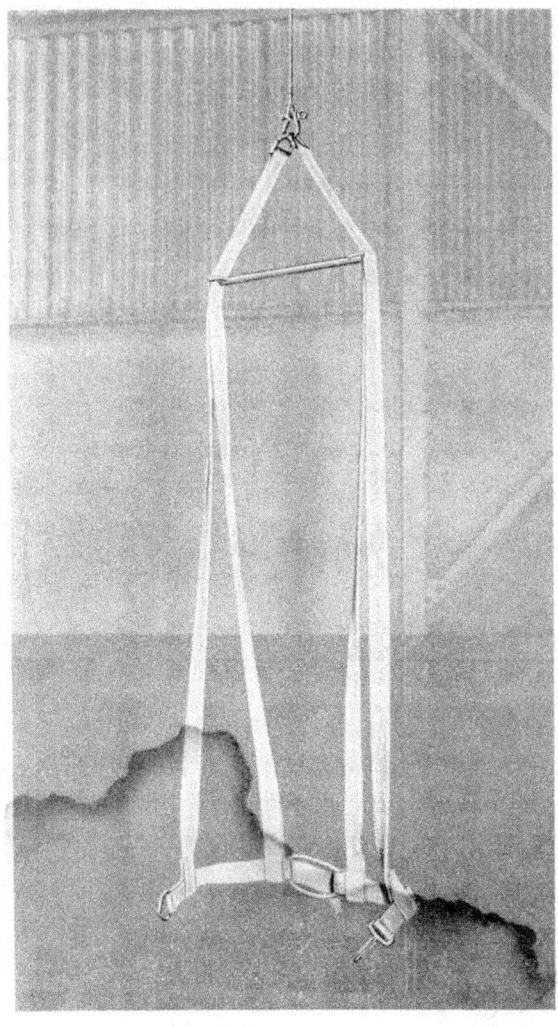

Fig. 4. Fan descent trainer harness

(2) Mount the platform, switch on the light and inspect the log card.

(3) Inspect the non-skid floor surface at the doorway.

(4) Inspect the attachment of the harness to the cable, the spreader bar, the harness, waist belt, snap-hook and 'D' ring for serviceability.

(5) Inspect the re-winding handle, the cable drum, the guide pulley and the fan blades for condition and security.

(6) Inspect the cable for fraying by lowering it to its full extent and, while doing so, allowing the full length of the cable to pass between his thumb and forefinger.

(7) Inspect the attachment of the cable to the drum for security.

RESTRICTED

F.S./3

A.P.4215, Sect. 3, Chap. 3
A.L.14, June, 61

apparatus is to be labelled with the UNSERVICEABLE board and the facts reported to the N.C.O.i/c Servicing section who is to ensure that the harness is removed immediately.

Outdoor exit trainer

12. The outdoor exit trainer consists of a wooden tower, 30ft. high, with a take-off platform approximately 10 ft. square at the top. The platform is surrounded by a safety rail 4 ft. high, in which two mock doors are built, one on each side of the platform. A steel cable is suspended close to and sloping away from each doorway; it is 200 ft. long and is supported by two tubular steel masts. The suspension point nearest to the door is 50 ft. high and the other, remote from the doorway, is 28 ft. high. A trolley is mounted on each cable and is fitted with two strops of equal length and a spreader bar.

13. The purpose of the outdoor exit trainer is to give the pupil practice in making exits from both port and starboard exit doorways, and holding and maintaining the exit position while he is being swung about on the cable in conditions which are approximately the same as those in the slipstream of an aircraft.

Safety precautions

14. The following precautions must be observed:—

(1) An officer instructor is to be present at all times when the apparatus is in use for training. He is to ensure that the tower and its equipment has been inspected, before use, and is serviceable.

(2) The cables and trolleys, with their harnesses attached, are to be checked when they are at the end of their travel, by two instructors swinging together on each harness.

Fig. 5. Composite mock fuselage

RESTRICTED

(3) On all occasions when instructors are despatching pupils from this trainer they are to wear the approved despatcher's safety belt with the hook and pin attached. The belt is to be adjusted to the shortest length which is consistent with safe despatching. Details of the safety belt are given in A.P.1182B, Vol. 1 and 6.

(4) An instructor is to give a demonstration of the exit technique before pupils use the apparatus.

(5) The safety cable/bar across each doorway is only to be removed on the command STAND IN THE DOOR, and is to be refitted immediately after an exit has been made.

(6) Steel helmets are to be worn; harnesses are to be correctly fitted.

(7) Supervision is to be strict to ensure that the drill is followed as though the pupils were jumping from an aircraft in flight.

Drill procedure

15. The pupils and the despatchers will follow the drill procedure given below :-

(1) The pupils on the platform awaiting, their turns to jump, will fit their harnesses and reserve packs.

(2) The No. 2 Despatcher will check the fitting of the harnesses and reserve packs.

(3) The No. 2 Despatcher will then retrieve the trolley and hook up the next pupil to make an exit; he will hold the spreader bar well above and behind the pupil's head.

(4) The No. 1 Despatcher will check the attachments of the trolley to the cable and the harness to the trolley and will ensure that the lift webs are disposed one on each side of the pupil's head with the spreader held as in (3).

(5) The No. 1 Despatcher will then order STAND IN THE DOOR and the pupil will adopt the correct postion.

(6) The pupil will make a normal exit on the command GO from the No. 1 Despatcher; at the same time the No. 2 Despatcher will move towards the door still holding the spreader above and behind the pupils' head and allowing it to follow through behind the pupil. He will release the spreader bar when the pupil is clear of the door.

(7) The pupil will free himself from his harness at the end of his descent and then land on the ground with his feet together and his arms held well above his head.

Fig. 6. Interior of Hastings fuselage

RESTRICTED

Note ...

A retrieval rope is to be attached to the lug on the leg strap of the harness prior to the pupil dropping to the ground; the harness will be returned to the platform by pulling the trolley along the cable with the rope.

Composite mock fuselage (*fig. 5*)

16. The composite mock fuselage is a skeleton structure made in sections so that it can be adjusted to approximately the same dimensions as the aircraft fuselage it represents. It is mounted on a platform two feet high and is fitted with safety belts, folding seats, static cables and strops; crash safety nets can also be fitted. Mats are provided below the doorways for the pupils to land upon.

17. The purpose of the apparatus is to enable a stick of pupils to perform a complete aircraft drill and exit technique under complete supervision from inside and outside the fuselage. The correct aircraft drill, as applicable to the type represented by the arrangement of the mock fuselage, must always be used as the basis for a training period; it is essential that good discipline and the most strict supervision are to be maintained to ensure the required results.

Sequence of instruction

18. The sequence of instruction is as follows:—

(1) The pupils are to enter the fuselage and familiarise themselves with the fastening, adjustment and releasing of safety belts. They are to practice the releasing, raising, lowering and the securing of the seats.

(2) The pupils will then stand up as port and starboard sticks (*of not more than three per stick*), and will practice the approach to the door. Emphasis will be given to the necessity for a slow and steady rhythm of the feet movements and the correct positions; excessive speed is unsafe and is not to be allowed.

(3) In this phase, reserve parachutes are to be fitted, strops given out and the drill in sub-para. (2) is to be repeated, with emphasis on the correct grip and carrying of the strop. This is to be followed by practice in releasing the strop at the No. 2 position, the STAND IN THE DOOR and the exit positions. As each stick moves through the doorway each pupil is to pause momentarily as he comes to the STAND IN THE DOOR position before making his exit.

(4) The complete sequence of the particular aircraft drill will then be practiced.

Fig. 7. Eight-cable stick exit training interior

RESTRICTED

Fig. 8. Eight-cable stick exit trainer—in use

(5) Dummy 'X' Type and reserve parachutes are to be fitted, the pupils lined up in stick order, numbered off and emplaned. The static lines will be placed over the correct shoulders of the pupils by the instructor, the strops will be given out and practice will be made of hooking up and inserting and fastening the locking pin. The instructor will emphasise this phase of the drill.

(6) The complete sequence of the particular drill will then be practiced.

Aircraft fuselage (*fig.* 6)

19. This apparatus is representative of the aircraft in flight and is completely fitted out with the equipment required for parachuting. The fuselage is mounted on trestles with mats below the doors for the pupils to land upon. The drill, sequence of instruction and notes for instructors are to be applied as for the mock fuselage. As the apparatus is an actual fuselage the drills can be practiced in more realistic conditions and are to progress gradually from training to operational drills.

Eight-cable stick exit trainer (*fig.* 7 *and* 8)

20. The apparatus consists of a tower on the top of which a wooden cabin is built, an arrangement of eight suspended travel cables on each of which a travelling trolley is mounted and a suspension harness for each trolley. There is a four-flight stairway within the structure of the tower leading to an access hatch in the cabin floor. The cabin

RESTRICTED

is provided with two exit doorways and observation windows and the floor is 30 ft. above ground level. Each doorway and the slot in the side of the cabin, through which the trolley harness suspension cables are passed, can be closed by a removable wooden panel. The travel cables are suspended from standards which are 10 ft. higher at the departure end of the installation, than at the arrival end. The standards are 300 ft. apart and this, coupled with the deep curve of the slack in each cable, provides each pupil with an effective run of approximately 250 ft. When using this apparatus the pupils are to wear training harnesses; their harnesses are attached to the spreader bar, fitted between the lower ends of the trolley suspension cables, by two lift webs, one on each side.

21. The purpose of the apparatus is to provide the pupils with practice in :-

(1) Making exits from port and starboard doorways and floor apertures.

(2) Approaching an exit as a member of a stick.

(3) Maintaining the exit position while being suspended and swung about in conditions which are approximately the same as those in the slipstream of an aircraft.

22. Additionally, the use of the apparatus increases the pupils' confidence in their equipment. Considerable realism is imparted to the exercise because the pupils experience a short free fall before their weight is arrested by their trolley suspension harness, which is followed by a rapid descent down the highest slope of the travel cable. The momentum of each pupil will carry him part of the way up the reverse slope of his cable, on which he will eventually come to a stop and then his trolley will run backwards to the lowest point of the cable. It should be noted here that the pupil swings at right angles to the travel cable during his descent, the degree of his swing depending on the vigour and manner with which he makes his exit. When the pupil reaches the lowest point of his travel cable he is steadied by a recovery man, releases himself from his harness and drops to the ground.

Safety precautions

23. The use of the stick exit trainer necessarily involves the participants in operations undertaken at a considerable height and serious accidents can occur unless there is strict disciplinary control. The use of the trainer is regulated by detailed Local Orders which must be complied with, in addition to taking the following precautions:-

(1) An Officer instructor is to be present while the trainer is in use. He is to ensure that the tower and its equipment has been inspected before use and is serviceable.

(2) The travel cables and trolleys with their suspension cables attached are to be checked when they are at the end of their travel, by two instructors swinging together on each trolley harness.

(3) On all occasions when instructors are despatching pupils from this trainer they are to wear the approved despatcher's safety belt with the hook and pin attached. The belt is to be adjusted to the shortest length which is consistent with safe despatching. Details of the safety belt are given in A.P.1182 B, Vol. 1 and 6.

(4) An instructor is to give a demonstration of the exit technique before pupils use the apparatus.

(5) The No. 1 Despatcher on the port and on the starboard side is to be a qualified instructor and is responsible for the giving of all orders to, and the safe and correct despatching of, the pupils in the sticks on their respective sides.

(6) The platform is not to be overloaded, i.e., it is not to be carrying more than 20 men altogether at any one time.

(7) Training harnesses are to be correctly fitted and steel helmets are to be worn. Spreader bars are to be held well above and behind the pupils' heads.

(8) The safety bar across each doorway is only to be removed when the command STAND IN THE DOOR is given and while a stick is making an exit. The safety bar is to be re-fitted as soon as an exit has been completed by a stick.

(9) Supervision is to be strict to ensure that the drills are followed as though the pupils were jumping from an aircraft in flight.

(10) After freeing themselves from their harnesses at the end of their descent the pupils are to land with both feet together and with their arms held above their heads.

Drill procedure

24. The stick exit trainer is provided with eight cables which permits practice in the despatching of sticks, of four pupils in each stick, from each side doorway. When the despatchers and pupils under instruction have mounted to the platform the drill procedure is as follows :-

(1) Each stick of four pupils is to stand in single file facing its respective doorway. The No. 1 Despatchers will retrieve the harnesses and pass them in turn to the No. 4, 3, 2 and 1 of their respective sticks assisted by the No. 2 Despatchers.

(2) The No. 2 Despatchers are then to assist the pupils in their sticks to fit their harnesses.

(3) When harness fitting has been completed the sticks are to stand as far back as their harnesses will allow and No. 1 Despatcher will check that each man's harness is correctly fitted.

(4) Each pupil is to pass his own spreader bar and lift webs over his head; the bar is to be held by the pupil behind him. A fifth pupil will hold the spreader bar of the No. 4 of each stick; pupils in the port stick will hold the spreader bars in their left hands, those in the starboard stick will hold the bars in their right hands. To ensure that the lift webs and cables are clear of the heads of the men in front of them, the holders are to retain the bars close to their chests.

(5) Each pupil is to check the attachment of his reserve parachute and the security of his quick-release box; for the man in front of him he will check the security of the lift web 'D' rings on the spreader bar snap-hooks and ensure that the lift webs have been passed correctly over the man's shoulders.

Tell-off for equipment check

25. When the checks in para. 24 have been completed the sticks are to 'tell-off' in the approved manner.

Action stations

26. The drill procedure is as follows :-

(1) The No. 2 Despatcher is to take over the spreader bar, from the pupil following No. 1, as the No. 1 man takes up his position on the command STAND IN THE DOOR.

(2) The No. 2 Despatcher is to pull the bar back to ensure that the lift web are well behind the No. 1; he is also to check that the trolley harness suspension cables are clear and that the trolley is free to move on the travel cable.

(3) When he has completed these checks he will inform the No. 1 Despatcher that the pupil can be despatched.

(4) He will repeat this procedure for No. 2, 3 and 4 of his stick in their respective turns.

(5) The No. 1 Despatcher and each pupil in turn are to follow normal drill procedure when the command STAND IN THE DOOR is given. The No. 2 Despatcher is to retain his grip on the spreader bar and move forward to allow the No. 1 of the stick to stand in the door.

(6) The No. 1 of the stick will make a correct exit on the command GO. The No. 2 Despatcher will move forward, retaining his grip on the spreader bar and allowing it to follow through with the pupil as he makes his exit and will release the bar when the pupil is clear of the doorway.

(7) This procedure will be repeated as the command GO - No. 1, No. 2, No. 3 is given in the correct sequence.

(8) The pupil will free himself from his harness at the end of his descent and then land on the ground with his feet together and his arms held above his head.

Note . . .

A retrieval rope is to be attached to the lug on the leg strap of the harness prior to the pupil dropping to the ground: the harness will be returned to the platform by pulling it along the cable with the rope.

A.P. 4215, Sect. 3, Chap. 3
A.L. 14, June, 61

CHAPTER 4

RESTRICTED

Look up (fig. 1)

5. On completion of the exit, the parachutist will look up to check the development of his parachute.

All round observation (fig. 2)

6. The parachutist is to grip the front lift webs and look around him to ascertain his position in the air in relation to other parachutists. To ensure maximum coverage he is to push away with his right hand when turning to the left and with his left hand when turning to the right; he must also look above and below.

Seat strap (fig. 3)

7. The seat strap should be eased off the buttocks by parting the legs and pulling it back with both hands sufficient to allow full movement of the hip joints.

Parachuting position (fig. 4)

8. The parachuting position is as follows:—

   (1) Feet and knees together, legs bent slightly and hanging below the body.

   (2) Back rounded, head forward, chin on chest and with the eyes looking at the ground.

   (3) Arms fully extended above the head, with the hands grasping the forward lift webs in a comfortable and secure grip. The grip should be with the little finger uppermost and the thumb to the front.

   (4) The whole body should be relaxed.

Fig. 3. Seat strap

Fig. 4. Parachuting position

RESTRICTED

Assessing drift

9. A parachutist is to assess his drift by looking at a stationary object on the ground in front of him. If he is going towards it, he is drifting forwards and if he is moving away from it, he is drifting backwards. Drift to the right or left can be assessed in a similar manner. Care must be taken not to confuse drift with oscillation.

Damping oscillation (*fig.* 5)

10. Oscillation, which is the pendulum swing of the body below the parachute, is damped out by pulling down on one set of lift webs to distort the parachute canopy either forwards or backwards according to the direction of the drift. The primary object of pulling down on the left webs is to damp out the oscillation and by selecting the correct lift webs, the drift can be decreased.

(1) When drifting forwards, the parachutist is to pull down on the back lift webs and maintain the pull until the feet are about to touch the ground; he should then let up, keeping the parachute canopy under control and with his body in the accepted landing position.

(2) When drifting backwards, the parachutist is to pull down on the front lift webs. As he approaches the ground, he is to reach back with his legs from the hips to ensure that the soles of his feet make first contact with the ground. He is to maintain the pull down throughout the fall.

(3) When drifting sideways, the parachutist is to pull down on the front lift webs, and when he is about 30 ft. from the ground, he is to let up on the side to which he is drifting.

(4) In the condition of no positive drift, the parachutist is to pull down on the front lift webs. If he finds that he has created a forward drift, he is to let up at approximately 30 ft. from the ground and adopt the correct landing position.

(5) If the wrong lift webs have been selected, the drift will be increased. When the error is discovered, if sufficient height ▶◀ remains, the parachutist is to change to the opposite lift webs and pull down, but if he is close to the ground, he is to let up and adopt the correct landing position.

Fig. 5. Pull down on front lift webs

Fig. 6. Reach high on correct lift webs

A.P.4215, Sect. 3, Chap. 5
A.L.14, June 61

CHAPTER 5

PARACHUTE FLIGHT TRAINING APPARATUS

RESTRICTED

Chapter 5

PARACHUTE FLIGHT TRAINING APPARATUS

LIST OF CONTENTS

	Para.		Para.
Introduction	1	Block and tackle flight and landing trainer	8
Elementary flight trainer	2	Sequence of instruction	11
Sequence of instruction	4	Static flight and twist trainer	12
Harness swing flight trainer	5	Sequence of instruction	14
Sequence of instruction	7	Double-arm descent training tower	15
		Sequence of instruction	17

LIST OF ILLUSTRATIONS

	Fig.		Fig.
Elementary flight trainer in use	1	Static flight and twist trainer	4
Harness swing flight trainers	2	Ready for descent from tower	5
Block and tackle flight and landing trainer	3	Landing after descent from tower	6

RESTRICTED

Introduction

1. All training apparatus is to be inspected as detailed in Unit Standing Orders. Before use it must be ensured that all working parts of any apparatus are serviceable, any suspension points to be used are secure and that the matted areas have a smooth and continuous surface. Parachute training aids are described in detail in A.P.2655, Vol. 1, (*2nd Edn.*,) Sect. 5. The following apparatus is available for the training of pupils in parachute flight training techniques (*Chap.* 4):-

(1) Elementary flight trainer.
(2) Harness flight trainer.
(3) Block and tackle, flight and landing trainer.
(4) Static flight and twist trainer.
(5) Tower.

Elementary flight trainer (*fig.* 1)

2. This item of training apparatus is made of webbing straps which are suspended from a platform to form a simple harness and to simulate the lift webs of an 'X' Type parachute when the parachute has developed. Elastic cords are fitted between the ends of one pair of lift webs and their points of attachment to the platform.

3. The elementary flight trainer is designed to teach a pupil the rudiments of flight technique, i.e. familiarisation with the swing of an oscillating parachute and the manipulation of the lift webs to damp out oscillation and to control drift.

Sequence of instruction

4. The sequence of instruction is as follows:-

(1) An instructor demonstrates the use of the apparatus.

(2) The pupil is assisted into the harness and the position of the four lift webs is pointed out to him, the webs with the elastic cords being to his front.

(3) The effect of 'pulling down' is explained to the pupil who then adopts the parachuting position and practices pulling down on the front lift webs.

(4) After pulling down the pupil is instructed how to regain his parachuting position.

(5) The pupil then practices pulling down on the back lift webs by sitting in the harness with the lift webs with the elastic cords behind him and continues with (4).

Harness swing flight trainer (*fig.* 2)

5. The principal components of this apparatus are:-

(1) A suspension tube or strut with ball-joints on its upper and lower ends which is suspended, at its upper end, from a strong point such as a hangar roof girder.

(2) A steel framework mounted on the lower ball-joint of the suspension tube.

(3) Four steel wire cables, suspended one from each corner of the framework.

(4) A parachute training harness, suspended by its lift webs from the cables.

(5) A jumping platform approximately 12 ft. high.

Fig. 1. Elementary flight trainer in use

6. In training, the pupil climbs up on to the platform, and with assistance, fits the training harness on himself. He then stands at the edge of the platform in the parachuting position grasping the lift webs of the harness. On the command from the instructor the pupil takes a slight lift on the lift webs and launches himself into the swing and, being suspended in the harness, swings to and fro. The length of the cables is such that the pupil swings clear of the matted area. The arrangement of the suspension tube and framework is such that the typical yield characteristics of parachute lift

webs during descent are simulated as the pupil practices pulling down. This is explained in detail in A.P.2655, Vol. 1, (2nd Edn.), Sect. 5, Chap. 12.

The apparatus is used as follows:-

(1) To provide the pupil with a first experience of an appreciable height from the ground, and the means of learning and practising flight technique.

(2) To give realistic instruction in the control of the body position and of the parachute, in the various phases of flight during a parachute descent.

(3) To familiarise the pupil with the swing of an oscillating parachute.

(4) To teach the methods of avoiding entanglement with other parachutists or their rigging lines during descent.

(5) To give more advanced training in the use of the lift webs in the damping out of oscillation and the control of drift.

Sequence of instruction

7. The sequence of instruction is divided into the following stages:-

(1) Introduction to the apparatus and demonstrations by the instructors of harness swings which are to include:-
  (a) Exit position.
  (b) Check parachute.
  (c) Observation.
  (d) Seat strap and parachute position.

(2) Practice by the pupils of 1(a) to (d) which is to include at least one repetition with maximum corrections.

(3) Introduction into the training of the wearing of reserve parachutes and progress in training in the checking of drift by pulling down on lift webs.

(4) As for (3) but demanding quicker reactions from the pupils and the more efficient execution of the drills.

Fig. 2. Harness swing flight trainers

Fig. 3. Block and tackle flight and landing trainer

RESTRICTED

(5) A demonstration and practices of the complete flight drill, followed by the practising of all emergency drills.

(6) A demonstration of P.W.C. drill during flight, followed by practice by the pupils in this drill with the maximum corrections.

(7) The practice of the complete flight drills with P.W.C., and repetition which is to include the emergency drills.

Block and tackle flight and landing trainer

8. The principal components of this apparatus are:-

(1) A training harness which is suspended from the four corners of a special frame.

(2) A pair of steel wire suspension cables to which the frame is attached: the cables pass over two pairs of pulleys which are mounted on the hangar roof girders and run downwards to a spacer bar which connects the cables together.

(3) A block and tackle, anchored to the floor to which the spacer bar is connected.

9. The design of the frame and the method of attachment of the suspension web is such that the typical yield characteristics of parachute lift webs are simulated as the pupil practices pulling down. The suspension webs can be attached to the frame so that the pupil can be made to swing backwards and forwards, or from side-to-side.

10. The trainer is used to teach the pupils the flight technique which follows after making an exit and, subsequently, landings. Emergencies such as spread-eagling, steering and disentangling can also be taught and practised.

Sequence of instruction

11. Under the supervision of an instructor the pupil fits the harness on himself and is hauled up by the block and tackle to about two feet above the floor. The instructor sets the pupil swinging, takes over the hauling rope of the block and tackle and instructs the pupil while he is still swinging.

(1) Instruction is first given in the flight technique after making an exit; this must be done fairly quickly while the pupil retains sufficient momentum in his swing to make a realistic landing.

(2) At a chosen point during the swing the instructor slackens his hold on the rope of the block and tackle and allows it to run so that the pupil descends to the matted area at approximately parachuting descent speed.

(3) The pupil lands in the manner appropriate to the direction of his approach to the ground, i.e., forwards or backwards, to the left or to the right.

(4) When the stage is reached where the apparatus is being used for training in landings, the pupils will already have been taught the complete clean fatigue flight technique which they can practice on this trainer.

(5) The pupils then practice the emergency drills (*para.* 10).

Fig. 4. Static flight and twist trainer

Fig. 5. Ready for descent from tower

RESTRICTED

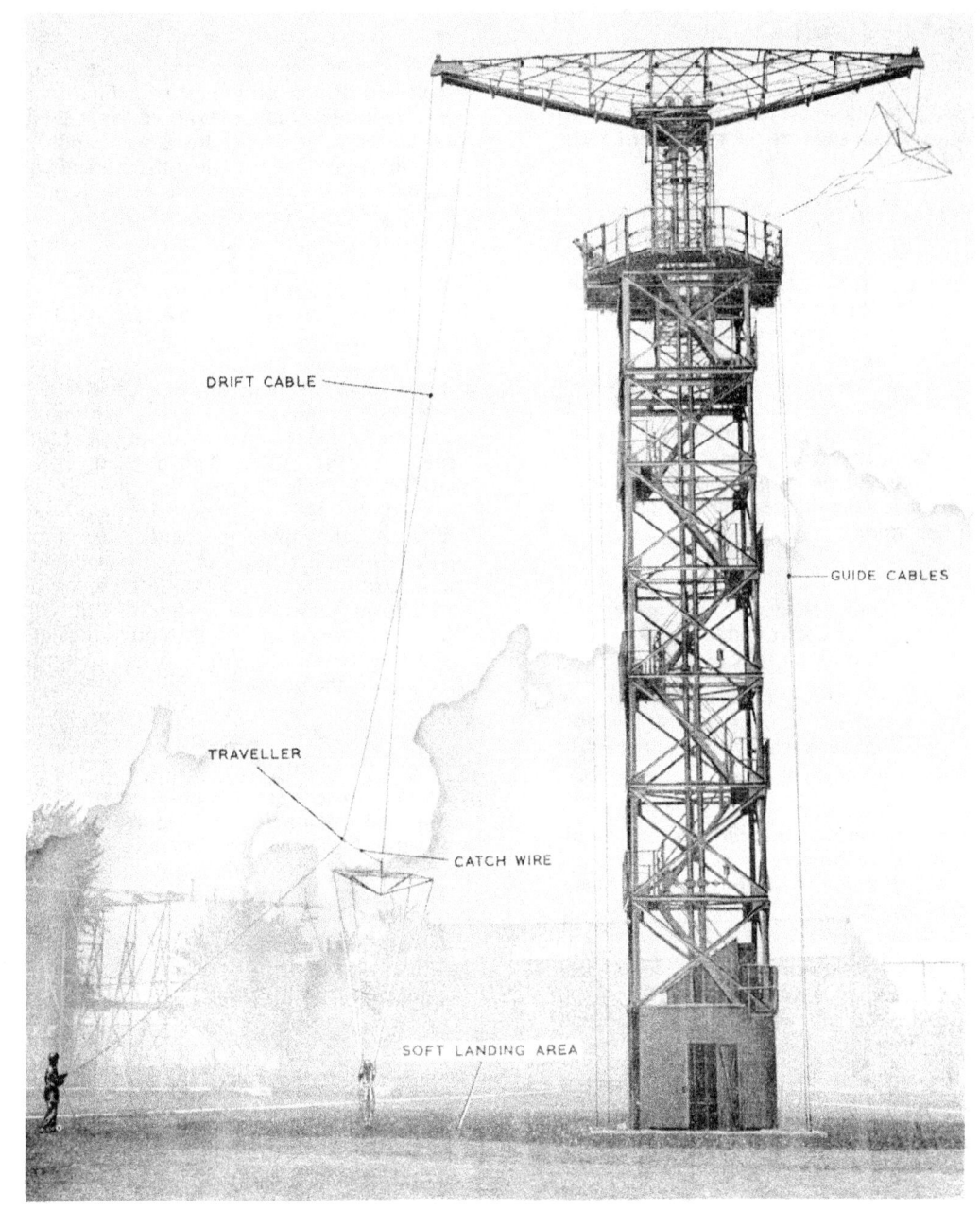

Fig. 6. Landing after descent from tower

Static flight and twist trainer (*fig.* 4)

12. The principal components of this apparatus are :-

(1) A training harness with two extra lift webs fitted between the normal front and back lift webs.

(2) A spacer bar, connecting the upper ends of the centre lift webs, which is suspended from a single point by a steel wire cable.

(3) A set of four ropes or cords with their upper ends spaced well apart and secured to the hangar roof girders; their lower ends are provided with elastic loops which support the normal lift webs of the harness.

13. The ropes, and the angle at which they suspend from the roof, simulate the rigging lines of a developed parachute. When the pupil pulls down the effect of the elastic loops is to simulate the typical yield characteristics of parachute lift webs during descent. When the pupil is in the harness his feet are about one foot clear of the ground and his weight is taken by the centre pair of lift webs. The single-point suspension makes it possible to turn the pupil round so that his rigging lines become twisted. A bench, about two or three feet high, for the pupil to stand on while fitting the harness, should be placed a short distance from the trainer.

Sequence of instruction

14. All flight techniques can be taught on this trainer as well as the correction of twists. The sequence of instruction is as follows :-

(1) The pupil fits on, and sits in, the harness. For elementary flight training he pulls down on the lift webs as directed by the instructor to correct oscillation or drift.

(2) For twist correction exercises the instructor rotates the pupil so that the lift webs and simulated rigging lines become twisted. The pupil is then instructed in how to look up and check his canopy and decide which way the rigging lines are twisted.

(3) The pupil is then shown how to correct the twists by vigorous kicking with feet or by making a stirring motion with his legs held together.

(4) As the last twist is about to unwind the pupil is taught to spread the lift webs apart to prevent any further twisting.

Double-arm descent training tower (*fig.* 5 *and* 6)

15. This apparatus is described in detail in A.P. 2655, Vol. 1, (2*nd Edn*,), Sect. 5, Chap. 22, and consists principally of the following components :-

(1) A main tower with a stairway giving access to a working platform 72 ft. above the ground.

(2) An upper tower which supports a double-arm rotating jib.

(3) A descent cable, for each arm of the jib, which passes over the necessary arrangement of pulleys and is connected to a pneumatic machine which controls the rate of descent of the pupils.

(4) A suspension frame, at the free end of the descent cable, with four suspension webs to which the pupil's lift webs are attached by snap-hooks.

(5) A drift cable which is connected by a traveller and a catch wire to the suspension frame so that the latter follows the run of the drift cable as the pupil descends.

16. The tower provides experience at a height which affords a pupil valuable familiarisation with the conditions that prevail during the critical final stages of a parachute descent and developes his confidence. As with other training devices the suspension arrangements are such that the typical yield characteristics of the lift webs of a developed parachute are simulated. The rate of descent is controlled by the discharge of air, at a fixed rate, from the pneumatic system. Therefore the rate at which individual pupils descend will vary according to the weight of the individual as in an actual parachute descent. The jib is rotated so that it is as nearly as possible at right-angles to the direction of the wind; drift is adjusted and controlled by an instructor at ground level using the drift cable. The pupil ascends to the platform, fits his harness and his lift webs are attached by the snaphooks to the suspension webs. A safety gate is opened, the pupil takes up the correct position and on the command from the instructor, takes a slight lift on his lift webs and allows himself to swing off the platform. When his swing is sufficiently regulated the instructor releases a cable brake and the pupil descends to the ground.

Sequence of instruction

17. The tower provides the nearest approach in training to an actual parachute descent; on this apparatus the pupils can be taught the full flight procedure and when this is completed, be lowered to the ground at a regulated speed as if in the final stages of a descent. During the descent the pupils are instructed in maintaining good parachuting positions and to watch the ground. The sequence of instruction is as follows :-

(1) Take-off holding lift webs, look up, observe, seat strap, parachuting position, descend and land.

(2) As in (1), but additionally practising pulling down on front and back lift webs and detailed checks of parachuting position, descend and land.

(3) Complete drill from exit position to landing.

(4) Repeat (3) but additionally practice all emergency drills.

(5) Training with P.W.C., exit position, lowering of P.W.C., descend and land.

(6) Repeat (5) with full flight drills.

(7) Repeat (6) but additionally practice all emergency drills.

RESTRICTED

CHAPTER 6

PARACHUTE LANDING TECHNIQUE

Chapter 6

PARACHUTE LANDING TECHNIQUE

LIST OF CONTENTS

	Para.		Para.
Introduction	.. 1	*Direct sideways landing*	.. 8
Objective	.. 3	*Diagonal backward landing*	.. 9
The landing position	.. 6	*Diagonal forward landing*	.. 10
Directional landings	.. 7	*Change of direction*	.. 11

LIST OF ILLUSTRATIONS

	Fig.		Fig.
Direct sideways landing	.. 1	*Diagonal forward landing*	.. 3
Diagonal backward landing	.. 2		

Introduction

1. Parachute landing is the third and final phase of the descent. It begins when the body first makes contact with the ground and ends when the parachutist is at rest and the parachute canopy is completely deflated.

2. If a landing is made correctly, even in unfavourable weather conditions, injury is improbable; but if a landing is made incorrectly it is more than probable to result in an injury. It has been said that a landing technique need not be taught because a supple man will never hurt himself, but military parachutists cannot all be supple, and experience gained in training many thousands of normal soldiers has proved beyond doubt that a simple landing technique is necessary and will prevent injury to the average parachutist if faithfully carried out.

Objective

3. The two main objects that a landing technique aims to achieve are:—
    (1) To absorb the impact shock by distributing it evenly over the body.
    (2) To allow only those parts of the body which are best suited to absorb the impact shock to come in contact with the ground.

4. The object of absorbing the impact shock is achieved by allowing the body to flex at the ankles, the knees, the hips and the back, then to collapse and roll, so that the shock is progressively absorbed by the maximum surface of the body coming in contact with the ground.

5. The second object is achieved by allowing the body to fall so that the impact shock is taken along the side of the leg, the thigh, the buttocks and diagonally across the rounded back to the opposite shoulder. In this way, the vulnerable parts of the body are kept clear of the ground.

The landing position

6. To achieve a landing in the correct manner the body must be in the correct position when the initial contact is made with the ground; this is called the landing position. It is basically the parachuting position, differing slightly in accordance with the direction of the approach to the ground, i.e.,
    (1) Feet together and parallel to the ground, legs slightly bent with the knees together.
    (2) Back rounded, head forward, chin on chest and with the eyes watching the ground.
    (3) Hands grasping the lift webs with a secure grip.
    (4) The whole body semi-relaxed to allow the landing to be made without resistance to the ground, yet sufficiently tense to maintain control.

Directional landings

7. The actual direction of landing is often unpredictable during conditions of oscillation so a parachutist must learn to land in any direction. For this reason the sequence of instruction is as follows:—
    (1) Direct sideways landing.
    (2) Diagonal backward landing.
    (3) Diagonal forward landing.

The detailed technique for each of these landings is described in para. 8 to 10, and progressively illustrated in fig. 1 to 3.

Direct sideways landing (*fig.* 1)

8. A direct sideways landing is often very comfortable to perform and one that can be undertaken by a parachutist with confidence. When approaching the ground in a sideways direction a parachutist must let up on the side to which he is drifting, i.e., the right or left arm will be fully extended. He should then watch the ground by looking under his extended arm. The legs are pushed slightly into the line of drift just before the touch down; this helps to make touch down on the flat of the soles with the feet together. This is the chief difficulty in an otherwise comparatively easy landing. As the feet touch the ground the upper part of the body should be turned so that the end of the roll may be taken on the back of the rounded shoulders.

Diagonal backward landing (*fig.* 2)

9. When approaching the ground in a backward direction, a parachutist should be pulling down on his forward lift webs and the rest of his body should be in a parachuting position. As the ground is approached his legs should reach slightly backwards from his hips to take the initial shock. If, as the feet touch the ground the direction is slightly diagonal to left or right of the line of drift, a landing will be made in that direction. His head should be kept well forward and the upper half of his body turned so that the normal roll can be made. If the approach is directly backward his lower limbs should be turned slightly off the line of drift so that a successful backward landing can be made.

Diagonal forward landing (*fig.* 3)

10. The term forward direction throughout this section means an obliquely forward direction. When approaching the ground in a forward direction a parachutist should be pulling down on his back lift webs and the rest of his body should be in the parachuting position. If, as the feet touch the ground, the direction is slightly diagonal to left or right of the line of drift, a landing will be made in that direction. The upper half of the body is turned and the subsequent roll is made so that the rounded back takes its full share of the landing shock. If the approach is directly forward the legs should be turned slightly off the line of drift so that a successful forward diagonal landing can be made.

Change of direction

11. It must be fully understood that a change of direction can take place during the last stages of flight and that the direction of landing should not be decided upon until the feet are about to make contact with the ground. If the body is held in a perfect parachuting position a late adjustment can easily be made and a smooth landing will follow.

RESTRICTED

Fig. 1. Direct sideways landing

Fig. 2. Diagonal backward landing

RESTRICTED

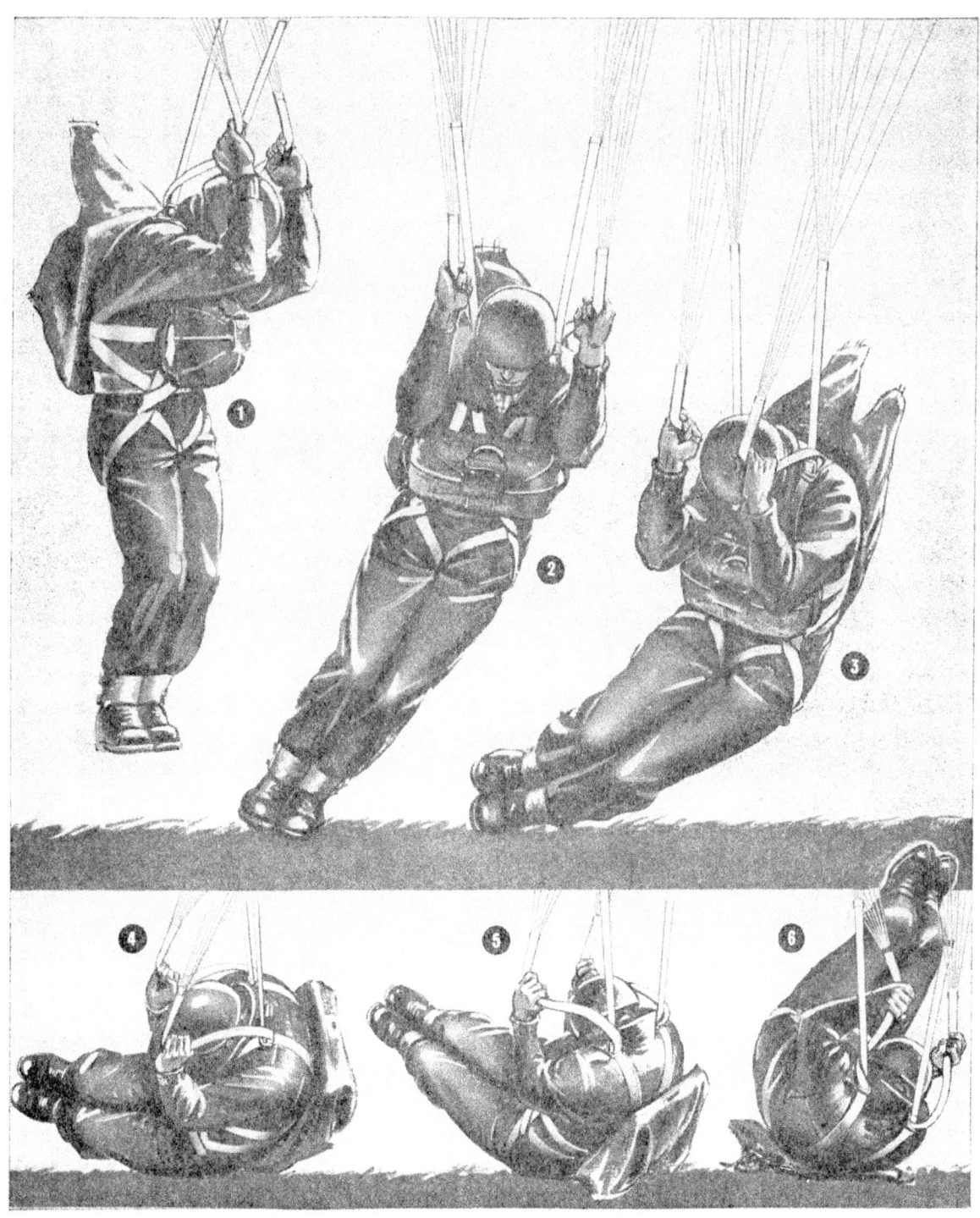

Fig. 3. Diagonal forward landing

A.P.4215, Sect. 3, Chap. 7
A.L.14, June 61

CHAPTER 7

**PARACHUTE LANDING
TRAINING APPARATUS**

RESTRICTED

F.S./1 A.P.4215, Sect. 3, Chap. 7
A.L.14, June, 61

Chapter 7

PARACHUTE LANDING TRAINING APPARATUS

LIST OF CONTENTS

	Para.		Para.
Introduction	1	Progressive landing trainer	11
The matted area	2	Sequence of instruction	12
Sequence of instruction	3	Slide landing trainer	13
Elastic fall trainer	4	Sequence of instruction	14
Sequence of instruction	6	Wheel landing trainer	15
Jumping platforms	7	Sequence of instruction	16
Sequence of instruction	8	Block and tackle flight and landing trainer	17
Ramps	9	Fan descent trainer	18
Sequence of instruction	10	Double-arm descent training tower	19

LIST OF ILLUSTRATIONS

	Fig.		Fig.
Elastic fall trainers	1	Progressive landing trainer	5
Jumping platforms	2	Slide landing trainers	6
Low ramp	3	Wheel landing trainer	7
High ramp	4		

RESTRICTED

Introduction

1. All training apparatus is to be inspected as detailed in Unit Standing Orders. Before use it must be ensured that all working parts of any apparatus are serviceable and that the matted landing areas form a smooth and continuous surface. Parachute training aids are described in A.P. 2655, Vol. 1, (2nd Edn.), Sect. 5. The following apparatus is available for the instruction of pupils in parachute landing training technique (*Chap.* 6):-

   (1) The matted area.
   (2) Elastic fall trainer.
   (3) Jumping platforms.
   (4) Ramps.
   (5) Progressive landing trainer.
   (6) Slide landing trainer.
   (7) Wheel landing trainer.
   (8) Block and tackle flight landing trainer.
   (9) Fan descent trainer.
   (10) Double-arm descent training tower.

The matted area

2. A large part of a hangar floor is thickly and continuously covered with landing mats, or mattresses overlaid with landing mats, in the area where the landing positions and the elementary falls are practised to develop the technique of landing in all directions.

Sequence of instruction

3. The sequence of instruction is as follows:-

   (1) Sideways landing positions.
   (2) Sideways landings with support, i.e., with an instructor holding the wrist of the pupil to assist him through the fall, and keep his shoulder clear of the ground.
   (3) Sideways landings with support, i.e., pupil assisting pupil.
   (4) Sideways landings without support.
   (5) Backward landings followed by forward landings in the sequence of (2) to (4).
   (6) Landings in all directions, with and without support, wearing a dummy reserve parachute, when all pupils have attained a reasonable standard of performace.

Elastic fall trainer (*fig.* 1)

4. The elastic fall trainer consists of two loops of webbing or rope, separated to shoulder width by a spacer bar and suspended from a beam. The length of the loops depends on the height of the beam from the ground. A loop of $\frac{5}{16}$ in. dia. elastic cord, approximately 4 ft. long, is attached to the bottom of each webbing or rope loop, and terminates in another loop of double webbing to form a hand-grip which simulates a parachute lift web. The hand-grips should be some 5 ft. from the ground but this may be varied to suit individual pupils.

5. The purpose of the apparatus is to provide support for the pupil when practising elementary landings and to assist him in keeping his shoulder away from the ground.

Fig. 1. Elastic fall trainers

Fig. 2. Jumping platforms

Sequence of instruction

6. The sequence of instruction is as follows:-

(1) The pupil stands directly under the beam, grips the lift webs and adopts a sideways landing position. He is to practise sideways landings and is to retain his grip on the lift webs throughout each practice fall.

(2) The pupil will then practice backward and forward landings as in (1).

(3) Landings in all directions are then to be practised, wearing the dummy reserve parachute, when the pupils have attained a reasonable standard of performance.

(4) The trainer can be used, in the sequence of instruction for the matted area, between the practices of landing with support (*pupil assisting pupil*) and landings without support (*para. 3, sub-para. (3) and (4)*).

Jumping platforms (*fig. 2*)

7. These are wooden platforms, approximately one and two feet high which are placed round the matted area. They are used when teaching the pupils the execution of a landing from a height and how to fall in any direction. The instruction is given initially from the lower platform and subsequently from the higher platform.

Sequence of instruction.

8. The sequence of instruction is as follows:-

(1) The pupil, wearing a dummy reserve parachute, is to stand on the lower platform in a sideways landing position and then step off the platform in the landing position. When practising landings to the right he is to step off with the right foot leading and bring his feet together before touching the ground. When practising to the left the left foot will lead.

(2) When the landing position has been practised and correctly performed, the fall will be practised with support, i.e., with an instructor assisting the pupil. There is to be a slight pause between the pupil's landing on the mat and the execution of the fall, to allow the instructor to observe and correct faults in the landing position. As the pupil's performance improves the pause is to be reduced, until a continuous movement of stepping off, landing and falling is achieved in practice.

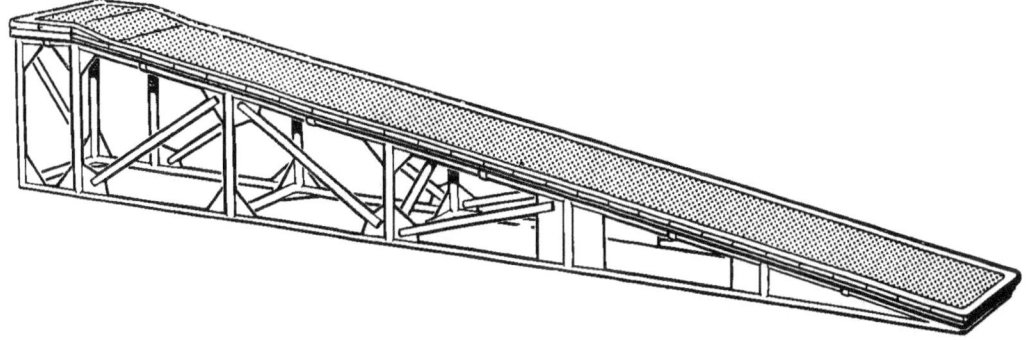

Fig. 3. Low Ramp

RESTRICTED

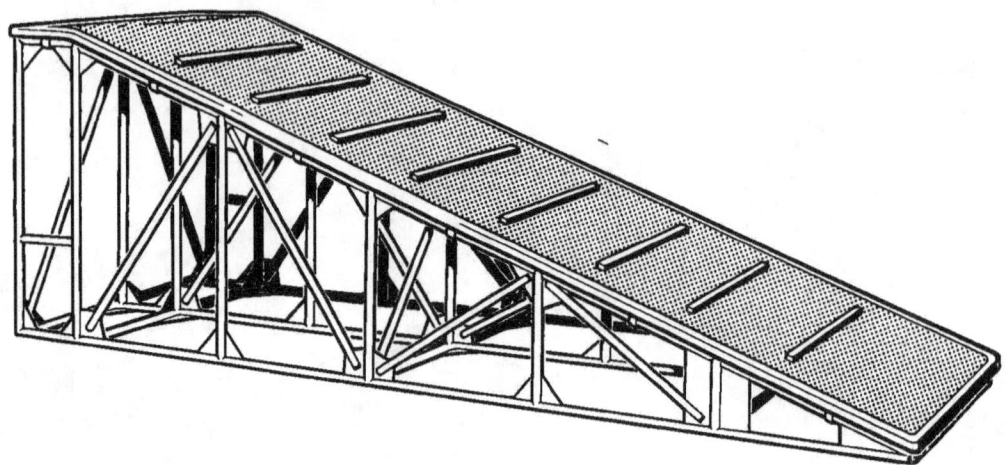

Fig. 4. High ramp

(3) Sideways landings and falls without support are then to be practised.

(4) Backward, followed by forward landing positions and falls are to be practised in a similar sequence to (1) to (3).

(5) All directional landings and falls are then to be practised, with and without support, from the higher platform.

Ramps (*fig.* 3 *and* 4)

9. The 'low' and 'high' ramps, 2 ft. and 4 ft. high respectively, each have a level area at the top as a jumping platform. The wooden upper surface of the ramps is covered with coir matting. The purpose of the ramps is to provide a means of attaining progressively increasing height and momentum during the training in landing and falling.

Sequence of instruction

10. The sequence of instruction is as follows:—

(1) The pupil is to wear a dummy reserve parachute, walk up the low ramp and step off the platform; the right foot is to lead, for forward and sideways landings to the right, and the left foot for forwards and sideways landings to the left.

(2) As the pupil steps off the ramp he is to adjust his body so that he lands in the correct attitude for the fall being practised. The instructor is to assist the pupil by holding the pupil's wrist which is nearest to the line of fall. All falls are to be made along a line parallel to the line of the ramp.

(3) The pupil is then to practise forward and sideways falls without support.

(4) The pupil is to progress to running gently up the ramp and practising forward and sideways falls without support.

(5) The pupil's run up the ramp is to be made increasingly faster as his performance improves.

Fig. 5. Progressive landing trainer

RESTRICTED

Fig. 6. Slide landing trainers

(6) Further progression is to be made by introducing the high ramps.

(7) Backward landings are to be practised as in para. 7 and 8.

Progressive landing trainer (*fig.* 5)

11. The apparatus consists of two lengths of webbing, separated to shoulder width by a spreader bar, and suspended from the hangar roof by a single cable. The two lengths of webbing below the spreader form hand-grips which represent parachute lift webs and terminate approximately 6 in. above the floor. Steps are positioned at a predetermined distance from the suspended apparatus. The space below the suspended apparatus which constitutes the landing area must be completely covered with matting which must extend, without gaps, to the foot of the steps. The purpose of this apparatus is to enable forward landings to be practised from progressively higher take-off positions. By standing on a step, grasping the lift webs and then stepping off the pupil will automatically be pulled through the forward fall.

RESTRICTED

Fig. 7. Wheel landing trainer

Sequence of instruction

12. The sequence of instruction is as follows:—

(1) The pupil, wearing a dummy reserve parachute, is to stand on the first step, grasp the lift webs and adopt a forward landing position.

(2) He is to step off as in para. 7 and retain his grasp of the lift webs. As he swings near to the ground the cable will pull him forward through the fall.

(3) When a reasonable standard of performance has been attained the pupil will progress to the second step and continue to practise forward landings.

(4) When the pupil has progressed as far as the third and higher steps he will find it necessary to take-off differently, and will swing off by pulling on the lift webs. At this stage, when a pupil swings off the steps the instructor must ensure that the pupil lands with his legs directly underneath his body.

Slide landing trainer (*fig. 6*)

13. The slide component of this apparatus is similar to a water chute, sloping downwards from a platform approximately 12 ft. high and terminating approximately 5 ft. above the landing area. Two bold white lines (*progression marks*), are painted on the sides of the slide to indicate the training starting positions. Directly above the slide a spacer bar attachment with two handgrips (*lift-webs*), is suspended from a cable. The cable passes over the bottom pulley on a carrier and the free end is anchored to a roof girder above the lower end of the slide. The carrier runs, on its top pulley, on a fixed horizontal cable also anchored between the roof girders above the slide. A rope is attached to the carrier and passes through a block and tackle arrangement suspended from a roof girder above and behind the platform of the slide. The bottom sheave of the block and tackle is anchored by a cord elastic bridle. As a pupil, holding the lift webs, slides down the chute, the spacer bar cable carrier is drawn forward along the fixed cable against the effort exerted by the cord elastic bridle. When the pupil lands and releases the lift webs the bridle draws the carrier and the spacer bar back to, and above, the top of the slide platform. The landing area must be completely covered with mattresses overlaid with landing mats. The purpose of the slide trainer is to provide practise in supported forward falls; three exercises are performed on this trainer according to the progress of the pupil. It should be noted that landings are practised with support, either from the instructor or by using the lift webs.

Sequence of instruction

14. The sequence of instruction is as follows:—

(1) The pupil, wearing a dummy reserve parachute, is to sit on the slide with his feet on the lowest progression mark and with his hands gripping the sides of the slide. His feet and legs are to be together, knees slightly bent, the upper part of the body leaning well forward, shoulders rounded, head forward with his chin on his chest and his eyes looking at the landing area.

(2) For a forward right landing the pupil is to extend his right arm forward and his left arm upwards. As the pupil's feet leave the end of the slide the instructor is to grasp the pupil's right hand. The pupil is to turn the lower part of his body across the line of drift; he is to complete his fall with the instructor assisting in turning his shoulder away from the ground. For forward left landings the positions of the arms are reversed.

(3) After practice, progress is made by starting from the higher progression mark on the slide.

(4) After (3), when starting from the top of the slide, the lift webs are used for support during the landing. The pupil is to sit in the starting position, grasping the lift webs and with his arms slightly bent. As he moves down the slide he is to extend his arms fully upwards, and is to retain his grip on the lift webs throughout the fall.

Wheel landing trainer (*fig. 7*)

15. This apparatus consists of an octagonal ring or wheel, approximately 21 inches in diam., of welded steel tube suspended from a hangar roof girder by a pair of four-wire bridles. The height of the wheel above the hangar floor can be varied to suit individuals and the landing area

RESTRICTED

below it is to be covered with mattresses overlaid with landing mats. The trainer provides practice in landings in all directions, with and without support. The pupil jumps up and grasps opposite sides of the wheel with his hands; he is then pushed by other pupils so that he swings to-and-fro. By changing his grasp to other sides of the wheel the pupil can face in different directions, relative to the direction of the swing of the wheel.

Sequence of instruction

16. The sequence of instruction is as follows:-

(1) The pupil, wearing a dummy reserve parachute, is to hang by his hands from the wheel as directed by the instructor.

(2) The instructor is to position himself so that he can grasp the pupil's wrist nearest to the line of the fall and so assist him to keep his shoulder clear of the ground.

(3) The pupil is to be swung sideways and, on the command from the instructor, is to release his grip on the wheel and complete his landing.

(4) In the earlier stages of this practice the pupil is to release his hold on the wheel at the end of the directional swing. As progress is made towards more dfficult landings the release of the hold on the wheel is to be made progressively earlier in the swing.

(5) The pupil is to change positions on the wheel so that all directional landings can be practised, with and without support.

Block and tackle flight and landing trainer

17. This apparatus, and its use in training in parachute flight techniques, is described in Chap. 5. It is also used for the practising of all directional landings, with particular emphasis on the preparation for directional landings. The sequence of instruction is as detailed in Chap. 5 but with the following additions:-

(1) Sideways landings are to be practised, the pupil being instructed to prepare for a landing in a specific direction.

(2) The pupil is to make progress by adjusting his landing position as he swings in turn to each side, i.e., he prepares for a right side landing as he swings to the right and vice-versa. At this stage the pupil will not be told on which side he is to release his hold on the wheel.

(3) Forward and backward landing progressions are as practised for the sideways landings. The instructor is to ensure that the pupil receives practice in presenting both the left and right sides of his body to the ground.

(4) In all landings, the point at which the hauling line of the block and tackle is released is to be such that the pupil lands in the centre of the landing area. Progression is achieved by releasing the pupil at increased speeds as the practises continue.

Fan descent trainer

18. This apparatus and its use are described in Chap. 3. When in use as a landing trainer the aim is to accustom the pupil to a vertical approach to the ground. The sequence of instruction is as follows:-

(1) On the command STAND IN THE DOOR, the pupil, wearing a steel helmet, and a dummy reserve parachute, will adopt the correct position except that he will grasp the lift webs of the harness.

(2) On the command GO he is to step forward clear of the take-off platform and immediately adopt the landing position.

(3) As the pupil approaches the ground he is to move his legs to the correct position for the direction of the landing being practised.

Double-arm descent training tower

19. This apparatus and its use are described in Chap. 5. During training on this apparatus the instructor is to ensure that each pupil is given instruction in all directional landings. This is to be achieved by rotating the parachute harness on the lift web attachment points.

RESTRICTED

A.P.4215, Sect. 3, Chap. 8
AL.6, Nov. 60

CHAPTER 8

PARACHUTE HARNESS RELEASE AND DRAGGING

RESTRICTED

Chapter 8

PARACHUTE HARNESS RELEASE AND DRAGGING

LIST OF CONTENTS

	Para.		Para
Introduction	1	*Other methods of release*	3
Main method of release	2	*Emergency measures*	4

LIST OF ILLUSTRATIONS

	Fig.		Fig.
Main method of release	1	*Releasing the harness*	3
Running to leeward of the parachute	2	*Emergency method*	4

RESTRICTED

Fig. 1. Main method of release

Introduction

1. When a parachutist has completed his fall his immediate action must be to release himself from his parachute harness, primarily to get into action quickly, and secondly to avoid being dragged along the ground by a wind inflated parachute canopy.

Main method of release (*fig.* 1)

2. A parachutist is to lie on his back and release one hook of the reserve parachute, then turn and press the quick release box (Q.R.B.). He is then to roll over, face the canopy and pull the rigging lines nearest to the ground, hand over towards him, thus collapsing the canopy. Having pulled the canopy to him he is to roll over on to the canopy to prevent re-inflation. He can then remove the reserve parachute, pull his weapons container to him and remove his parachute harness.

Other methods of release

3. Two other methods of release are taught to parachutists and they are:—
   (1) Regaining his feet and running around the canopy (*fig.* 2), so that he is to leeward of the parachute canopy. In this position the parachute canopy will deflate. The parachutist is then to lie on the conopy and remove his reserve parachute and parachute harness.
   (2) The parachutist is to lie on his back, (*fig.* 3 *Detail* 1), release one hook of the reserve parachute, then turn and press the Q.R.B., free his leg straps (*fig.* 3, *Detail* 2), and free one arm from his harness (*fig.* 3, *Detail* 3). He is then to turn away from his reserve parachute on to the front of his body, raise his other arm and allow the parachute to pull his harness clear (*fig.* 3, *Detail* 4).

Fig. 2. Running to leeward of the parachute

RESTRICTED

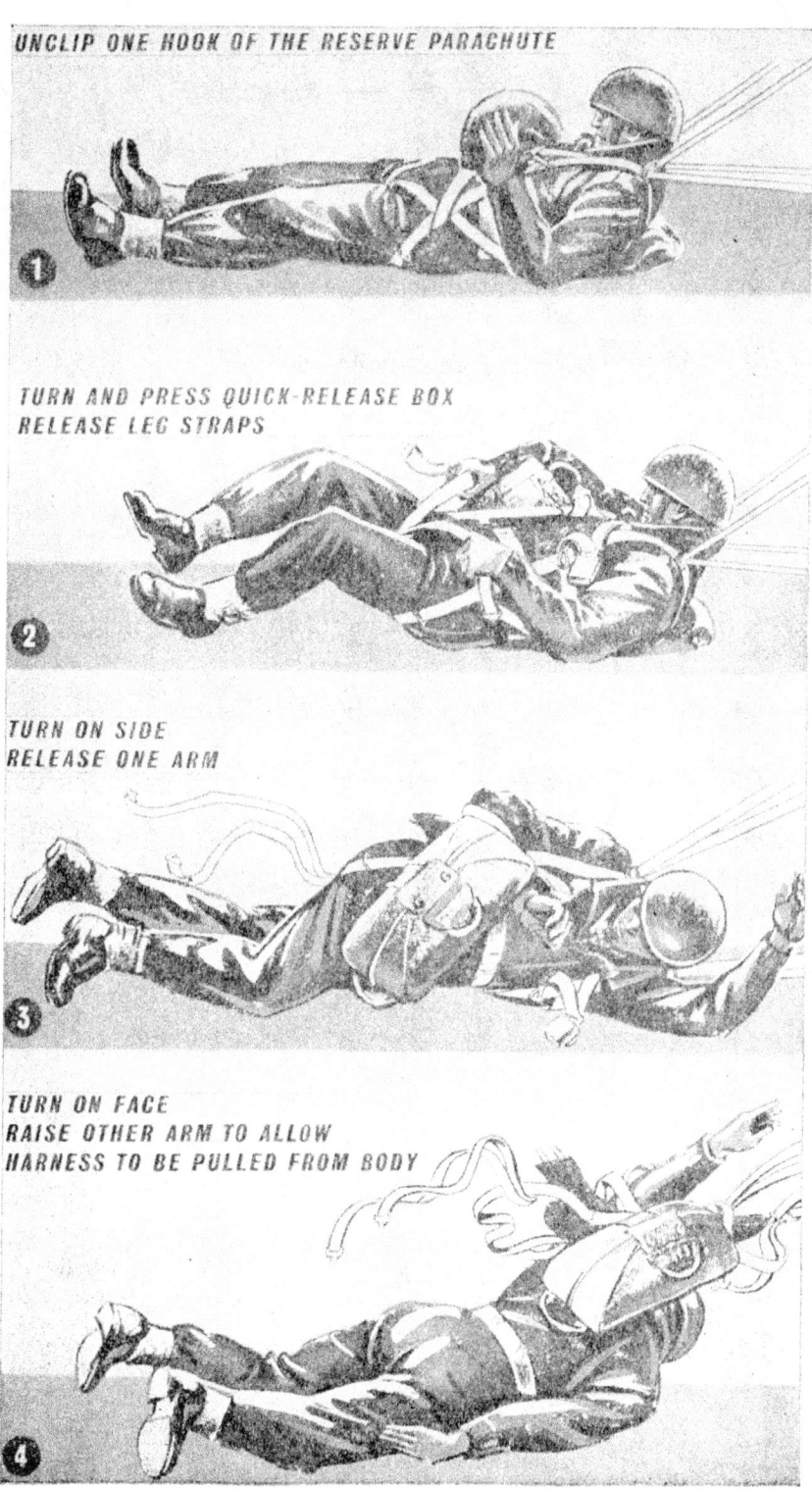

Fig. 3. Releasing the harness

Fig. 4. Emergency method

Emergency measures (*fig.* 4)

4. In addition to the methods outlined in para. 2 and 3 the following emergency methods are also taught:—

(1) To assist an injured man or to recover a container the peripheral band or apex of the parachute is to be grasped and the canopy pulled into wind. This will deflate the canopy and prevent further dragging.

CHAPTER 10

LECTURES AND FILMS

Chapter 10

LECTURES AND FILMS

LIST OF CONTENTS

	Para		Para
Introduction	1	*The weapons and personal equipment container*	16
Essential lectures	2	*Airfield procedure*	17
Opening address	3	*Parachutist's life-jacket*	18
Syndicate officer's introductory address	4	*Containers, other than suspended loads*	19
Exit technique	5	*The history of parachuting*	20
Flight technique	6	*Final address*	21
Landing technique	9	*Additional activities*	22
Aircraft drill	12	*List of essential films*	23
Emergency aircraft drills	13	*List of film strips*	24
The parachute assembly	15	*Miscellaneous films of general interest*	25

Introduction

1. Parachuting is a practical activity, and is best taught by practical methods and physical practise in the skills and techniques involved. In practical activities and the teaching of physical movements, the best results will be obtained when the practical work is based upon sound theoretical knowledge. Therefore, lectures are a fundamental part of the scheme of training at a Parachute Training School (*P.T.S.*). It is the task of the syndicate officer or other officer concerned to deliver these lectures, which all instructors concerned with a particular syndicate or course are to attend.

Essential lectures

2. These lectures cover all aspects of parachute training and parachuting applicable to Airborne Forces, and are designed in content and sequence of delivery, to give the maximum degree of foundation to the practical work and a natural progression of training. The position of the lectures in the sequence of training is given in the Transport Command Standard Syllabus for Parachute Training. All lectures are to be adequately prepared and, where applicable, should be illustrated by films and the various other visual training aids, listed at paragraphs 23 to 25. The lectures detailed below, and outlined in subsequent paragraphs, are to be given to the pupils under training at the appropriate phase of the course:—

   (1) Opening address
   (2) Syndicate officer's introductory address
   (3) Exit technique
   (4) Flight technique (*Parts* 1 *and* 2)
   (5) Landing technique
   (6) Aircraft drills
   (7) Emergency aircraft drills
   (8) The parachute assembly
   (9) The weapons container
   (10) Airborne life-jacket
   (11) Airfield procedure
   (12) C.L.E. containers
   (13) History of parachuting
   (14) Final address

Opening address

3. This is delivered by the Officer Commanding, or the Squadron Commander responsible for the intake. The content of the address is normally to be as follows:—

(1) A welcome to the Parachute Training School (*P.T.S.*) and to the Station, on behalf of the Station Commander and the Royal Air Force generally.

(2) An outline of the organization of the Station, showing how the P.T.S. is dependent on the other Wings which provide the necessary services required for parachute training.

(3) A brief outline of the courses held at the School, with particular emphasis on the type of course concerning those present.

(4) An outline of the organization of the course Staff—Squadron Commander, Syndicate Officers and N.C.O. and Section instructors.

(5) The development and importance of the close link between the pupil and the instructor.

(6) The standard of discipline required—on and off duty.

(7) The factors affecting training:—
   (a) Ground training:—repetition
   (b) Parachuting:—weather and availability of aircraft.

(8) An affirmation that the aim of everyone on the school staff and on the Station is solely to produce capable and confident parachutists.

Syndicate officer's introductory address

4. After the opening address, each Syndicate Officer of the course is to give an introductory address to his respective syndicate, covering the following points:—

(1) *Standing Orders:*—As applicable to the trainees, bounds, access to aircraft, smoking, dress and general discipline.

(2) *Ground training hangar:*—Emphasis that the ground training hangar is out of bounds during non-working hours, and that training apparatus is not to be used unless under the supervision of an instructor.

(3) *Medical:*—The importance of the pupil's physical fitness, that the section instructor must be informed of any injuries sustained prior to the course, and of any other injury or ailment sustained during the course.

(4) *Discipline:*—That self-discipline is the keynote of behaviour, both off and on duty. An explanation that control is the secret of success in parachuting.

(5) *Punctuality:*—That all parades will be attended punctually. Unpunctuality may result in the omission of training and the delaying of parachuting programmes.

(6) *Details of Course:*—The breakdown of training, system of progression and the necessity for repetition. The allocation of instructors to small sections and an introduction of the syndicate staff.

(7) *Questions:*—The invitation of questions from the trainees.

Exit technique

5. The lecture on exit technique will normally follow the "Exit Technique" film and will deal with side door and floor aperture exits; it should include the following:—

(1) Aim of exit
(2) Achieving the aim
(3) Side door exits (*port and starboard*)
   (a) STAND-IN THE DOOR positions
   (b) The physical actions of exit
   (c) The compact exit position
(4) Floor aperture exit. Detail as for side door exits.
(5) Apparatus to be used during exit training
   (a) Mock doors
   (b) Fan exit trainer
   (c) Balloon car (*floor aperture*)
   (d) Stick exit trainer

Flight technique

6. The lecture on flight technique will be in two parts. The first will follow the "Flight Technique" film and deal with the theory of flight technique as applicable to a normal straight-forward descent; the second will follow the film "The Reserve Parachute", and will deal with the various additional drills necessitated by double door jumping and emergencies.

7. *Part* 1. This should include the following:—
(1) Aim of flight technique
(2) Describe factors affecting flight:—
   (a) Vertical descent
   (b) Drift
   (c) Oscillation
(3) Achieving the Aim:—
   (a) Damping oscillation—primary factor
   (b) Reducing drift
   (c) Correct lift webs for various directions of drift
   (d) Pulling down—high and controlled
   (e) Preparation for landing—body position
(4) Other Factors:—
   (a) Conditions of no positive drift
   (b) Changes of direction
(5) Sequence of drill:—
   (a) Look up
   (b) All round observation
   (c) Seat strap
   (d) Parachuting position
   (e) Assess drift
   (f) Correct lift webs—pulling down
   (g) Prepare for landing

8. *Part* 2. This should include the following:—
(1) Reason for additional flight drill:—
   (a) Introduction of double door aircraft
   (b) Avoidance of collisions—all round observation, steering.
   (c) Collisions—spread eagle—disentanglement
(2) Emergencies:—
   (a) Twists
   (b) Landing in trees
   (c) Landing in water
   (d) Abnormal main canopy, recognition of blown periphery and reasons for blown peripheries.
(3) Sequence of drill, including additional drill:—
   (a) Look up
   (b) Action for abnormal main canopy
   (c) All round observation
   (d) Action to prevent entanglement
   (e) Action if entangled
   (f) Kicking out of twists
   (g) Steering—avoiding action
   (h) Seat strap
   (j) Parachuting position
   (k) Assess drift
   (l) Correct lift webs—pulling down
   (m) Prepare for landing

Landing technique

9. The lecture on landing technique will normally follow the "Landing Technique" film and be given after the pupils have completed a number of landing training periods.

10. The aim of the landing technique is to avoid injury; this is achieved by:—

(1) Learning to absorb the impact shock by distributing it evenly over the maximum length of the body.

(2) Learning to allow only those parts of the body best suited to absorb the shock to come into contact with the ground.

11. The lecture should include the following:—
   (1) Aim of landing technique
   (2) Achieving the aim:—
      (a) Comparison of the technique with a gymnastic fall, and explain why the latter is unsuitable
      (b) Spreading the impact shock
      (c) Directional landings
      (d) Landing positions
      (e) Landing training apparatus

Aircraft drill

12. The lecture on aircraft drill will normally follow the "Aircraft Drill" film and will outline the drill for the particular types of aircraft from which the pupils will jump. The purpose of the lecture is to emphasise to the pupil the necessity for controlled actions in the aircraft, to ensure the safety of all concerned, and to enable good exits and even sticks to be achieved. Explain the following drill procedures with emphasis as necessary:—
   (1) Inspection of aircraft by instructors
   (2) Emplaning drill
   (3) Take-off—necessity for safety belts
   (4) PREPARE FOR ACTION—hooking up
   (5) "STAND-UP"—clearing strops
   (6) "CHECK EQUIPMENT"—strop holding
   (7) "TELL-OFF"
   (8) "ACTION STATIONS"—strop carrying and shuffle step
   (9) "GO"—movement forward and correct release of strops
   (10) Differences for port and starboard sticks for side door exits
   (11) Differences for port and starboard sticks for floor aperture exits

Emergency aircraft drills

13. The lecture on emergency aircraft drills is to be given in conjunction with the "Emergency Aircraft Drill" film before the first air-experience flight of the course; it should cover the following drills for the types of aircraft to be used:—
   (1) Introduction—Explain why the drill is necessary, but emphasise that emergencies are rare occurrences. Quote examples from incidents in the 1939-45 war.
   (2) Ditching drill
   (3) Crash landing drill
   (4) Abandoning aircraft in the air

14. Full details of the emergency drills for the Beverley and Hastings aircraft will be found in Section 5.

The parachute assembly

15. The lecture on the parachute assembly is to be given at an early stage in the training in order to familiarize the pupils with the correct handling of the parachutes, and to demonstrate the method of deployment of the main and reserve parachutes. The lecture should include the following:—
   (1) The title of the assembly—Parachute, assembly, Type "X", Mk. 4
   (2) A demonstration of correct handling of parachutes
   (3) A demonstration of how the parachute and harness should be worn and the main points which will ensure a correctly fitting harness.
   (4) A demonstration deployment of a main parachute
   (5) A demonstration deployment of a reserve parachute
   (6) The details of the canopy and harness construction of the main parachute
   (7) The details of the canopy and attachments of the reserve parachute

The weapons and personal equipment container

16. The lecture on the Container, weapons and personal equipment, parachutist, commonly known as the "weapons container", is to be given in conjunction with the "Weapons Container" film and after the pupils have completed at least one descent from an aircraft. The lecture should include the following:—
   (1) The purpose of the container
   (2) A description
   (3) The equipment that can be carried in the container
   (4) The inspection of the container before packing
   (5) The packing of the container—the centre section and the weapons sleeve
   (6) Servicing the container
   (7) Fitting the container
   (8) Exit
   (9) The flight—emergencies and jettisoning
   (10) Landings
   (11) Action after landing

Airfield procedure

17. The lecture on airfield procedure is to be based on information contained in Transport Command Standard Operational Procedure (*T.C.S.O.P.*) and the current Airborne Directives. It is delivered to all pupils to familiarize them with the organization at the take-off airfield, and is to include information and/or explanations concerning the following:—
   (1) *Airfield Control:*—How the Airborne Control Officer (*A.C.O.*) in charge of the Airborne Control Section (*A.C.S.*) is linked with the R.A.F. and Army units, and issues the necessary airfield procedure for M.T. as detailed in Appendix H, Section 3 of Airborne Directives.
   (2) *Duties of A.C.O:*—As detailed in Appendix G, Section 3 of Airborne Directives.

(3) *Report Centres:*—How these are directly linked with the Air Traffic Control Section (*A.T.C.*), and are manned by A.C.O. staff and unit representatives. How and why all requests for assistance are to be made to Report Centres.

(4) *Dispersal Areas:*—How these are normally organized on a Squadron basis for the disposal of aircraft

(5) *Marshalling Areas:*—The arrangements which are made for aircraft which will normally be marshalled in these areas prior to take-off.

(6) *Aircraft Parking Plans:*— Explain how an aircraft parking plan is prepared by the A.C.S., and that a copy is issued to each Stick Commander. How each aircraft is marked with a "Chalk number" corresponding to the number of the stick that it will carry

(7) *Vehicle Markings:*—How vehicles are marked with the "chalk number"

(8) *Action at Airfield:*—

(a) *Bombing-up containers:*—Why this is normally done one day before the day of jumping (*i.e. Jumping day minus one* = $D-1$), and that this is the responsibility of the R.A.F. assisted by working parties from Units. That if containers are not bombed-up on $D-1$ they will be carried to the airfield in the same vehicle as their aircraft load.

(b) *Fitting parachutes:*—That this is also normally done on $D-1$, and that care must be taken to ensure that parachutists wear all their equipment at that time to avoid last minute alterations to harness etc. How stick commanders are to supervise the fitting of harnesses and parachutes, and ensures when this task is completed that the parachutes are stacked under arrangements made by A.C.O'S. How parachutes are marked with the user's name and stick number, and that a spare parachute is to be available for each aircraft.

(c) *Spare aircraft:*—That Stick Commanders must know the location of the spare aircraft, what to do if their aircraft becomes unserviceable and the policy concerning the priority of loads. That the final responsibility for transferring loads rests with the A.C.O.

(d) *Sanitary arrangements:*—That ground and airborne arrangements are the responsibility of the A.C.O.

(e) *Blankets:*—Why parachutists must be kept warm during flight, and that one blanket per man must be carried in the aircraft on flights in winter or of long duration.

(f) *Organised rest:*—To provide for the maximum rest for all concerned for the 24 hours prior to take-off, how the programme for $D-1$ must be organised.

(g) *The duties of the Stick Commander:*—That the Stick Commander is responsible for the following:

(i) Supervising the issue and fitting of parachutes and equipment.
(ii) Flight manifests.
(iii) Inspection of the stick, parachutists and equipment.
(iv) Explanation how and order that men jump on the green light signal.

(v) The delivery of the sticks, ready for inspection and emplaning, to the No. 1 Parachute Jumping Instructor (*P.J.I.*) at the aircraft.

Parachutist's life-jacket

18. The lecture on the life-jacket is to be given to all pupils on basic training, to parachutists prior to a flight over water and to parachutists making planned descents into water. The lecture should include the following:—

(1) The purpose of the life-jacket
(2) Description
(3) Inspection and servicing
(4) Fitting
(5) Method of inflation
(6) Action in emergencies. (Ditching and abandoning the aircraft)
(7) Action in making planned descents into water
(8) Action in the water

Containers, other than suspended loads

19. The lecture on containers is to be given to all pupils on basic training, and is to include the following:—

(1) The purpose of the C.L.E. Container
(2) A description of container and parachutes used
(3) Packing the container
(4) Fitting the parachute
(5) Loading the container
(6) Types of loads
(7) System of dropping the containers
(8) The use of the delay-opening device

The history of parachuting

20. The lecture "History of Parachuting" is to be given to all R.A.F. trainees as Parachute Jumping Instructors; it may also be given to Army trainees when time permits. Officers preparing this lecture should refer to the books and papers listed below; the substance of the lecture should be as indicated in sub-para. (1) to (4):—

Parachutes in Peace and War .. Low
Parachuting .. .. .. Dixon
Prelude to Glory .. .. .. Newham
The History of Parachuting .. J. C. Tristen

(1) *Introduction:*—
(a) The definition of the word "parachute" in the Oxford dictionary
(b) Earliest records—sketches by Leonardo da Vinci
(c) The first recorded parachute descents
(d) The introduction of balloons and parachute descents from them

(2) *Early descents from balloons:*—
(a) Records of descents from balloons
(b) Personnel who made the earliest descents
(c) Inventors of parachutes

RESTRICTED

(d) Main points of progress from 1783 to the first descents from aircraft

(e) Varied construction and success of different types of parachutes

(3) *Early descents from aircraft:*—

(a) Record of the early use of parachutes, as a means of escape from aircraft

(b) Personnel who experimented from aircraft

(c) The construction of early types of parachutes used from aircraft

(d) Acceptance of parachutes for use by Air Forces

(4) *Military parachuting:*—

(a) First recorded use of parachute troops by Russia

(b) Large scale manoeuvres by Russia in 1936

(c) The build-up of the German Parachute Corps from 1936 to 1939

(d) The use of German Parachute Troops early in the war 1939 to 1945

(e) The formation of the British Airborne Forces

(f) Requirements for, and design of the statichute

(g) The formation of the Central Landing Establishment (*C.L.E.*) at Ringway

(h) Early descents

(j) Types of aircraft and balloons used

(k) Introduction and improvement of exit, flight and landing techniques

(l) Introduction of various types of aircraft with different types of exits

(m) Introduction of weapon—and equipment—carrying personnel

(n) The build-up of the British Airborne Units

(o) Operations during the war 1939 to 1945

(p) Introduction of new aircraft and equipment from 1945 to the present day

Final address

21. The final address will follow the presentation of "Wings" to the successful pupils and will be delivered by the Officer Commanding the Parachute Training School. It should include the following:—

(1) A summary of the results

(2) Reiteration of the necessity to treat parachutes and parachuting with respect, and at all times to follow the basic drills that have been taught

(3) Explanation that there is a close link between the Parachute Training School Staff and the various airborne formations, and that there is an R.A.F. Detachment with all airborne formations to supervise continuation training, exercises and operational work.

Additional Activities

22. Where it is necessary to introduce additional subjects of interest the following lectures, films and visits, may be arranged:—

(1) *Lectures of general interest:*—

(a) Meterology—By Meterological Office Staff

(b) Pilot's Lecture—By an experienced pilot

(2) *Parachuting films of general interest:*—

(a) Airborne Soldier

(b) Operation Market

(c) Operation Varsity

(d) Test Drop

(e) Pegasus

(f) German Training Film

(3) *Visits:*—

(a) To Transport Command Parachute Servicing Unit (*T.C.P.S.U.*) R.A.F., Upper Heyford, for demonstrations of servicing, maintenance and packing of parachutes.

(b) To R.A.F., Watchfield, for demonstrations of supply dropping, and the servicing, and packing of supply dropping equipment by the R.A.S.C.

List of essential films

23.

Ref. No.	Title	Running time mins.
14L/5254	The Parachute	10
14L/5254	Landing Technique	20
14L/5254	Hastings Aircraft—Drill	10
14L/5254	Hastings Aircraft—Emergency Drills	10
14L/5941	Introductory Film	20
14L/5943	Suspended Loads (Weapons Container)	20
14L/6355	The Reserve Parachute	10
14L/6357	Exit Technique	20
14L/6359	Parachute Flying Technique	20

List of film strips

24.

Ref. No.	Title	Running time mins.
14J/466	The Reserve Parachute	20
14J/468	Personal Parachutist Equipment—(*Weapons Container*)	20
14J/532	Double Door Exit Technique	20
14J/533	Parachute Flying Technique	20
14J/534	Parachute Landing Technique	20
14J/535	Hastings Aircraft—Parachute Drill	10
14J/N.I.V.	The Parachute	20

25. Miscellaneous films of general interest

Ref. No.	Title	Running time mins.
—	Invasion of The Lowlands	20
—	Test Drop (*American*)	10
2873	Operation Market	10
4555	Operation Varsity	20
6297	Airborne Soldier	30
14L/5254	Hastings Aircraft—Stick Commander's Duties	10
14L/5395	Pegasus	40
14L/5641	Jungle Operations—Air Supply in Malaya 1949-50	20

A.P.4215, Sect. 4

SECTION 4

PRACTICAL PARACHUTING

RESTRICTED

A.P.4215, Sect. 4

SECTION 4

PRACTICAL PARACHUTING

List of Chapters

1 Introduction

2 Balloon descents

3 Aircraft descents

4 Night descents

5 Water descents

6 Free fall descents

CHAPTER 1

INTRODUCTION

Chapter 1

INTRODUCTION

LIST OF CONTENTS

	Para.		Para.
General	1	*The descents*	6
The Weather	2	*Dress*	8
Wind speeds	3	*The parachuting programme*	9
Ground surface	4	*Implementing the programme*	14
Availability of aircraft or balloon	5		

General

1. It is a natural progressive sequence for the first parachute descent to follow instruction on the advanced ground training apparatus, as it is at this stage of instruction that the pupil parachutist should have reached the peak of his proficiency on ground training apparatus. The instructor must satisfy himself that each pupil is ready to make a parachute descent, and that his proficiency during the ground training phase has reached the required standard. Several factors are involved in the conducting and control of the parachuting programme; some of these factors can produce undesirable physical and mental strain on the pupils. The one that effects pupils most directly is delay. This results in tiredness and emotional fatigue, which in turn affects morale and the standard of performance. Factors which may cause delay are as follows:—

   (1) The weather

   (2) Availability of balloon or aircraft

The weather

2. For the first time during the training of a pupil parachutist, the weather begins to exert a controlling influence on the training programme. It is important during the first few descents that the weather conditions should be as favourable as possible, therefore accurate weather forecasting becomes very important, as does a strict and thoughtful appreciation of "On the Spot" weather conditions. The effects of weather conditions on parachuting will be dealt with in Sect. 1, Chap. 3.

Wind speeds

3. The following maximum ground wind speeds are to be applied to parachute descents made during basic and refresher courses:—

   (1) First four descents—10 m.p.h. (8.7 *knots*)

   (2) Descents from aircraft or balloons at night—10 m.p.h. (8.7 *knots*)

   (3) All other descents from aircraft or balloons—15 m.p.h. (13 *knots*)

Ground surface

4. Frost or drought cause hard surfaces which produce an increased injury rate, and if the dropping zone (*D.Z.*) is frozen or sun baked, allowance must be made for these conditions when assessing the favourability of conditions for parachuting.

Availability of aircraft or balloon

5. Although the availability and servicing of aircraft and balloons is not the direct responsibility of the Parachute Training School. Instructors, they have their parts to play in ensuring that aircraft and balloons are ready for parachuting at the correct time. Instructors are to check the aircraft detailed and are to satisfy themselves that it is serviceable for parachuting. Similarly the balloon should be checked for serviceability before parachuting is due to commence. In this way, much can be done to ensure that unnecessary delays and long periods of stand-by are avoided. Details of aircraft and balloon checks are outlined in Section 5.

The descents

6. The number of descents required for qualification as a parachutist is eight, normally consisting of two descents from a balloon and six from an aircraft. One of the descents from an aircraft is to be made at night, and two descents are to be made carrying suspended loads. The Territorial Army Courses consist of seven descents, four of which may be balloon descents. There is no night descent on the Basic Territorial Army Course. The sequence of and details of descents are outlined in Chapter 3.

7. There is a great temptation, when weather conditions are suitable, to permit pupils to carry out two, or even three descents in one day, particularly if a course is behind its schedule. However, experience has shown that this practice of hastening jumps is not a good policy to pursue. Instruction is not assimilated, co-ordinations are inaccurate and the incidence of injury shows a marked increase, as the pupils are in a state of

RESTRICTED

physical strain and mental weariness. A period of discussion and briefing, in addition to corrective ground training, should follow each parachute descent and not more than two descents should be made in any twenty-four hour period.

Dress

8. The Army pupils' dress for all parachute descents is to be as follows:—

(1) Army pattern boots (*Commando type with rubber soles and heels*)
(2) Gaiters or puttees
(3) Denim trousers
(4) Jumping smock
(5) Waist belt (*worn under smock*)
(6) Steel helmet (*Parachutist type*)

The parachuting programme

9. When planning a parachuting programme, consideration must be given to an alternative programme, so that in the event of parachuting being postponed or cancelled, little or no training time is wasted. When the normal training subjects have been exhausted, additional film displays and ground training revision should be given. A list of suitable films and lectures is detailed in Sect. 3, Chap. 10. Further activities which may be used are as follows:—

(1) Visit to a parachute packing section
(2) Visit to a heavy drop and air despatch sections
(3) Recreational training

10. Having considered the weather forecast, the Squadron Commander is to plan the parachuting programme for his course, in close liasion with the Support Squadron Commander, who is responsible for the allocation of the available aircraft and/or balloons. The Squadron Commander is to brief the Syndicate Officers, who then complete their syndicate programmes on the operations board. Syndicate Officers will in their turn brief the instructors and pupils for a particular descent in accordance with the briefing instructions detailed in Sect. 3, Chap. 11.

11. The Operations Officer is to arrange for the publication of the programme and is to ensure that the following detail is completed:—

(1) That the unit providing the aircraft or balloon is informed of the emplaning and the take-off times, and in the case of ballooning, the time at which the balloon is to be positioned on the D.Z., and whether the car is to be prepared for door or aperture exits.

(2) That the parachute section is notified of the number of parachutes required and the time that they are to be issued.

(3) That the Medical Officer is notified of the dropping time and the D.Z. to be used.

(4) That the D.Z. Safety Officer is informed of the dropping time, stick composition and the number of lift from aircraft and/or balloon.

(5) That the Parachute Training School Warrant Officer is given the details of the programme

12. The Parachute Training School Warrant Officer is to arrange for the following:—

(1) The detailing of the Marshaller, Despatchers, Parachute fitters, Drifter and the D.Z. party (*for aircraft programmes only*).
(2) Transport as required.
(3) Early and late meals, if and when required.

13. When the parachuting programme is arranged for early morning, it may be necessary in view of uncertain weather conditions to have a further weather forecast prior to the parade time of the parachutists and aircrew. In this instance, an Officer Parachute Jumping Instructor is to be detailed to examine the forecast and to decide if parachute jumping is to take place or not. The decision made is to be passed on to the following sections:—

(1) The duty Supervisor P.B.X. (*Telephone exchange*)
(2) Air Traffic Control
(3) Station Sick Quarters
(4) Main Guardroom
(5) Operations

Implementing the programme

14. When a course parades for parachuting, the Squadron Commander is to check with the D.Z. Safety Officer, as to the actual weather conditions at the D.Z. If the weather conditions are suitable, the D.Z. Safety Officer is to prepare the D.Z., as required, for a balloon and/or an aircraft parachuting programme. Details of D.Z. signals and lay-outs are dealt with in Section 7. If weather conditions are unsuitable, the Squadron Commander is to arrange for the alternative programme to be implemented. The Marshaller is to inform the sections detailed in para. 13, of any changes in the published programme.

RESTRICTED

CHAPTER 2

BALLOON DESCENTS

Chapter 2

BALLOON DESCENTS

LIST OF CONTENTS

	Para.		Para.
Introduction	1	Recording N.C.O.	17
Door and aperture descents	2	The balloon programme	18
Staff responsibilities	8	Demonstration descents	19
Equipment	9	Pupils' descents	20
Inspection of balloon	10	Control of descents	21
D.Z. Duties	11	Balloon cable angle	22
Officer in charge of Parachuting	12	Pupils' balloon descent details	23
Syndicate Officer	13	First descent	24
Flight Sergeant in charge of D.Z. Duties	14	Second descent	25
N.C.O. in charge of Signal Flags	15	Balloon passengers, other than pupils	26
Despatcher	16		

Introduction

1. The balloon fills the important role of providing the pupils with their first parachute descent in conditions of exit and flight similar to, but easier than, those met with in descents from aircraft. The pupil is under the control of the Instructor in the balloon car, until after he has made his exit and then because of the lack of noise he is able to absorb the instruction given him from the ground. The absence of slipstream reduces the possibility of loss of body position during the exit. By virtue of the fact that the points of release and landing are known, the Syndicate Officer is able to position the loud hailer so that the pupil receives the maximum instruction throughout his descent.

Door and aperture descents

2. The pupils are mustered in their normal sections of eight, then each section is divided into sticks. Pupils then fit their parachutes and are inspected by the Despatcher, who checks the fitting of their harness, the main parachute and the reserve parachute. The Despatching Instructor will wear a main parachute; his reserve parachute and jumping helmet will be stowed in the balloon car. The Instructor then marches the stick into the balloon car and ensures that the static lines are secured in the normal manner.

3 When all the pupils are hooked up and the safety bar secured in the safe position, the Despatcher is to call out to the winch driver, the number of feet the baloon is to be allowed to ascend to and the number of parachutists jumping, e.g., UP 800 FEET, FIVE MEN JUMPING. To ensure that there is no error, the winch driver is to repeat the order.

4. Once the balloon is at the dropping height, and the signal to start despatching is received, the Despatcher is to undo the safety bar and despatch the pupils. The pupils are to carry out the drills, as laid down, throughout their balloon descents. It cannot be stressed too strongly, that it is only during balloon descents, when only one parachutist need be in the air, that the Syndicate Officer can give his full attention to one man, thus ensuring that the maximum instructional value is gained from the descent.

5. During the first two descents, the pupil is spoken to on the loud hailer immediately after his exit and given instructions which call for quick reaction. A pupil must have an opportunity to carry out the flight technique he has learned during the ground training phase. A complete record of each descent should be made by the recording N.C.O., so that corrections can be given after the descent.

6. When a pupil has landed he must carry out his D.Z. drills, as instructed by the Syndicate Officer at the briefing. At this time, the pupil is usually greatly elated and a little confused, and is, therefore, liable to forget the ultimate aim of military training. The pupil must learn the necessity for immediate action after landing. Simple tasks must be set for him to carry out; to ensure immediate reaction and control. He must collapse his parachute canopy, remove his harness (*using the operational method*) and report to the Recording N.C.O. without delay. Tests of this nature accustom the pupil to the fact that parachuting is a means to an end, and that the end is not achieved when he arrives on the ground but that his military work then begins.

RESTRICTED

7. The pupils are debriefed by the Syndicate Officer, who makes use of the recording proformae to analyse individual faults. The ensuing ground training periods are planned to give practice in the parachuting phase which produced the most faults.

Staff responsibilities

8. When it is confirmed that a balloon parachuting programme is to be implemented, the Officer in charge of Parachuting is to arrange for the Syndicate Flight Sergeant to supervise the drawing and fitting of parachutes, the recording of parachute serial numbers by sections, and the movement of the sections and the equipment to the D.Z.

Equipment

9. The equipment required for use in the D.Z. is as follows:—
   (1) Loud hailer
   (2) Megaphone for emergency use
   (3) Velometer
   (4) Ambulance flag
   (5) Red, yellow and blue signal flags
   (6) Aldis lamp, complete with coloured glasses if required
   (7) An adequate supply of P.T.S. Form 8, (Sect. 1, Chap. 5)

Inspection of balloon

10. The Officer in charge of Parachuting is to carry out a check of the balloon car and balloon rigging, as detailed in Sect. 5, Chap. 4. The balloon is then to be run up to the operating height without troops in the car, to check the security of the balloon rigging and to assess the upper wind speed and direction.

D.Z. Duties

11. The personnel required to supervise a balloon parachuting programme are as follows:—
    (1) Officer in charge of Parachuting
    (2) Syndicate Officer
    (3) Flight Sergeant in charge of D.Z. duties
    (4) Section Instructors, allocated to the following duties:
        (a) N.C.O. in charge of Signal Flags
        (b) Despatchers
        (c) Recording N.C.O.

Officer in charge of Parachuting

12. The Squadron Commander is normally the Officer in charge of Parachuting, but in his absence the duty is undertaken by the Syndicate Officer whose syndicate is to parachute. He is responsible for all the parachuting and the organisation during the programme. He is to ensure that a Medical Officer and an ambulance are in attendance throughout the programme

Syndicate Officer

13. The syndicate Officer is responsible for giving the instructions to the pupils during descents, and is to ensure that the loud hailer is positioned and used in such a manner as to be of maximum benefit to the pupils. In the event of an injury or an abnormality, the Syndicate Officer is to ensure that necessary action as detailed in Chapter 3 has been taken.

Flight Sergeant in charge of D.Z. Duties

14. The Flight Sergeant in charge of D.Z. Duties is responsible to the Syndicate Officer for the supervision of the Section Instructors and the allocation of duties on the D.Z.

N.C.O. in charge of Signal Flags

15. The N.C.O. in charge of Signal Flags is responsible for giving the appropriate instructions to the N.C.O. in charge of the Balloon Crew and for controlling the jumping, by passing the appropriate signals to the Despatcher. The methods of controlling the descents from the balloon are outlined in para. 21 to 25.

Despatcher

16. The Despatcher is responsible for carrying out the Despatcher's Duties as detailed in Sect. 5, Chap. 4 and 5 (*Balloon Car Drills*).

Recording N.C.O.

17. The Recording N.C.O. is responsible for the completion of the P.T.S. Form 20 and ensuring that the details recorded are accurate, in order that the Syndicate Officer concerned will have a correct assessment of each pupil's standard of performance. In the event of an injury or an abnormality, the Recording N.C.O. is to take the necessary action as outlined in Chapter 3.

The balloon programme

18. When the Syndicate Officer has positioned the balloon and the loud hailer, and the various N.C.O. have been allocated to the duties outlined in para. 14 to 17, the Flight Sergeant in charge of D.Z. Duties is to marshall the pupils at the loud hailer position.

Demonstration descents

19. Before pupils make their first parachute descent from the balloon, the Officer in charge of Parachuting is to arrange for demonstration parachute descents to be made by Instructors. The Syndicate Officer is to describe to the pupils the various actions that are demonstrated. The Instructors are to jump in the following sequence, and carry out the actions as detailed:—
   (1) *No.* 1: Carry out the duties of a drifter, i.e., refrain from controlling the drift of his parachute except when preparing for his landing, or any appropriate emergency action. This will enable the Officer in charge of Parachuting to check the positioning of the balloon winch and make any corrections that he may consider necessary.
   (2) *No.* 2: A normal descent
   (3) *No.* 3: A descent including a demonstration of the spread-eagle position and steering
   (4) *No.* 4: A descent with a suspended load (*P.W.C.*)
   (5) *No.* 5: Operation of the reserve parachute

RESTRICTED

Pupils' descents

20. The Flight Sergeant in charge of D.Z. Duties is to marshall each section, as required, from the loud hailer position to the balloon winch position, where they are then handed over to the Despatcher. The Despatcher is to check, emplane and despatch the pupils as detailed in Sect. 5, Chap. 4 and 5.

Control of descents

21. Descents are controlled by the N.C.O. in charge of Signal Flags, who is to position himself in such a manner that he can assess the angle of the balloon cable, pass verbal instructions to the N.C.O. in charge of the Balloon Crew and be seen by the Despatcher. The three methods of passing signals to the Despatcher are as follows:—

(1) *Flags:*—These are used when visibility is good and the flags can be seen clearly by all concerned. The signal system is as follows:—

   (a) *Blue*—Clearance to despatch

   (b) *Yellow*—Do not despatch, stand by

   (c) *Red*—Do not despatch, the balloon is being close hauled

(2) *Loud hailer combined with flags:*—This combination is used when the Despatcher is unable to recognise the flag signals. It may be necessary to arrange a system whereby the N.C.O. in charge of Signal Flags, signals to the Syndicate Officer, who in turn passes the instructions over the loud hailer to the Despatcher.

(3) *Aldis Lamp:*—An aldis lamp is used when balloon descents take place at night. The signal colours are the same as for signal flags (*sub-para.* (1)).

Balloon cable angle

22. The N.C.O. in charge of Signal Flags is responsible for checking the balloon cable angle. In conditions of little or no wind, when there is insufficient angle to the balloon cable to permit descents to be made, he is to arrange for the winch chassis to be driven slowly into wind to create and maintain the necessary angle of the balloon cable. He is to ensure that the appropriate signals are made to the Despatcher, i.e., when the angle is insufficient, the "yellow" is to be shown and the "blue" only when it is safe for despatching. The winch chassis driver is not to be relieved without reference to the Syndicate Officer.

Pupils' balloon descent details

23. As only two balloon descents are allocated to each course, full use must be made of each descent to instruct the pupil in general descent technique as detailed in para. 24 and 25.

First descent

24. (1) *Exit:*—The pupils are to be despatched singly from the door at a height of 800 feet. Only one pupil is to be in the air at any one time, in order that he may receive the maximum instruction through the loud hailer.

(2) *Flight:*—After the parachute canopy has developed, the pupil is to carry out normal parachute flight technique with instruction from the ground.

(3) *Action after landing:*—After landing, the pupil is to release himself from his harness, using the operational method of harness release and dragging, (*Sect. 3, Chap. 8*), and report as quickly as possible to the Recording N.C.O. at the loud hailer position, and give his name and section number. He is then to recover his parachutes and return them to the parachute container.

Second descent

25. (1) *Exit:*—Details are similar to those for the first descent from the balloon, except that the exit will be made through the floor aperture.

(2) *Flight:*—In addition to normal parachute flight technique, the pupil is to practice steering and the spread-eagle positions.

(3) *Action after landing:*—After landing, the pupil is to release himself from his harness, using the operational method of harness release and dragging, and then continue as detailed for the first descent from the balloon.

Balloon passengers, other than pupils

26. The carriage of passengers, other than those on a recognised parachute training course, in a balloon car must be authorised by The Officer Commanding the Parachute Training School, who will decide whether Indemnity Forms are to be completed.

CHAPTER 3

AIRCRAFT DESCENTS

Chapter 3

AIRCRAFT DESCENTS

LIST OF CONTENTS

	Para.
Introduction	1
Details of descents	2
First descent	3
Second descent	4
Third descent	5
Fourth descent	6
Fifth descent	7
Sixth descent	8
Descents from Beverley aircraft—upper deck	9
The parachuting programme	12
Duties of D.Z. Party for day descents—	
Officer in charge of Parachuting	13
Syndicate Officers	14
Flight Sergeant in charge of D.Z. Party	15
Centre Signal N.C.O.	16
Recording N.C.O.	17
Transport N.C.O.	18
Equipment N.C.O.	19

	Para.
Duties of D.Z. Party for night descents—	
Officers in charge of Parachuting	20
Syndicate Officers	21
Flight Sergeant in charge of D.Z. Party	22
Centre Signal N.C.O.	23
Recording N.C.O.	24
Transport N.C.O.	25
Duties at take-off airfields, day and night descents	26
Marshaller	27
Parachute fitter	28
Drifter	29
Despatchers	30
Injuries in the D.Z.	31
Methods of signalling for the ambulance—	
Descents from balloon by day	32
Descents from aircraft by day	33
Descents by night	34
Abnormalities	35
Recording	39

Introduction

1. The six parachute descents from an aircraft can be considered as the final step towards the completion of the pupil's training, and as such should be undertaken with circumspection and with an understanding of the problems and the new sensations to be encountered by the pupil. Since there are six aircraft descents to be completed, it is necessary to ensure that the descents programme is progressive in all aspects. The sequence in which the qualifying parachute descents are made will depend on the type of aircraft available.

Details of descents

2. In order to achieve progression during the parachuting phase, the following specific actions are detailed for each descent. The details for exit are given as for a Hastings aircraft, or the lower deck of a Beverley aircraft. Details of the drills and sticks when the descents are from the upper deck of the Beverley aircraft are outlined in para. 9 to 11.

First descent

3. (1) *Exit:* The pupils are to be despatched at a height of one thousand feet in consecutive sticks of three, i.e., three pupils from the starboard side door followed two seconds later by three pupils from the port side door. On receipt of the "Green Light" despatching signal, the starboard stick Despatcher is to despatch his stick by ordering the first man GO, No. 2 GO, No. 3 GO at one second intervals. In addition to giving the command GO, he is to tap the man on the shoulder. Two seconds after No. 3 of the starboard stick is clear of the door, the port stick Despatcher will despatch the port stick in a similar manner to that of the starboard stick. Each pupil will make his exit on the executive word GO. As each pupil makes his exit, the man following is to move into the door and adopt the STAND IN THE DOOR position, ready to make his exit on hearing his number and the command GO.

(2) *Flight:*—For the first time, the pupils are in the air with other parachutists and may find it necessary to apply one or other of the

emergency techniques. Normal flight technique is to be applied but the pupils are to be aware of the proximity of other parachutists throughout the descent.

(3) *Action after landing:*—After landing, the pupil is to release himself from his harness using the operational method of harness release and dragging and then report as quickly as possible to the Recording N.C.O. He is then to recover his main and reserve parachutes and return them to the parachute container.

Second descent

4. (1) *Exit:*—The pupils are to be despatched at a height of one thousand feet in sticks of six, i.e., three pupils from the starboard side door simultaneously with three pupils from the port side door. On receipt of the "Green Light" despatching signal, the Despatchers are to despatch their sticks by ordering GO, "2", "3", at the same time tapping each man on the shoulder. No. 1 is to make his exit on the command GO and each successive pupil on hearing his number called. As each pupil makes his exit, the man following is to move into the door and adopt the STAND IN THE DOOR position, ready to make his exit on his number being called.

(2) *Flight:*—With simultaneous stick jumping, the pupils must be made to be aware of the greater danger of collision and are to be prepared to take avoiding action at an early stage of their descents.

(3) *Action after landing:* After landing, the pupils are to take similar action as detailed for the first descent.

Third descent

5. (1) *Exit:*—The pupils are to be despatched at a height of one thousand feet in sticks of 15, seven from one side door and eight from the other side door (*Hastings aircraft*) or ten from each side door (*Beverley aircraft*). Each pupil is to be despatched and is to make his exit as detailed for the second descent.

(2) *Flight:*—Action is as detailed for the second descent.

(3) *Action after landing:*—Parachute canopies are to be collapsed, using the operational method. Parachutists are to rendezvous (*R.V.*) on No. 4 starboard and double to the loud hailer position in stick order.

Fourth descent

6. (1) *Exit:*—The pupils are to be despatched at a height of one thousand feet at night, in single sticks of six, six from one side door and on a separate run-in of the aircraft, six from the other side door. After the equipment check has been completed, No. 1 Despatcher is to request the Captain of the aircraft to dim the interior lighting. On receipt of the "Green Light" despatching signal, the Despatcher is to despatch his stick by ordering GO, "2", "3", "4", "5", "6", at the same time tapping each man on the shoulder. No. 1 of the stick is to make his exit on the command GO, and each successive pupil on hearing his number called. As each pupil makes his exit, the man following is to move into the door and adopt the STAND IN THE DOOR position, ready to make his exit on his number being called. Parachutists are to be despatched at one second intervals.

(2) *Flight:*—Normal flight technique is to be applied but greater emphasis must be given to the landing position.

(3) *Action after landing:*—After landing, the pupils are to collapse their parachute canopies and release their harness, using the operational method. The pupils are to reply to the Syndicate Officer's check of the stick (*para.* 21), recover their parachutes, and return them to the container. Pupils are responsible for their own parachutes. To avoid losses, they must retain possession of them until they are handed in at the container.

Fifth descent

7. (1) *Exit:*—The pupils are to be despatched at a height of one thousand feet, in consecutive sticks of five, i.e., five from the starboard side door, followed two seconds later, by five from the port side door. Each pupil will be equipped with a personal weapon container (*P.W.C.*), with the weapon sleeves packed inside the body of the container. The pupils are to be despatched and are to make their exits as detailed for the second descent.

(2) *Flight:*—When each pupil is clear of other parachutists, he will lower his P.W.C. and then carry out normal flight technique.

(3) *Action after landing:*—After landing, the pupils will service their P.W.C. for carrying, roll up their parachutes and carry all equipment off the D.Z.

Sixth descent

8. (1) *Exit:*—The pupils are to be despatched at a height of one thousand feet, in sticks of 30 from a Hastings aircraft or in sticks of 40 from a Beverley aircraft. In the case of the Hastings aircraft, 15 from the starboard side door, simultaneously with 15 from the port side door. In the case of the Beverley aircraft 20 from the starboard side door simultaneously with 20 from the port side door. Each pupil will be equipped with a container packed with a weapon. The pupils are to be despatched and are to make their exits as detailed for the second descent.

(2) *Flight:*—As for fifth descent, but with more emphasis on steering and avoiding action prior to lowering their P.W.C.

(3) *Action after landing:*—After landing and collapsing their parachutes, the pupils are to service their P.W.C. for carrying, double to an R.V. with their P.W.C. on their backs and then carry out any ground exercise as detailed. The pupils will recover their parachutes after the detailed exercises have been completed.

RESTRICTED

Descent from Beverley aircraft—upper deck

9. The details of the descents are as follows:—

(1) *First and second descent:*—Single stick of six

(2) *Third descents:*—Single stick of ten

(3) *Fourth descent:*—A night descent in a single stick of six

(4) *Fifth descent:*—Single stick of ten with a P.W.C.

(5) *Sixth descent:*—Single stick of 15 with a P.W.C.

10. Actions to be taken in the aircraft are outlined as follows:—

(1) *First and second descent exits:* The pupils are to be despatched at a height of one thousand feet in sticks of six. The first stick of six from the aircraft is to consist of three men from the starboard side followed by three men from the port side, This action of taking three men from each side is to permit the seats near the aperture to be folded up and so give more space for the despatching of subsequent sticks. The remaining pupils are to be despatched in sticks of six from the starboard and port sides alternately. On receipt of the "Green Light" despatching signal, the Despatcher is to despatch the stick, No. 1 to No. 6 by shouting, each man's number followed by the word GO. e.g., "6" GO. Each pupil is to make his exit on the executive word GO. As each pupil makes his exit, the man following is to move forward and adopt the STAND IN THE DOOR position, ready to make his exit on the word GO.

(2) *Flight:*—Action in flight as detailed in para. 3 to 8 inclusive.

(3) *Action after landing:*—As detailed in para. 3 to 8 inclusive.

11. For the subsequent descents, the action to be taken is similar to that detailed in para. 3 to 9 inclusive.

The parachuting programme

12. When it is confirmed that an aircraft parachuting programme is to be implemented, the D.Z. party, consisting of the following personnel will proceed to the Dropping Zone.

(1) Officer in charge of Parachuting
(2) Syndicate Officers
(3) Flight Sergeant in charge of the D.Z. Party
(4) Centre Signal N.C.O.
(5) Recording N.C.O.
(6) Transport N.C.O.
(7) Equipment N.C.O. (*required only for descents with equipment*)

Duties of D.Z. Party for day descents

Officer in charge of Parachuting.

13. The Squadron Commander is normally the Officer in charge of Parachuting, but in his absence the duty is undertaken by the Senior Syndicate Officer on the course. He is responsible for all parachuting and organisation during the programme. He is to ensure that a Medical Officer and ambulance are in attendance throughout the programme.

Syndicate Officers

14. Syndicate Officers are responsible for giving instruction during descents, and are to ensure that the loud hailers are positioned and used in such a manner as to give the maximum benefit to the pupils. In the event of an injury or an abnormality, they are to ensure that the necessary action, as detailed in para. 31 to 34 inclusive, has been taken.

Flight Sergeant in charge of D.Z. Party

15. The Flight Sergeant in charge of the D.Z. Party is responsible to the Officer in charge of Parachuting for the supervision of the N.C.O. and their allocation to D.Z. duties.

Centre Signal N.C.O.

16. The N.C.O. at the centre signal is responsible for the recording of descents and any abnormalities on P.T.S. Form A.R.4, manning the field telephone and the passing of messages from or to the control tower. He is to inform the control tower if aircraft are dropping parachutists incorrectly.

Recording N.C.O.

17. The Recording N.C.O. are responsible for the completion of P.T.S. Form 20 and ensuring that the details recorded are accurate. It is essential that the recorded details are accurate so that the Syndicate Officer concerned will have a correct assessment of each pupil's performance. In the event of an injury or an abnormality the Recording N.C.O. is to inform the Officer in charge of Parachuting immediately.

Transport N.C.O.

18. The Transport N.C.O. is responsible for ensuring that transport is used in the most economical and efficient manner.

Equipment N.C.O.

19. The equipment N.C.O is responsible for the return of the equipment to the P.T.S. He is to ensure that all equipment is re-serviced correctly and that any unserviceable equipment is marked U/S and returned separately.

Duties of D.Z. Party for night descents

Officer in charge of Parachuting

20. Responsibilities are similar to those for day descents (*para.* 13).

Syndicate Officers

21. In addition to the responsibilities outlined for day descents (*para.* 14), the Syndicate Officers

are to check each stick after landing by calling each pupil's number in turn, e.g., NO 1 ARE YOU O.K. Each pupil, if uninjured, will reply in response to his number, e.g., NO. 1, O.K. When the check is complete and there are no injuries, the Syndicate Officer will report accordingly to the Officer in charge of Parachuting. When there are no injuries, the Officer in charge of Parachuting is to flash a green Aldis Lamp signal towards the control tower to indicate that the next stick may be dropped. The actions to be taken in the event of an injury requiring the ambulance are outlined in para. 31 to 34 inclusive.

Flight Sergeant in charge of D.Z. Party
22. Responsibilities are similar to those for day descents (*para.* 15).

Centre Signal N.C.O.
23. Responsibilities are similar to those for day descents (*para.* 16).

Recording N.C.O.
24. Recording N.C.O. are allocated, one per parachutist in each stick, and are responsible for contacting the parachutist when he lands. In the event of an injury, the Recording N.C.O. is to flash his torch in the dirction of the Officer in charge of Parachuting (*at the 'T'*), who will summon the ambulance. The Recording N.C.O. is to guide the ambulance to the casualty by flashing his torch. In the event of an abnormality he is to take the action as detailed in Para. 35 to 37 inclusive.

Transport N.C.O.
25. In addition to the responsibilities outlined for day descents (*para.* 18), the Transport N.C.O is to be in possession of a nominal roll for each syndicate jumping and is to check each pupil against the nominal roll as they hand in their parachutes at the container. This action serves as a check that all pupils are safely off the dropping zone.

Duties at take-off airfields, day and night descents
26. Whilst the D.Z. is being prepared and the D.Z. Party are on route to the D.Z., the following action is to be taken by the personnel allocated to the duties detailed in para. 27 to 30 inclusive.

Marshaller
27. The Marshaller is to be responsible to the Officer in charge of Parachuting for co-ordinating and supervising the programme at the take-off airfield, and recording details of the programme as required by P.T.S. Form 32. He is to inform the D.Z. of the details of loads and take-off times, and is responsible for co-ordinating transport requirements.

Parachute fitter
28. The Parachute fitter is to supervise the drawing and fitting of parachutes, and is responsible for recording the details of pupils and parachutes as required by P.T.S. Form 19. To enable the D.Z. Party to identify the sticks of parachutists in the air, the Parachute fitter is to arrange for the starboard stick to have white parachute canopies and the port stick to have khaki parachute canopies. For night descents all pupils must have khaki parachute canopies. He is to assemble the pupils in "stick" order and inspect their parachutes and equipment. On receipt of the instructions from the Marshaller, he is to march the pupils to the aircraft and pass details of the stick to No. 1 Despatcher.

Drifter
29. The Drifter is to draw and fit his parachute and emplane with the stick of pupils. He is to jump on his own at the start of each programme. The Drifter must be equipped in a similar manner as the pupils, i.e., with or without a P.W.C., and must conform to the standard aircraft drill and exit technique for the particular aircraft in use. He is to refrain from controlling his parachute flight except when preparing for his landing, or for any appropriate emergency action. After landing he is to recover his parachute and report to the N.C.O. in charge of the D.Z. Party for allocation to a D.Z. duty.

Despatchers
30. The number of Despatchers allocated will depend on the type of aircarft to be used. No. 1 Despatcher is to ensure that the aircraft is fully inspected and is servicable for parachuting in accordance with the inspection schedule which he is to sign. The duties of each Despatcher are detailed in Sect. 5, Chap. 1.

Injuries in the D.Z.
31. If a pupil slightly injures himself on landing but is capable of walking off the D.Z. without assistance, the Instructor nearest to him is to record the pupil's name and section, and then detail another pupil to escort him to the Medical Officer at the ambulance. As soon as possible after the incident, the Instructor is to check with the Medical Officer that the injured man did in fact report as instructed. If there is any doubt whatsoever as to the ability of the injured man to walk to the ambulance, the Instructor is to inform the Officer in charge of Parachuting who is to arrange for the Medical Officer and the ambulance to proceed on to the D.Z. The Instructor is to remain with the injured man until the casualty is taken over by the Medical Officer. The Instructor is to ensure that the injured man's parachute and equipment, if no abnormality has occurred, are removed from the dropping area. The action to be taken in the event of a fatal or serious accident is outlined in A.M.O. A.161/58.

Methods of signalling for the ambulance
Descents from balloon by day
32. When the attendance of the Medical Officer and the ambulance is required on the dropping area during descents from a balloon by day, the Officer in charge of Parachuting is to stop the parachuting, and authorise the ambulance to proceed to the dropping area by signalling with the ambulance flag (*white flag with red St. George's cross*) which is located at the loud hailer position.

RESTRICTED

Parachuting is to re-commence only when the ambulance has cleared the dropping area.

Descents from aircraft by day

33. To summon the Medical Officer and ambulance on to the dropping area during an aircraft programme by day, the request is to be passed to the Control Tower by the Officer in charge of Parachuting. The D.Z. Safety Officer will stop parachuting and authorise the ambulance to proceed to the dropping area. Parachuting is to re-commence only when the ambulance has cleared the dropping area.

Descents by night

34. To summon the Medical Officer and the ambulance on to the dropping area at night, the Recording N.C.O. with the injured man is to flash his torch towards the Officer in charge of Parachuting who is to inform the Control Tower by field telephone. The D.Z. Safety Officer will take action as for descent by day (*para*. 33). The Recording N.C.O. is to remain with the injured man and direct the ambulance to him by flashing his torch.

Abnormalities

35. All parachutes which show some form of abnormality are classified as follows:—

(1) *Grade 1:*—Slightly damaged canopies or non-persisting blown peripheries including complete inversions when the normal rate of descent is not noticeably increased.

(2) *Grade 2:*—Damaged canopies or persisting blown peripheries, e.g., simple two-lobe, when the rate of descent is so slightly increased that it can be considered as a safe rate of descent.

(3) *Grade 3:*—Badly damaged canopies or persisting blown peripheries with two or more lobes, when the rate of descent is considered to be unsafe, also when the opening of the canopy is delayed for a considerable time.

(4) *Grade 4:*—Severely damaged canopies, complete failure of squids, which would result in severe injury without the successful use of the reserve parachute.

36. All instructors on the dropping zone are to watch for abnormalities and make a mental note of the condition of the parachute and the actions of the parachutist.

37. When parachutes have been classified as Grade 1 or 2 abnormalities, the Recording N.C.O. is to instruct the pupil concerned to report with his parachute to the D.Z. Safety Officer.

38. All abnormalities which are graded 3 or 4 are to be assessed by the Officer in charge of Parachuting and/or the D.Z. Safety Officer; then after consultation with the Officer Commanding P.T.S. a decision will be reached as to whether or not a "PARAC" signal shall be sent and a Board of Inquiry initiated vide A.M.O. A161/58. If this action is taken, the parachutes and equipment if any are not to be disturbed and are to be left for investigation by the Board of Inquiry. The parachutist concerned is to be examined by the Medical Officer and made available for interview by the Board of Inquiry. All witnesses are to submit an individual written report as soon as possible after the incident. The aircraft, complete with all the parachuting equipment is to be impounded.

Recording

39. The D.Z. Safety Officer is to record the details of all abnormalities. The Centre Signal N.C.O. is to record the necessary information as required on P.T.S. Form A.R.4. Abnormalities are to be recorded by grade number, and if the reserve parachute was operated, the letter "R" in brackets is to be entered after the number, e.g., 2(R).

A.P. 4215, Sect. 4, Chap. 4
A.L.7, Dec. 60

CHAPTER 4
NIGHT DESCENTS

RESTRICTED

Chapter 4

NIGHT DESCENTS

1. The details of the Dropping Zone Party for night descents are detailed in Chap. 3, para. 20 to 25 inclusive.

2. Night descents are a practical proposition both operationally and under training, and are a requirement of The Parachute Regiment and The Special Air Service Regiment personnel. The amount of instruction that can be given is rather more limited in scope than in day descents, as it is more difficult to assess drift and the proximity to the ground.

3. If practised during training, it is an opportunity for the pupils to assess drift by the lights and any visible objects on the ground. In moonlight and on bright nights, the general outline of trees and large objects, and even the ground, are visible and since pupils only make night descents after completing four day descents, they should be sufficiently advanced to be able to use all visible aids to assess drift.

4. The Recording N.C.O. will position themselves close to the point where the pupils will be landing so as to be able to issue instructions and guidance during the last 100 feet of the pupil's descents.

5. It is important that the lights in the aircraft shall be dimmed as much as possible and particularly near the door. As soon as the stick is prepared for action, the lights should then be reduced to the minimum consistent with safe despatching. It is the duty of the No. 1 Despatcher to ensure that this is carried out.

6. Under training, night descents should not take place in winds in excess of 10 miles per hour.

7. Each parachutist will reply to his stick number when called upon to do so by the Syndicate Officer. This checks whether or not the parachutist is injured. Each parachutist will then maintain complete silence until he is clear of the D.Z.

CHAPTER 5

DESCENTS INTO WATER

Chapter 5

DESCENTS INTO WATER

1. The normal training of a parachutist does not require a descent into water to be included in the training syllabus, other than instruction on how to meet such an emergency should it arise.

2. It is, however, part of the duties of a Parachute Training School to be able to instruct in this aspect of parachuting and to be able to arrange a water dropping programme.

3. Water descents are required for trained personnel of the Royal Marine Corps, The Special Air Service Regiment and other specialist units. Instruction in the use of life-jackets, specialist suspended loads and the method of release from the parachute harness will be required (*Sect. 3, Chap.* 4).

4. The Dropping Zone must be carefully selected and it must obviously be clear of obstructions and surface craft. Retrieval boats must be available and a D.Z. Party provided. The system of D.Z. signals consists of a green winking Aldis Lamp on the control boat, which constitutes the release point for the aircraft which will be flying on a pre-determined run-in.

5. ◀ The number of parachutists in each stick is governed by the number of retrieval craft available. As a general rule there should be one retrieval craft available for each parachutist in the stick.▶ The aircraft shall not commence its next dropping run until the Officer in charge of Parachuting has signalled that the previous stick and their parachutes have been picked up and that the retrieval craft are clear of the D.Z.

6. The control boat is to be in R/T contact with the aircraft, and should this contact fail, Verey Lights can be substituted as follows:

 (1) *Green*—Clear to drop.
 (2) *Yellow*—stand-by, do not drop.
 (3) *Red*—Return to base, drop cancelled.

A.P.4215, Sect. 5

SECTION 5

AIRCRAFT AND BALLOON CAR DRILLS

RESTRICTED

A.P.4215, Sect. 5
A.L. 10, Apr. 61

Section 5

AIRCRAFT AND BALLOON CAR DRILLS

LIST OF CHAPTERS

1. Duties and responsibilities of despatchers
2. Inspections before emplaning
3. Inter-communication drill
4. Mk.3 Balloon car drill—Side door exit
5. Mk.3 Balloon car drill—Floor aperture exit
6. Valetta aircraft drill—Training
7. Valetta aircraft drill—Operational
8. Valetta aircraft—Emergency drill
9. Hastings aircraft drill—Training
10. Hastings aircraft drill—Operational
11. Hastings aircraft—Emergency drill
12. Beverley aircraft drill—Lower deck
13. Beverley aircraft drill—Upper deck
14. Beverley aircraft—Emergency drill
15. Twin Pioneer aircraft drill—Operational

RESTRICTED

CHAPTER 1

DUTIES AND RESPONSIBILITIES OF PARACHUTIST DESPATCHERS IN AIRCRAFT

Chapter 1

DUTIES AND RESPONSIBILITIES OF PARACHUTIST DESPATCHERS IN AIRCRAFT

LIST OF CONTENTS

	Para.		Para.
Introduction	1	Opening and removing parachutist exit doors	13
Complements of despatchers	5	Closing and replacing parachutist exit doors	14
Duties of despatchers	6	Strops	15
No. 1 despatcher	7	Methods of folding strops	16
Despatcher in charge of a stick	8	Intercom. drill in aircraft	17
Assistant Despatcher	9	Method of passing instructions	18
Duties of an Air Quartermaster	10	Example of intercom. sequence	19
Strop retrieval	11		

LIST OF ILLUSTRATIONS

	Fig.
Method of folding strops, Beverley aircraft (upper deck only)	1
Method of folding strops, Hastings aircraft	2

Introduction

1. In operational aircraft or aircraft employed on continuation training, the parachutist despatcher in charge of despatching operations will be a Parachute Jumping Instructor (P.J.I.); he may be assisted by an additional P.J.I. and/or an Air Quartermaster (A.Q.M.). In aircraft employed on basic parachutist training, the despatcher in charge of despatching operations will be a P.J.I.; he may be assisted by one or more P.J.I. and an A.Q.M.

2. The parachutist despatchers in any aircraft are responsible for the safety of the parachutists and for ensuring that the checks and drills are carried out as laid down for the particular aircraft concerned.

3. When carrying out despatching duties, despatchers are to bear in mind that pupil parachutists will be subject to nervous tension and may, particularly during their earlier descents, require considerable reassurance. This reassurance can best be given by an efficient and confident approach to the work in hand and by the despatcher showing consideration for the parachutists' comfort and safety.

4. All despatchers are to emplane wearing Back Type, Mk. 6 parachutes (Ref. 15A/612) and are to have a standard Safety Harness (Ref. 6F/282) available for immediate use. The safety harness is to be secured to a strong point in the aircraft and worn whenever a despatcher is working in the vicinity of an open door. The waist belt of the safety harness is to be worn over the parachute harness; the anchorage strap should be adjusted so that the despatcher's movements are restricted to positions short of the door/s.

Complements of despatchers

5. The complements of despatchers for aircraft in current use are as follows: —

(1) Operational Exercises and Continuation Training.

(a) Beverley aircraft	Full Parachutist Dropping Role		2 P.J.I. and 1 A.Q.M.
(b) Beverley aircraft	Heavy Drop/Upper Deck Parachutist Dropping Role		1 P.J.I. and 1 A.Q.M.
(c) Hastings aircraft	Parachutist Dropping Role		1 P.J.I. and 1 A.Q.M.

(2) Basic Training of Parachutists

(a) Beverley aircraft   Full Parachutist Dropping Role   { 5 P.J.I. or 4 P.J.I. and 1 A.Q.M.

RESTRICTED

(b)	Beverley aircraft	Heavy Drop/Upper Deck Parachutist Dropping Role	4 P.J.I. or 3 P.J.I. and 1 A.Q.M.
(c)	Hastings aircraft	Parachutist Dropping Role	5 P.J.I. or 4 P.J.I. and 1 A.Q.M.
(3)	Whirlwind helicopter	Parachutist Dropping Role	1 P.J.I.
(4)	Twin Pioneer aircraft	Parachutist Continuation and Conversion Training only	1 P.J.I.

Duties of despatchers

6. The duties of despatchers are divided into four groups as follows: —

(1) Duties of a No. 1 Despatcher.
(2) Duties of a Despatcher in charge of a stick.
(3) Duties of an Assistant Despatcher.
(4) Duties of an A.Q.M.

No. 1 Despatcher

7. A No. 1 Despatcher (P.J.I.), irrespective of rank, is to be in charge of all parachutists and all other despatchers in the aircraft, and is to supervise all aircraft checks and drills. In addition he is responsible for the following: —

(1) Inspection of the aircraft in accordance with current orders.

(2) Emplaning the parachutists.

(3) Wearing an intercom. headset and maintaining contact with the aircraft captain throughout the detail, and acknowledging all orders from the aircraft captain, when the A.Q.M. is not available.

(4) Ensuring that the parachutist fittings are reserviced for the next detail.

(5) Completing P.T.S. Form 15 and submitting it to the Officer Commanding the P.T.S. or the Detachment Commander.

(6) Submitting a written report concerning any abnormal incident which may have occurred during the detail.

Despatcher in charge of a stick

8. A Despatcher in charge of a stick is responsible for the following: —

(1) Ensuring that the parachutists in his stick are correctly seated for take-off and for checking the security of their safety belts.

(2) The correct positioning and clearance of static-lines.

(3) Checking the hooking up of each parachutist in his stick.

(4) Supervising the fastening back of seats.

(5) Giving the command for his stick to check equipment.

(6) Checking his stick in accordance with current orders.

(7) Checking suspended loads, if carried, in accordance with current orders.

(8) Giving the order for his stick to tell-off for equipment and ensuring that each parachutist answers in turn.

(9) Informing the No. 1 despatcher or the A.Q.M. that his stick is ready for action.

(10) Taking up his position to despatch his stick.

(11) Ensuring that his stick moves forward correctly on the command ACTION STATIONS.

(12) Watching the despatch signal lights, and when the red light comes on giving the command STAND IN THE DOOR; ensuring that the parachutists in his stick move into their correct positions.

(13) Despatching his stick when the green signal light comes on, and giving the commands appropriate to the particular descent as detailed in current orders. He is to ensure that each man adopts a good position at the aircraft exit, steadying him if necessary.

(14) Checking that the strops are clear of the parachutists' legs, arms, heads and equipment.

(15) Stopping the despatch of parachutists in his stick on receipt of the appropriate command from the No. 1 despatcher or on seeing the red signal light or in the event of any emergency. In the event of having to stop parachutists jumping, he is to stop the parachutist who is approaching the door and not the parachutist who is already in the door, unless he observes something that would be detrimental to his safe exit.

(16) Retrieving the trailing strops and bags as detailed in para. 11.

Assistant Despatcher

9. An Assistant Despatcher, who will be detailed for duty during basic or continuation training, is to assist the Despatcher in charge of a stick in all the duties detailed in para. 8. In addition he will be responsible for the following: —

(1) Issuing the correct strop to each parachutist in a stick.

(2) Following the last parachutist in a stick as far as the exit and observing the movement of the strops down the anchor cable. Being prepared, if necessary, to take action in the event of any obstruction to the correct movement of the strops down the anchor cable.

Duties of an Air Quartermaster

10. The duties of an Air Quartermaster are as follows: —

(1) Beverley aircraft (*lower deck*).
  (a) To be connected up to the intercom. position aft of the parachute exit doors and to be responsible for keeping the aircraft captain informed of the progress of the drills.

RESTRICTED

(b) Relaying all messages between the aircraft captain and the P.J.I. despatchers.

(c) Assisting the despatchers in the retrieval of the trailing strops and bags, and in any emergency.

(2) Beverley aircraft (*upper deck*)

(a) To be connected up to the intercom. position on the starboard side forward of the floor aperture.

(b) Similar duties as those quoted in sub-para. (1).

(3) Hastings aircraft

(a) To be connected up to the intercom. position aft of the port door and to be responsible for keeping the aircraft captain informed of the progress of the drills.

(b) Relaying all messages between the aircraft captain and the P.J.I. despatchers.

(c) Assisting the P.J.I. to open and close the parachute exit doors.

(d) Take up his despatching position at the port exit door five minutes before 'P' hour and on observing the green despatch light signal despatch the port stick of parachutists in accordance with current orders.

(e) To assist the P.J.I. in the retrieval of the trailing strops and bags, and in any emergency.

Strop retrieval

11. During parachute dropping training flights, when small sticks are dropped, the trailing strops and bags are to be retrieved after each dropping run. The trailing strops and bags, after small sticks have been dropped, may be retrieved manually as follows: —

(1) Side door exits—The despatcher in charge of a stick and the assistant despatcher are to grip all the trailing strops of their stick and move forward in the aircraft pulling the strops and bags through the door; alternatively a retrieval rope may be used.

(2) Floor aperture exits—The despatcher in charge of the stick and the assistant despatcher are to pull the retrieval strop from its securing clips and pull the strops to the forward edge of the floor aperture, where the trailing strops can be gripped and pulled into the aircraft.

12. When large sticks of parachutists are dropped, it may be necessary to use the retrieval winch to pull the trailing strops and bags into the aircraft. In this event the winch is to be used as follows: —

(1) The assistant despatcher is to operate the winch to pay out the cable.

(2) The despatcher in charge of the stick is to take the retrieval strop aft and attach it round the trailing strops of each stick.

(3) The assistant despatcher is to operate the winch to haul in the cable and so retrieve the strops.

(4) The despatcher in charge of the stick is to stand by the doorway to ensure that the strops and bags do not foul the doorway as they are being retrieved.

Note...

The emergency block and tackle carried in the aircraft may be used to retrieve the trailing strops if necessary.

Opening and removing parachutist exit doors

13. In some operational aircraft the doors can be opened, folded back, and secured; in other aircraft the doors have to be removed and securely stowed. The various methods of opening and securing the doors are dealt with in the relevant aircraft drill chapters in this section. The opening of parachutist exit doors is only to take place when approved by the captain of the aircraft and ordered by the No. 1 despatcher.

Closing and replacing parachutist exit doors

14. The actions of closing or replacing parachutist exit doors are only to take place when approved by the captain of the aircraft and ordered by the No. 1 despatcher. The methods of closing or replacing the doors in the various aircraft are dealt with in the relevant aircraft drill chapters in this section.

Strops

15. In British aircraft, each strop is attached by one end to the aircraft anchor cable and a snap-hook, complete with safety pin, is attached to the other end. The purpose of the strop is to act as an extension to the parachute static line, which is attached to the snap-hook on the free end of the strop, and so permit the parachute canopy to deploy without interference from any part of the aircraft. The lengths of the strops vary according to the aircraft being used and on occasion their location in an aircraft as follows: —

(1) Hastings aircraft—11 ft. strops (Ref. 15A/579) are used.

(2) Beverley aircraft upper deck—4 ft. 6 in. strops (Ref. 15A/798) are used.

(3) Beverley aircraft lower deck—3 ft. 6 in. strops (Ref. 15A/935) are used.

Methods of folding strops

16. Strops are folded in such a manner that the folds can be retained in retaining bungees (Ref. 15A/507) and that when extended, the strop pays out from the centre. Typical methods of folding strops are shown in Fig. 1 and 2.

Intercom. drill in aircraft

17. No. 1 despatcher or the A.Q.M. is responsible for maintaining contact with the aircraft captain throughout a sortie. This contact is maintained by means of the intercom. system. If at any time the

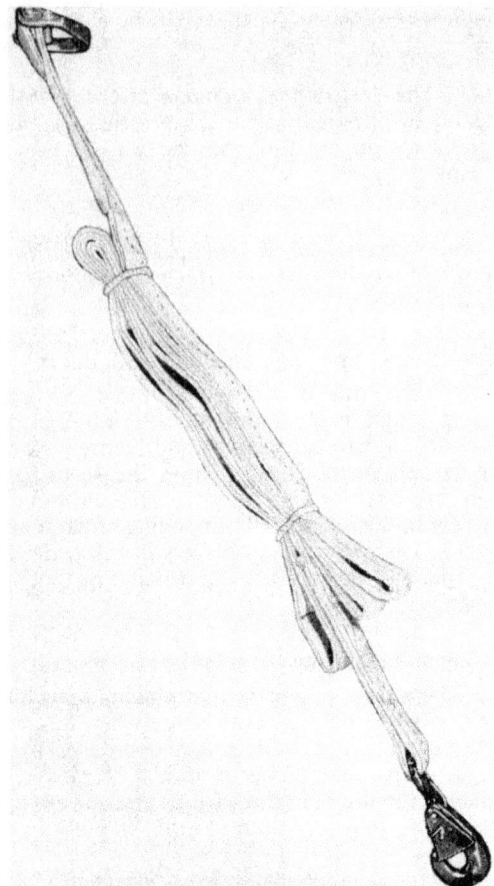

Fig. 2. Method of folding strops, Hastings aircraft

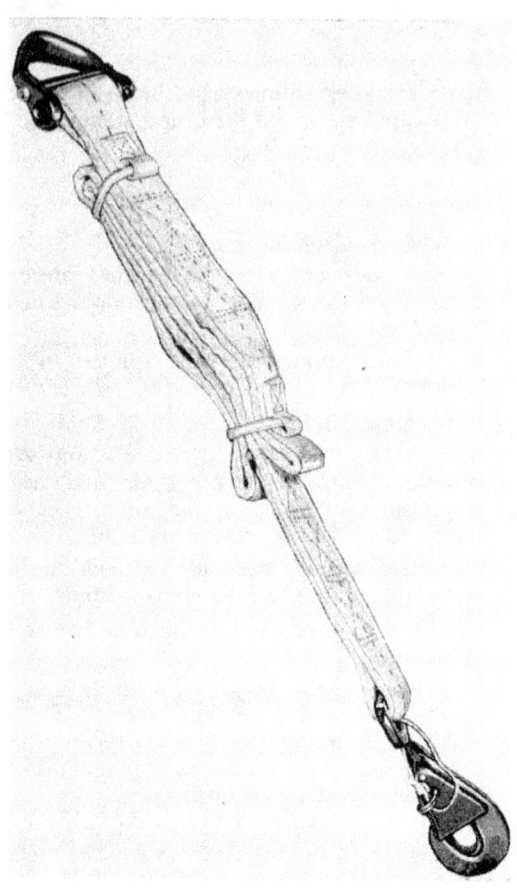

Fig. 1. Method of folding strops, Beverley aircraft (upper deck only)

duties of No. 1 despatcher require him to leave his intercom. station, he must advise the captain accordingly.

Method of passing instructions

18. All instructions passed over the intercom. system must be preceded by details of from whom, and to whom, the call is being made, e.g., DESPATCHER TO CAPTAIN or CAPTAIN TO DESPATCHER. All instructions are to be acknowledged by the receiver repeating the instruction, e.g., CAPTAIN TO DESPATCHER—PREPARE FOR ACTION—DESPATCHER TO CAPTAIN—PREPARE FOR ACTION. The despatcher is to ensure that his microphone is switched off when not in use.

Example of intercom. sequence

19. The following is an example of the intercom. drill for a training flight in a Hastings aircraft carrying a drifter and 30 parachutists with weapons containers, jumping in simultaneous sticks of five:—

Despatcher to Captain	Test intercom.—test lights—Red on—Red off—Green on—Green off—lights O.K. (*The captain will call on intercom. as each light is switched on and off*).
Captain to Despatcher	Acknowledge
Despatcher to Captain	One drifter and thirty parachutists with weapons containers jumping on four runs, one drifter followed by three simultaneous sticks of five. Dropping height 1,000 feet above ground level (A.G.L.)
Captain to Despatcher	Acknowledge
Despatcher to Captain	Steps in ready to taxy
Captain to Despatcher	Acknowledge
Captain to Despatcher	Fasten safety belts—Prepare for take-off
Despatcher to Captain	Acknowledge
Despatcher to Captain	Safety belts fastened—Ready for take-off
Captain to Despatcher	Acknowledge
Captain to Despatcher	Prepare for action
Despatcher to Captain	Acknowledge (*No. 1 despatcher relays the command* PREPARE FOR ACTION *to the other despatchers who prepare the parachutists. No. 2 and 3 despatchers advise No. 1 despatcher when the parachutists are ready*)

Despatcher to Captain	Permission to remove starboard door
Captain to Despatcher	Acknowledge
Despatcher to Captain	Starboard door removed and parachutists ready for action
Captain to Despatcher	Acknowledge
Captain to Despatcher	Action stations
Despatcher to Captain	Acknowledge (*No. 1 despatcher relays the command* ACTION STATIONS *to the parachutists and the other despatchers*)
Navigator or Captain to Despatcher	Red on
Despatcher to Navigator or Captain	Acknowledge
Navigator or Captain to Despatcher	Green on
Despatcher to Navigator or Captain	Green on 1, 2, 3, 4 et seq. (*count out parachutists to keep the captain informed as to progress*). Parachutists gone
Navigator or Captain to Despatcher	Acknowledge
Despatcher to Navigator or Captain	Bags in
Navigator or Captain to Despatcher	Acknowledge

Preparation for landing

Captain to Despatcher	Fasten safety belts
Despatcher to Captain	Acknowledge
Despatcher to Captain	Safety belts fastened and clearing intercom.
Captain to Despatcher	Acknowledge

CHAPTER 4

Mk.3 BALLOON CAR DRILL—SIDE DOOR EXIT

Chapter 4

Mk.3 BALLOON CAR DRILL—SIDE DOOR EXIT

LIST OF CONTENTS

	Para.		Para.
Introduction	1	*Descents with equipment*	9
Inspection of balloon cars and equipment	2	**Emergency procedures—**	
Side door exit drill	5	*Refusals to jump*	10
Inspection of pupils' parachute assemblies and equipment	6	*Suspended parachutist*	11
Emplaning	7	*Balloon breaking free*	12
Despatching	8	*Winch failure*	13

LIST OF ILLUSTRATIONS

	Fig.
Balloon car and pupils' positions	1

INTRODUCTION

1. Officers in charge of parachuting from balloons are to comply with current Flying Orders. The responsibilities of personnel detailed for duties at a Balloon Dropping Zone (*D.Z.*), are detailed in Sect. 4, Chap. 2 and reference should also be made to Sect. 4, Chap. 1.

Inspection of balloon cars and equipment

2. The Officer or N.C.O. in charge of the Balloon Car Crew is to inspect balloon cars before flight or at weekly intervals i.e., the inspection is to be carried out at least once per week. On completion of the inspection (*para. 4*), the Balloon Car Maintenance Pro-Forma attached to Form 1332 (*Balloon Record and Maintenance*), is to be completed (*noting any unserviceability*) and signed accordingly.

3. The Pro-Forma is to be brought to the notice of the Officer in charge of parachuting at the D.Z., who before flight, is to inspect the balloon car and rigging (*para. 4*), note any unserviceability and sign the Pro-Forma accordingly.

4. The following items are to be inspected:—
  (1) Joints for springing.
  (2) Metal frame for security.
  (3) Light fittings.
  (4) Guard rails for security.
  (5) Well cover for fit etc.
  (6) Canopy lashings.
  (7) Canopy generally.
  (8) Static beam for security.
  (9) Static bar for security.
  (10) Static strops for wear.
  (11) Static line hooks, safety catches and springs.
  (12) Door safety bar and fittings.
  (13) Lifting ropes.
  (14) Car legs and metal plates for security.
  (15) Rubber floor covering for wear and security.

SIDE DOOR EXIT DRILL

5. The Despatcher is to ensure that the fittings listed below are serviceable: —
  (1) Strops.
  (2) Hooks and locking devices.
  (3) Static beam and static bar.
  (4) Door safety bar and fittings.
  (5) Non-slip floor surface.
  (6) Balloon emergency rip-cord.

Inspection of pupils' parachute assemblies and equipment

6. The pupils are to be formed up in one rank in stick order; each pupil is to unfasten the 'Lift the Dot' fasteners on the flap of his reserve parachute pack, place both hands beneath the pack and raise it up. The Despatcher will then inspect each pupil, from the front and rear, and ensure that: —

(1) The eyelet, grommet and release pin system is serviceable and that the two release pin retaining threads are tied securely.

(2) There are six reserve parachute pack retaining elastics and that they are correctly fastened.

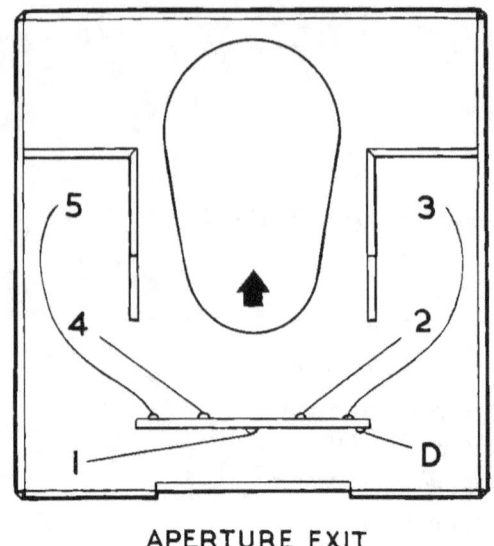
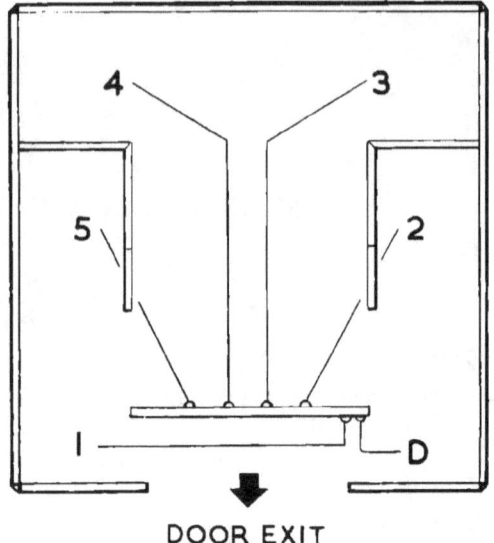
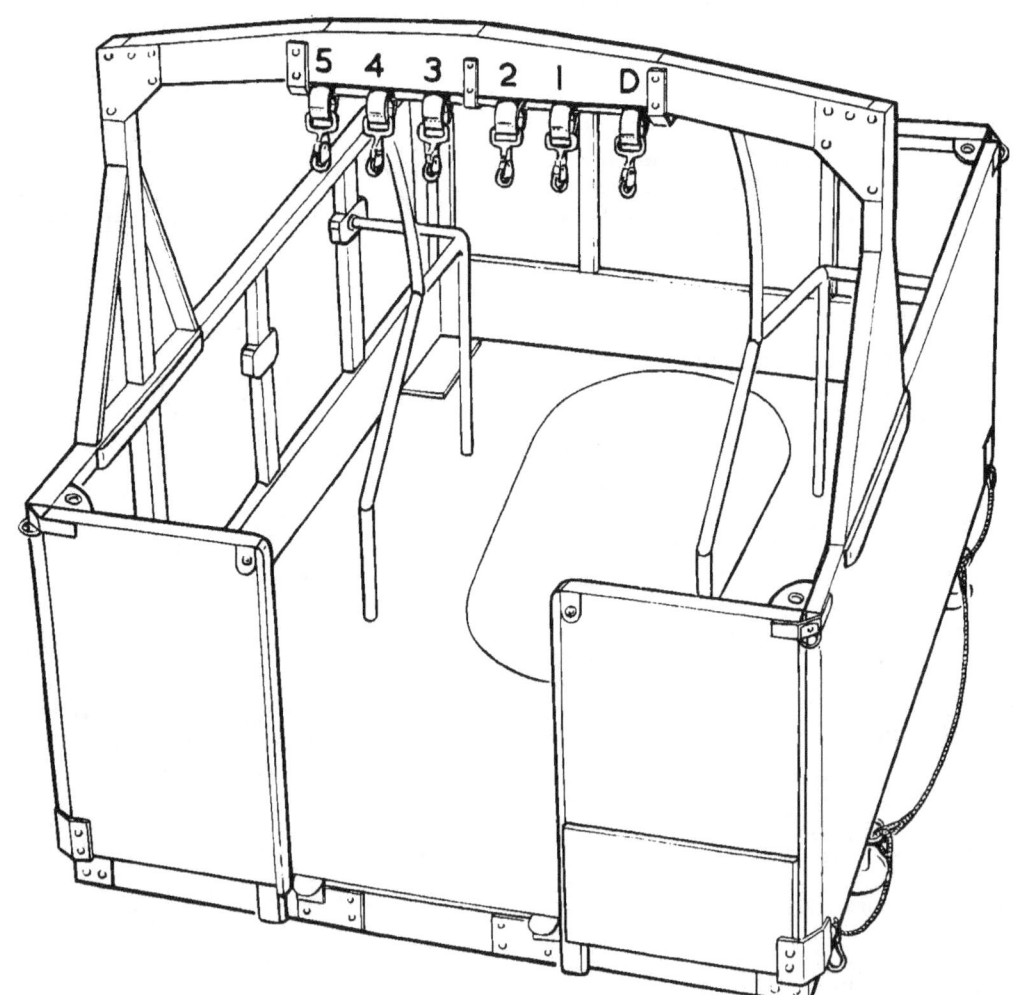

Fig. 1. Balloon car and pupils' positions

RESTRICTED

(3) The 'Lift the Dot' fasteners on the flap of the reserve parachute are correctly re-fastened.

(4) The Red rip-cord handle is uppermost.

(5) The reserve parachute pack is securely attached to the upper 'D' rings of the harness.

(6) The pupils quick-release box is locked (*by pressing it*).

(7) The locking buckles on the front lift webs are adjusted down to the shoulder buckles (*which should be evenly placed on the shoulders*).

(8) The harness is a comfortable fit and the main parachute is high on the back.

(9) The steel helmet is securely fastened.

(10) The fitting and servicing of the weapons container (*if carried*), is correctly completed.

(11) The three visible ties, the static line and the 'D' ring of the main parachute are serviceable and correctly disposed.

Emplaning

7. The Despatcher is to enter the balloon car first and will hang up his reserve parachute on the hook provided. The drill procedure is then as follows: —

(1) The Despatcher is to order the stick to EMPLANE, NO. 5 LEADING, and as each pupil enters the car, he will direct him to his respective position (*fig.* 1).

(2) The Despatcher is then to hook up each pupil, in the order in which they emplaned. He will pull out only sufficient of each pupil's static line to enable him to hook it up on the appropriate hook.

(3) The Despatcher will ensure that all static lines are free from twists and that none pass under or between lift webs.

(4) The Despatcher will hook up his own static line after the pupils are hooked up.

(5) The Despatcher will then do a final check of the hooking up and the equipment (*if carried*); each pupil in turn will answer to the check by replying to the Despatcher, NO. 5 O.K., NO. 4 O.K., and so on.

(6) The Despatcher is then to fasten the safety bar across the door.

(7) He is then to order, to the N.C.O. in charge of Signal Flags, UP 800 FEET—FIVE MEN JUMPING, or such details as are appropriate.

(8) The N.C.O. in charge of Signal Flags is to repeat the order to the N.C.O. in charge of the Balloon Crew, who will acknowledge the order by repeating it.

Despatching

8. When the Despatcher receives, or observes the Signal to Despatch, the procedure is as follows: —

(1) The Despatcher is to remove the door safety bar and order NO. 1 STAND IN THE DOOR.

(2) He is then to check the No. 1 man's position at the door, and ensure that his static line runs unobstructed from the centre of his pack to the strong point.

(3) The Despatcher is to grip the No. 1 man's static line with one hand and pull it taut against the hook, and with his other hand steady the man holding his lift web close to the shoulder buckle.

(4) The Despatcher will ensure that the balloon is in a safe position for despatching and that the Signal to Despatch is still being given; he will then order NO. 1 GO and at the same time tap the No. 1 man on the shoulder.

(5) The No. 1 man will then immediately make his exit.

(6) The Despatcher is to observe the pupil's exit and the deployment and development of his parachute; he will then retrieve the trailing line and bag and stow them on the hook provided so that they do not obstruct the approach of the remaining pupils to the door.

(7) The Despatcher is to despatch the remaining pupils in a similar manner to that for No. 1, whilst ensuring that: —

(a) The Signal to Despatch is being given or shown.

(b) The trailing static lines and bags are retrieved in turn.

(c) Not more than one pupil is in the air at a time, unless otherwise ordered by the Officer in charge of the parachuting.

(8) When all the pupils have been despatched the Despatcher is to replace the safety bar and roll up the retrieved static lines and bags.

(9) The N.C.O. in charge of Signal Flags, having observed that all the pupils have jumped, is to give the order to CLOSE HAUL to the N.C.O. in charge of the Balloon Crew who is to acknowledge this order by repeating it.

(10) The N.C.O. in charge of Signal Flags is to signal to the Despatcher with the Red flag, which is to remain displayed throughout the descent of the balloon.

(11) The Despatcher is to cease any action at the height of 400 feet and steady himself in the balloon car so as to guard against any violent movements of the balloon.

(12) The balloon car is to be cleared of all retrieved lines and bags before the next stick emplanes.

Descents with equipment

9. The drill procedure for descents with equipment is as detailed in para. 5 to 8, excepting that only four pupils are to be carried in the balloon car.

RESTRICTED

EMERGENCY PROCEDURES

Refusals to jump

10. In the event of any pupil refusing to jump the following action is to be taken by the Despatcher: —

(1) If the No. 1 man refuses to jump he is to be taken away from the door and is to exchange positions with the No. 2 man. The normal despatching sequence and drill is to be continued.

(2) If any of the other pupils refuse they are to be taken away from the door and returned to their own positions.

(3) If there is more than one refusal, the pupils concerned are to be taken away from the door and returned to positions which will allow the safe despatching of the remaining pupils.

(4) When the despatching is completed the Despatcher is to order, CLOSE HAUL.

(5) The N.C.O. in charge of Signal Flags will display the Red flag and will repeat the order CLOSE HAUL to the N.C.O. in charge of the Balloon Crew, who will acknowledge the order by repeating it.

(6) When there are pupils in the balloon during descent, static lines are not to be unhooked until the car is on the ground. During descent action is to be taken as in para. 8, sub-para. (11), by the Despatcher and any pupils in the balloon car.

Suspended parachutist

11. If a parachutist is caught up outside the balloon car and is suspended by his strop, the following action is to be taken : —

By the Despatcher: —

(1) Ensure that the other pupils (*if any*) in the car remain in their respective positions.

(2) Lower the free end of the retrieval rope to the suspended pupil.

(3) Instruct the pupil to secure the rope round his body.

(4) Give the order to CLOSE HAUL the balloon when he is satisfied that the pupil has securely tied the rope round himself.

By the N.C.O. in charge of Signal Flags: —

(1) Await the Despatcher's order to CLOSE HAUL.

(2) Order the N.C.O. in charge of the Balloon Crew to CLOSE HAUL as slowly as possible.

(3) Observe the descending balloon and give the order to stop close hauling as soon as the suspended pupil makes contact with the ground.

(4) Supervise the releasing of the pupil from the rope and his harness and ensure that he is taken to the Medical Officer for examination.

By the Officer in charge of parachuting: —

(1) Investigate the reason for the suspension of the pupil before the parachute is disconnected from the balloon car and before any balloon drill is recommenced.

(2) Ensure that full reports are submitted, by all concerned, to the Officer Commanding, The Parachute Training School.

Balloon breaking free

12. In the event of the balloon breaking free the Despatcher is to take the following action: —

(1) He is to ensure that there is sufficient height for the pupils to jump and that the area below the balloon is such that they can land safely.

(2) He will then despatch all pupils as quickly as possible and as is consistent with safety.

(3) He will then fit his own reserve parachute.

(4) Pull the Red-painted release line on the starboard side of the balloon car to remove the balloon tear-off panel. (*Four distinct pulls of the line are required to remove the panel.*)

(5) Check that his static line is clear and then jump.

Winch failure

13. If a failure of the winch occurs during the ascent or descent of the balloon with pupils in the car, the Officer in charge of parachuting is to take the following action: —

(1) Check the height at which the balloon is flying.

(2) Ascertain the time that is required to rectify the failure.

(3) If the delay will be prolonged he is to: —

   (a) Consider the experience of the pupils in the balloon car.

   (b) Check the balloon cable angle.

   (c) If the balloon is at a safe jumping height, i.e., not less than 600 feet, order the Despatcher to despatch the pupils.

(4) Order the Despatcher to jump if he considers it advisable for him to do so (*otherwise the Despatcher is to remain in the balloon car*).

(5) Alternatively, if the balloon is not at a safe jumping height, he is to order STAND BY until it is possible to close haul or continue.

CHAPTER 5

Mk.3 BALLOON CAR DRILL—FLOOR APERTURE EXIT

Chapter 5

Mk.3 BALLOON CAR DRILL—FLOOR APERTURE EXIT

LIST OF CONTENTS

	Para.		Para.
Introduction	1	Emergency procedures—	
Inspection before emplaning	2	*Refusals to jump*	6
Emplaning	3	*Suspended parachutist*	7
Despatching	4	*Balloon breaking free*	8
Descents with equipment	5	*Winch failure*	9

INTRODUCTION

1. Officers in charge of parachuting from balloons are to comply with current Flying Orders. The responsibilities of personnel detailed for duty at a Balloon Dropping Zone (D.Z.), are detailed in Sect. 4 Chap. 2 and reference should also be made to Sect. 4, Chap. 1.

Inspection before emplaning

2. The Officer in charge of parachuting and the Despatcher are to make the inspection of the balloon car, the pupils' parachute assemblies and their equipment as detailed in Chap. 4.

Emplaning

3. The emplaning drill is as detailed in Chap. 4, with the exception that the door is secured in position after the pupils have emplaned. The details of their positions and hooking up are as shown in fig. 1, Chap. 4.

Despatching

4. When the Despatcher receives the order or observes the Signal to Despatch he is to give the order NO. 1 STAND IN THE DOOR, and then perform the Despatcher's duties as detailed for Side Door Exit Drill in Chap. 4.

Descents with equipment

5. The drill procedure is as detailed in Chap. 4, but only four pupils are to be carried in the balloon car.

EMERGENCY PROCEDURES

Refusals to jump

6. In the event of any pupil refusing to jump the following action is to be taken by the Despatcher:—

(1) If either No. 1, 2 or 4 has refused to jump the man concerned is to be placed in the No. 1 position.

(2) If No. 3 or 5 has refused to jump the man concerned is to be returned to his normal position.

(3) In the event of more than one refusal the pupils concerned are to be placed in such positions that will allow the safe despatching of the remainder.

(4) The procedure then remaining to be followed is as detailed in Chap. 4.

Suspended parachutist

7. If a parachutist is caught up outside the balloon car and is suspended by his strop the action to be taken is as detailed in Chap. 4.

Balloon breaking free

8. In the event of the balloon breaking free the Despatcher is to follow the drill as detailed in Chap. 4.

Winch failure

9. If a failure of the winch occurs during the ascent or descent of the balloon with pupils in the car, the Officer in charge of parachuting is to take the action as detailed in Chap. 4.

CHAPTER 9

HASTINGS AIRCRAFT DRILL—TRAINING

Chapter 9

HASTINGS AIRCRAFT DRILL—TRAINING

LIST OF CONTENTS

	Para.		Para.
Introduction	1	*Prepare for action*	19
Despatchers' duties—		*Equipment check*	20
		Action stations	21
General	2	*Red despatch signal lights*	22
No. 1 Despatcher	3	*Green despatch signal lights*	23
No. 2 Despatcher—port side	4	*Strop retrieval*	24
No. 3 Despatcher—starboard side	5	**Jumping with P.W.C. and similar loads**	25
No. 4 Despatcher—port side	6	*Before emplaning*	26
No. 5 Despatcher—starboard side	7	*Emplaning*	27
Repetition of orders	8	*Before take-off*	28
Strop retrieval	9	*Prepare for action*	29
Removal and replacement of doors	10	*Equipment check*	30
Training drill—		*Action stations*	31
Before emplaning	13	*Red despatch signal lights*	32
Aircraft inspection check list	14	*Green despatch signal lights*	33
Inspection of the pupils	15	**Emergency procedures—**	
Emplaning	16	*Refusals*	34
Before take-off	17	*Sickness*	35
After take-off	18	*Retrieval of a suspended parachutist*	36

INTRODUCTION

1. In the parachutist training role the flying crew will normally consist of the Captain, Second Pilot, Navigator/Supply Aimer, Flight Engineer and the Signaller Air. Five Parachute Jumping Instructors (*P.J.I.*), are to be carried as Despatchers. The maximum number of parachutists to be carried in the aircraft during training is 30 (*two sticks of* 15), plus one P.J.I. as Drifter, on the first sortie of each programme. For training purposes the number of trainee parachutists in one stick (*up to the maximum of* 15) may be varied so that several short sticks may be dropped instead of two sticks of full strength. There are seats and safety belts for 32 parachutists only in the parachutists' compartment; any personnel carried above that number are to be accommodated in crash belts for take-off and landing. As distinct from the dropping of parachutists only, mixed loads can be dropped in any one of the following sequences:—

(1) Containers followed by parachutists.

(2) Containers and parachutists together; in this role the container parachutes must be fitted with delayed-action devices set at 3·0 seconds delay.

(3) Parachutists followed by containers.

(4) Parachutists followed by containers, followed by parachutists.

Note...

(a) *When mixed loads of containers and parachutists are being dropped the Captain of the aircraft is to ensure that the Aircrew, Despatchers and parachutists are carefully briefed as to the sequence to be followed.*

(b) *Reference must be made to A.P.4203A, Vol. 1 (War office Code No. 8478), for detailed information concerning the Hastings Aircraft and its equipment when employed in the parachutists' role.*

DESPATCHERS DUTIES

General

2. The five P.J.I. Despatchers carried for double door jumping training are to implement the Hastings Aircraft Drill—Training, and will emplane wearing back-type parachutes. They will comply with the instructions detailed in the Hastings Aircraft Drill—Operational (*Chap.* 10), for the wearing of back-type parachutes and safety harnesses.

No. 1 Despatcher

3. The No. 1 Despatcher, whatever his rank, is to be in charge of all parachutists and the other Despatchers, and is to supervise the aircraft drills and checks. He is to :—

(1) Wear an intercommunication headset and is to maintain communication with the Captain of the aircraft during the whole of the time that he is in the aircraft.

(2) Inform the Captain of the composition of the sticks and the height from which they will be dropped.

(3) Acknowledge all orders from the Captain of the aircraft, repeat the orders to the Despatchers and the parachutists, and keep the Captain informed as to the progress of the checks, the aircraft drill and the jumping detail.

(4) Confirm with the Navigator/Supply Aimer when the Red or Green despatch signal lights are showing.

(5) Inform the Captain of the progress of each stick during jumping.

(6) Submit a written report to the Officer Commanding, The Parachute Training School, concerning any abnormal incident that has occurred during flight.

No. 2 Despatcher—port side

4. The No. 2 Despatcher is in charge of the port stick in the aircraft. He is to :—

(1) Check the hooking up of the port stick.

(2) Supervise the equipment checks of the port stick, assisted by the No. 4 Despatcher.

(3) Position himself aft of the port door.

(4) Watch the despatch signal lights and despatch the port stick on the appearance of the Green despatch signal light.

(5) Stop the stick jumping immediately, if the Red despatch signal light shows " on " while the stick is leaving the aircraft, or in an emergency such as a jammed strop.

(6) Give his commands in a loud clear voice, and supervise the parachutists' actions which follow his commands.

No. 3 Despatcher—starboard side

5. The duties of the No. 3 Despatcher are similar to those detailed in para. 4, but are applied to the starboard stick of parachutists and the starboard side of the aircraft.

No. 4 Despatcher—port side

6. The No. 4 Despatcher is to assist the No. 2 Despatcher in the following duties :—

(1) Checking the hooking up of the port stick.

(2) Supervising the equipment checks of the port stick.

(3) Supervising the stick to ensure that the drill procedure is followed correctly, ensuring that the strops move freely along the cable and following the last man to the exit door as the stick leaves the aircraft.

No. 5 Despatcher—starboard side

7. The duties of the No. 5 Despatcher are similar to those detailed in para. 6 but are applied to the starboard stick of parachutists and the starboard side of the aircraft.

Repetition of orders

8. The orders given by the No. 1 Despatcher are to be repeated, as necessary, to the parachutists by No. 2, 3, 4 and 5 Despatchers, who are then to supervise the parachutists' actions which follow.

Strop retrieval

9. The strops and bags will be retrieved by the No. 2, 3, 4 and 5 Despatchers after each stick has jumped ; they will use the winch, if required, as follows :—

(1) No. 5 Despatcher is to operate the winch to pay out the cable.

(2) No. 4 Despatcher is to take the cable and the retrieval strop aft to No. 2 and 3 Despatchers and then return forward to the winch.

(3) No. 2 and 3 despatchers are to attach the retrieval strop to the cable and secure it round the trailing strops.

(4) No. 4 Despatcher is to assist No. 5 Despatcher to operate the winch until the cable is wound in fully.

(5) The anchor strop is then to be fitted and the procedure is to be repeated until all strops have been retrieved.

Note...
When short sticks are dropped during training, it will be possible to retrieve the strops by hand ; No. 2, 3 or 4 Despatchers are to combine as necessary to pull in one set of strops at a time.

Removal and replacement of doors

10. During air experience flights in Hastings Aircraft the parachutists' exit doors are to be closed after the pupils have emplaned. The doors are to remain closed until it is necessary to open or remove them to follow the aircraft drill, or to obtain practice in door removal and replacement in flight. The No. 1 Despatcher (*or when applicable the A.Q.M.*), is to advise the Captain of the aircraft when it is intended to remove a door or doors in flight, and is to obtain the Captain's permission before any door is removed. Normally doors are removed and replaced by the No. 2 and 3 Des-

patchers; if two other personnel are detailed for these duties their functions are to correspond relatively to those of the No. 2 and 3 Despatchers, as shown in the following paragraphs dealing with the door removal and replacement procedures.

11. The procedure for the removal of a parachutists' exit door in flight is as follows :—

Starboard door :—

(1) The No. 2 Despatcher (*or No. 1 man detailed*), is to position himself forward of the door, grasp the bottom door handle with both hands and hold it firmly in position.

(2) The No. 3 Despatcher (*or No. 2 man detailed*), is to position himself aft of the door, and when No. 2 Despatcher is ready, is to push the door securing lever forward.

(3) The No. 3 Despatcher is then to turn facing outboard, square with the door, grasp each of the two upper handles and pull the top of the door towards himself and into the aircraft.

(4) The door is to be lowered in this way until it is at an angle of 30 degrees or less to the aircraft floor when it can be withdrawn into the aircraft. The lugs on the bottom of the door are not to be disengaged from their recesses in the door sill until the door has been lowered sufficiently.

(5) The door is then to be stowed correctly on its own side of the fuselage aft of the exit.

Port door :—

The removal procedure is similar to that for the starboard door, except that the No. 2 Despatcher's position is aft of the door and he performs the duties of the No. 3 Despatcher; the No. 3 Despatcher's position is forward of the door and he performs the duties of the No. 2 Despatcher.

12. The procedure for the replacement of a parachutists' exit door in flight is as follows :—

Starboard door :—

(1) The No. 2 Despatcher is to position himself forward of the door and, with the No. 3 Despatcher, remove the door from its stowage and place it in position facing, and aligned with, the exit aperture.

(2) From his forward position the No. 2 Despatcher is to grasp the bottom door handle with both hands, while the No. 3 Despatcher holds the door firmly by the upper handles.

(3) Together the Despatchers are to carefully align and engage the lugs on the bottom of the door with their recesses in the door sill.

(4) When the No. 2 Despatcher is satisfied that the lugs are correctly and securely located, No. 3 Despatcher is to raise the top of the door into the exit aperture and then lock the door by pulling the door securing lever aft.

Port door :—

The replacement procedure is similar to that for the starboard door except that the Despatchers are to change positions.

TRAINING DRILL

Before emplaning

13. Prior to emplaning :—

(1) The No. 1 Despatcher is to carry out an inspection of the aircraft before each flight, as detailed in Appendices 1 and 2 of the Hastings Aircraft Drill-Operational (*Chap.* 10). This entails the completion and signature of a proforma, on which the inspection groups are listed in the same order as that in which they are detailed in the following paragraph.

(2) The P.J.I. detailed for marshalling and parachute fitting duties is to carry out the inspection of the pupils, number them off (*para.* 15), and give the orders to emplane (*para.* 16), as detailed in the Hastings Aircraft Drill-Operational (*Chap.* 10).

Aircraft inspection check list

14. The No. 1 Despatcher is to ensure that :—

(1) The intercom. system is serviceable between his and the A.Q.M. positions and the Captain's and the downward observation positions.

(2) The Red and Green despatch signal lights at both exit doors function correctly by switching each light ON and OFF in turn, and by checking with the Navigator/Supply Aimer from the downward observation position.

(3) It is confirmed with the Navigator/Supply Aimer, LIGHTS AND INTERCOM. O.K., when the intercom. system and despatch signal lights check have been completed.

(4) The cargo door hinges are efficiently masked and the lower hinge fairing is masked with fabric if necessary.

(5) Any sharp edges or obstructions, inside or outside the aircraft, that might damage or interfere with parachutes or their static lines, are made good or are masked.

(6) The anti-skid matting is serviceable and secure.

(7) The toilet outlets under the fuselage are of soft rubber.

(8) The bar on the forward edge of the cargo door is withdrawn fully and the securing screw is tightened.

RESTRICTED

(9) The handle inside and aft of the port exit door is securely masked.

(10) The floor surfaces and door sills are safe.

(11) The parachutists' anchor cables are serviceable, that both ends of each cable are secure and the tensioning turnbuckles are locked by pins.

(12) The parachutists' anchor cables are correctly tensioned.

(13) The Despatchers' anchorage cables are serviceable, that both ends of each cable are correctly secured to the aircraft structure and the tensioning turnbuckles are wire-locked.

(14) There are sufficient strops, of the correct number on each side, that the strops are serviceable, folded in the correct manner and attached to the anchor cables so that the tongues of the snap hooks face forward when the strops are fully extended.

(15) All snap hooks, pins and "D" rings are serviceable (*strops are to be secured at the forward ends of the anchor cables when not in use*).

(16) The requisite number of parachutists' seat safety belts are installed with their quick-releases facing in the correct direction, i.e., so that the releases pull aft on the port side and forward on the starboard side to unfasten.

(17) The seat units can be folded up and that the seat securing fittings are serviceable.

(18) The requisite number of serviceable crash belts (*fourteen double and four single*) are stowed correctly and that their lashing units are not obstructed.

(19) The lashing point blanking plate adjacent to the starboard exit door has been removed if the aircraft has been converted from the personnel carrying role.

(20) The strop retrieval winch and its mounting are serviceable and that the retrieval and anchor strops are available in the aircraft.

(21) A supply of vomit bags is available in the aircraft.

(22) The seats and their retaining straps are serviceable.

Inspection of the pupils
15. The P.J.I. detailed for marshalling and parachute fitting duties is to line up the sticks in two ranks on the port side of the aircraft, forward of the exit door and facing the tailplane. He is then to, inspect each parachutists' equipment for the serviceability and correct fitting of the following items:—

(1) The parachute harness.

(2) The quick-release box on the parachute harness.

(3) The parachute pack and all visible ties.

(4) The parachute static line and "D" ring.

(5) The steel helmet and helmet straps.

(6) The airborne life-jacket, if worn, ensuring that the physical inflation valve is closed and that the CO_2 bottle is inserted correctly.

(7) The weapons and equipment carried.

(8) The packing and security of all suspended loads paying particular attention to the security and attachments of the suspension rope or cord and quick-release fitting.

(9) The authorised weight and bulk of the suspended loads.

(10) The efficient functioning of the jettison devices. (*These are to be checked physically*).

Emplaning
16. The Despatchers are to supervise the sticks as they emplane. The P.J.I. marshaller/parachute fitter is to give the following orders to the sticks:—

(1) STARBOARD STICK—NUMBER
The starboard stick (*front rank*) is to number from left to right.

(2) PORT STICK—NUMBER
The port stick (*rear rank*) is to number from right to left.

(3) LEFT TURN
Both sticks are to turn to the left and face the port door of the aircraft.

(4) EMPLANE
The order is to be given from the door of the aircraft. The first parachutist of the starboard stick is to lead into the aircraft, his stick following him forward along the port side of the parachutists' compartment, under the forward end of the anchor cables and back along the starboard side of the compartment. The last man of the port stick is to follow the last man of the starboard stick, and all parachutists' are to occupy the seats to which they have been detailed. The parachutists' exit doors are then to be closed (*para.* 10), and secured after the steps have been removed.

(5) The No. 1 Despatcher will inform the Captain AIRCRAFT READY TO TAXY.

Before take-off
17. Before take-off:—

(1) The Captain is to order SECURE SAFETY BELTS and the No. 1 Despatcher is to give the order to the parachutists.

(2) The No. 4 and 5 Despatchers are to check the security of the safety belts and report to No. 2 and 3 Despatchers when all safety belts are secured; the latter are to inform the No. 1 Despatcher.

(3) The No. 1 Despatcher is then to inform the Captain READY FOR TAKE-OFF.

After take-off
18. The Despatchers are to prevent any unnecessary movement of the parachutists after the aircraft is airborne.

RESTRICTED

Prepare for action

19. For training flights, the Dropping Zone (*D.Z.*) is usually only a short distance from the Departure Airfield and therefore the command PREPARE FOR ACTION is given soon after take-off. The drill procedure is as follows: —

(1) The Captain is to give the order PREPARE FOR ACTION to the No. 1 Despatcher, who is to repeat the order to the parachutists and Despatchers.

(2) No. 4 and 5 Despatchers are to unfasten the strops at the forward end of the static cables and pass them to the last man of each stick.

(3) The strops are to be passed aft from man to man, each man in turn retaining the last strop (*i.e. the most forward strop*), as he does so.

(4) Each man is to ensure that his static line is over his correct shoulder, i.e.,

(a) On the port side, over the left shoulder.

(b) On the starboard side, over the right shoulder.

(5) Each man is then to hook up his static line to his strop, insert and fasten his safety pin (*Sect. 3, Chap.* 2), and then unfasten his safety belt.

(6) At the appropriate time, after the hooking up has been completed, the No. 1 Despatcher is to give the order STAND UP.

(7) All parachutists in the first sticks are to stand up, release the sliding bolts securing the seats to the floor, then fold up the seats and secure them with their retaining straps.

Note...
Before the seats are raised it must be ensured that the snap hooks on the safety belts are not connected to the " D " rings at the back of the seats, and that the belts are neatly folded and stowed. When the parachutists are jumping in short sticks the seats are not to be raised until the first stick on each side has left the aircraft.

(8) The parachutists are then to turn facing aft, forming a single line on each side of the aircraft.

Equipment check

20. The drill procedure for the equipment checks is as follows: —

(1) When the Preparation for Action is completed, the No. 2 and 3 Despatchers are to order respectively, PORT (OR STARBOARD), STICK—CHECK EQUIPMENT.

(2) Each man is then to check: —

(a) His helmet for security.

(b) The hooking up of his static line to his strop and the security of the safety pin.

(c) The security of his reserve parachute.

(d) The security of his quick-release box.

(e) The position of his static line and the freedom of his strop on the static cable.

(f) The static line and all visible ties on the parachute of the man in front of him.

(3) No. 4 and 5 Despatchers are then to check the hooking up of each man, ensure that all static lines are free from obstruction, that all strops move freely on the static cable and that all seats are folded and secured (*Note, para.* 19, *sub-para.* (7)).

(4) No. 2 Despatcher is then to order PORT STICK, TELL-OFF FOR EQUIPMENT CHECK, and after the check has been correctly and completely effected, the men in the port stick are to call out in succession, NO. 15 O.K., NO. 14 O.K., etc., back to No. 1, who will then call out NO. 1 O.K., STICK O.K.

(5) After the port stick Tell-off, the No. 3 Despatcher is to order, STARBOARD STICK, TELL-OFF FOR EQUIPMENT CHECK, and the procedure is to be similar to that for the port stick.

(6) After the starboard stick Equipment Check has been completed, the No. 2 and 3 Despatchers are to inform the No. 1 Despatcher PORT AND STARBOARD STICKS READY FOR ACTION.

(7) The No. 1 Despatcher is then to inform the Captain TROOPS READY FOR ACTION.

Action stations

21. The command ACTION STATIONS is given soon after the Captain has been informed that the parachutists are Ready for Action, for the reason given in para. 19. The drill procedure is as follows: —

(1) The Captain is to give the order ACTION STATIONS to the No. 1 Despatcher, who is to repeat the order to the parachutists and the Despatchers.

(2) The sticks are to move towards their respective exit doors, until the No. 1 of each stick has reached the position where he can place his aft hand above his exit doorway.

(3) The No. 2 and 3 Despatchers are to take up positions aft of their respective doorways and watch the despatch signal lights.

Red despatch signal lights

22. The appearance of the Red despatch signal lights is the signal for the No. 1 parachutists of each stick to STAND IN THE DOORS. The drill procedure is as follows: —

(1) The Navigator/Supply Aimer is to switch ON the Red despatch signal lights and call out RED-ON, five seconds before arrival at the

Ground Dropping Signal. The No. 1 Despatcher is to confirm RED-ON.

(2) The No. 2 and 3 Despatchers are to order, immediately, STAND IN THE DOOR, and No. 1 of each stick is to take up his correct position in his respective exit doorway.

(3) The remainder of each stick are to take up their appropriate positions and prepare for an immediate exit in the correct sequence.

Green despatch signal lights

23. The appearance of the Green despatch signal lights is the signal for the No. 1 parachutists to make their exits, followed by the remainder of their sticks. The drill procedure is as follows:—

(1) The Navigator/Supply Aimer is to switch ON the Green despatch signal lights and call out GREEN-ON, when the aircraft is directly over the Aiming Signal.

(2) Immediately the Green lights appear:—

(a) The No. 1 Despatcher is to confirm GREEN-ON.

(b) The No. 2 and 3 Despatchers are to tap on the shoulders of their respective No. 1 men and shout GO.

(c) The No. 1 man of each stick is to make an immediate exit.

(3) The remainder of each stick is to follow its No. 1 man in the correct sequence while the Green lights are ON.

IMPORTANT...

(a) As the sticks move towards the exits each man is to grasp the strop of the man preceding him and guide it along the static cable, releasing it as he himself comes to the No. 2 position at the doorway. The last man of the stick is to carry his own strop in addition to that of the man in front of him.

(b) If a parachutist finds that the strop of the man preceding him in the stick is jammed, he is to prevent him from jumping; the whole stick affected is to cease to jump until the strop is cleared.

(4) The No. 1 Despatcher is to count off the parachutists as they make their exits; if a Red light appears while the aircraft is over the D.Z., the No. 2 and 3 Despatchers are to call out RED-ON immediately, and are to prevent any further jumping.

(5) The Navigator/Supply Aimer is to switch ON the Red despatch signal lights and call RED-ON as soon as the aircraft is over the D.Z. Ground Limit Signal.

(6) No. 2 and 3 Despatchers are to repeat RED-ON and are to prevent any remaining parachutists from jumping.

(7) No. 1 Despatcher is to inform the Captain if, and why, any members of a stick have been prevented from jumping.

Strop retrieval

24. The strops are to be retrieved as detailed in para. 9. The remainder of the drill procedure is as follows:—

(1) The Captain will fly the aircraft as slowly as possible while the strops are being retrieved.

(2) The No. 1 Despatcher is to inform the Captain when the strop retrieval is completed.

(3) The Navigator/Supply Aimer is to switch OFF the despatch signal lights and call RED OFF, MASTER SWITCH OFF.

(4) The Second Pilot is to place the Master Switch to the OFF position and confirm MASTER SWITCH OFF.

JUMPING WITH P.W.C. AND SIMILAR LOADS

25. The normal complement of parachutists carrying personal weapons containers (*P.W.C.*), or similar loads, consists of 30 men. When this type of training is undertaken, the procedure detailed in para. 26 to 33 are to be followed in addition to the standard training drills (*para. 2 to 24*).

Before Emplaning

26. The P.J.I. detailed for marshalling and parachute fitting duties (*para. 13, sub-para.* (2)), is to inspect all P.W.C. for serviceability, packing and security (*para. 15*).

Emplaning

27. Each man is to carry his own equipment into the aircraft and when seated is to place his equipment between his feet. The Despatchers are to assist any heavily laden parachutists.

Before take-off

28. After safety belts are secured, the Despatchers are to ensure that the parachutists with heavy equipment keep it resting on the floor and between their legs; this position is to be maintained until the order PREPARE FOR ACTION is given.

Prepare for action

29. On the command PREPARE FOR ACTION the No. 4 and 5 Despatchers are to distribute the strops to the parachutists who are then to proceed as follows:—

(1) Hook up their static lines and strops.

(2) Release their safety belts.

(3) Stand up, remove their reserve parachutes and place them at the back of their seats, with the red handles down and to the rear.

(4) Sit down and transfer the quick-release hooks from their harnesses to the suspension plates on their load containers or P.W.C.

(5) Fit their jettison devices and their leg straps.

(6) Stand up on the command STAND UP, secure their load containers or P.W.C. to their lower

RESTRICTED

"D" rings, replace their reserve parachutes on their upper "D" rings and tighten their leg straps.

(7) Fold up and secure their seats (*Note, para. 19, sub-para.* (7)).

Equipment check

30. When the order CHECK EQUIPMENT is given the parachutists are to check their equipment, their quick-release snap hooks, their jettison devices and leg straps in addition to the items detailed in para. 20.

Action stations

31. Each man with a P.W.C. or similar load is to grasp it in the correct manner and move to his correct position.

Red despatch signal lights

32. When the Red lights appear and the order STAND IN THE DOOR is given, each man is to take up his correct stick position in as normal a manner as his equipment will permit.

Green despatch signal lights

33. When the Green lights appear and the order GO is given, the parachutists are to make their exists in the correct sequence and in as normal a manner as their equipment will permit.

EMERGENCY PROCEDURES

Refusals

34. *During flight*: —

If a parachutist refuses to jump during the flight to the D.Z., he is to be unhooked by the No. 4 or 5 Despatcher, as appropriate, and taken forward in the aircraft. The Despatcher concerned is to re-service his strop and hand it to the next man in the stick, who is then to carry it in addition to the strop of the man preceding him in the stick.

During jumping: —

If a parachutist refuses to jump at the exit door, he is to be removed to the rear of the aircraft, aft of the exit doors, by the No. 2 or 3 Despatcher so that the remainder of the stick can jump without further delay.

Sickness

35. If a parachutist becomes too sick to jump he is to be unhooked by the nearest Despatcher and taken forward, or if necessary, laid on a seat or the floor of the aircraft. His strop is to be re-serviced and carried by the next man in the stick.

Retrieval of a suspended parachutist

36. A standard procedure for the retrieval of a suspended parachutist who is being towed behind an aircraft is defined in A.P. 4200, Sect. 3, Chap. 3 (*War Office Code No.* 8297). If a parachutist is suspended outside a Hastings Aircraft the emergency procedure detailed in sub-para. (1) to (6) is to be followed without delay.

IMPORTANT...

A suspended parachutist can suffer serious injury through being buffeted against the aircraft. It is imperative that this series of operations is performed with the maximum speed and efficiency, particularly during the final stages of retrieval. Despatchers who are assisting the parachutist over the door sill must have their safety harnesses secured to aircraft floor tie-down rings or the overhead cable.

(1) The No. 1 Despatcher is to inform the Captain that a parachutist is suspended outside the aircraft, and is to state from which side of the aircraft.

(2) The Captain will fly the aircraft as slowly as possible, on a circuit towards the side from which the parachutist is suspended.

(3) The No. 5 Despatcher is to operate the winch and pay out the cable.

(4) The No. 4 Despatcher is to take the retrieval strop and cable aft to the appropriate doorway and then return forward to assist No. 5 Despatcher in winding the winch.

(5) The No. 2, or No. 3, Despatcher is to attach the retrieval strop to all the parachute strops trailing at the doorway, and then give the signal to wind in the cable.

(6) The No. 2, or No. 3, Despatcher is to be near the exit doorway to assist the man in getting back into the aircraft. The No. 1 and No. 3 (*or No.* 2), Despatchers are to assist as much as possible.

RESTRICTED

CHAPTER 11

jettisoned by the No. 1 and 2 men of the port stick and No. 3 and 4 of the starboard stick.)

(6) The parachutists who are the odd numbers, in both sticks, are to remove the crash belts from their stowages and secure the belts to the floor *(para. 3)*, assisted by the nearest even-numbered parachutists.

(7) As the crash belts are installed the parachutists are to take up their crash landing stations *(fig. 1)*. Each man is to be seated on the floor facing aft, with his knees bent and his feet flat on the floor; the hands are to be clasped behind the neck, holding the head firmly down to the chest.

(8) At this stage those parachutists who may still be wearing parachutes are to turn and release the quick-release boxes, remove their leg straps and place their reserve parachutes beneath their knees.

(9) When all the parachutists *(and the Flying crew members concerned)*, are at their stations, the A.Q.M. will take up his own crash landing station. He is to remain on intercom, and is to inform the Captain as soon as all personnel in the compartment are ready for crash landing.

(10) The Captain is to call out the decreasing altitude of the aircraft as it descends, and at 500 ft. he will press the call light button. At 100 ft. he will call out over the intercom. BRACE–BRACE and press the call light button as a signal to the parachutists to BRACE themselves.

(11) As soon as the A.Q.M. hears the Captain's order he is to shout BRACE–BRACE to all in the compartment.

Action on crash landing

12. When the aircraft touches down there may be more than one phase of the impact or a violent change of direction. It is essential that the BRACE position is maintained until the aircraft has come to rest.

Action after crash landing

13. When the aircraft has come to rest the drill procedure is as follows:—

(1) The A.Q.M. and the Navigator/Supply Aimer, assisted by the P.J.I. Despatcher, are to remove the port and starboard parachute exit doors respectively.

(2) The parachutists are to lower the seats at the escape window positions.

(3) The parachutists and the Flying Crew are to make their exits as quickly as possible in a cool and disciplined manner and in the order detailed in para. 8, 9, and 10.

ABANDONING THE AIRCRAFT IN THE AIR

14. If it is necessary to abandon the aircraft in the air the drill procedure is as follows:—

(1) The Captain is to order over the intercom. PUT ON PARACHUTES—PREPARE TO ABANDON AIRCRAFT. He will flash P–P–P on the call light in morse (·— — · ·— — · ·— — ·), and switch ON the Red despatch signal lights.

(2) The A.Q.M., P.J.I. Despatcher and the Flying crew will acknowledge the order in turn from aft to forward. If the operation takes place at night the compartment lights are to be switched ON.

(3) The Flying Crew are to follow the drill procedure detailed in A.P. 4203A, Vol. 1, Sect. 3, Chap. 5.

(4) The parachutists are to release their safety belts and attach their static lines to their respective strops; they will take up their normal STAND IN THE DOOR positions *(Chap. 9 and 10)*, and will commence to jump on receiving the Captain's order JUMP—JUMP which he will give as he switches on the Green despatch signal lights.

(5) The A.Q.M. and the P.J.I. Despatcher are to despatch their respective sticks; the latter is to jump after the last man of the starboard stick.

(6) The A.Q.M. is to inform the Captain when all the parachutists and the P.J.I. Despatcher have jumped, disconnect his intercom. plug and then jump from the port parachute exit door.

(7) The Captain is to disconnect his intercom. plug after hearing that all personnel have left the aircraft and make his exit through the flying crew emergency hatch.

Note . . .

Survival on land or at sea is dealt with in Air Ministry Pamphlets No. 214, 224, 225 and 226, and in Air Diagrams No. 3992 to 3996.

CHAPTER 15

TWIN PIONEER AIRCRAFT DRILL—OPERATIONAL

A.P.4215, Sect. 5, Chap. 15
A.L.20, Mar. 62

Chapter 15

(Completely revised)

TWIN PIONEER AIRCRAFT DRILL—OPERATIONAL

LIST OF CONTENTS

	Para.		Para.
Introduction	1	Action stations	11
Despatcher	2	Red light ON	12
Before emplaning—		Green light ON	13
Inspection of the aircraft	4	Strop carrying	14
Inspection of the parachutists	5	Movement to the door	15
Load manifests	6	Exits	16
Emplaning	7	Dropping Zone limit	17
Aircraft drill—		**Emergency procedures**	
Prepare for action	8	Refusals	18
Equipment check	9	Sickness	20
Tell off for equipment check	10	Retrieval of a suspended parachutist	21

LIST OF ILLUSTRATIONS

	Fig.		Fig.
Ready for take-off—clean fatigue	1	Ready for take-off—carrying equipment	4
Preparing for action—clean fatigue	2	Preparing for action—carrying equipment	5
Prepared for action—clean fatigue	3	Prepared for action—carrying equipment	6

INTRODUCTION

1. With a flying crew of two persons the parachuting complement of the Twin Pioneer Aircraft is as follows: —

(1) One despatcher and ten parachutists in clean fatigue dress (*i.e. not carrying additional equipment*),

or

(2) One despatcher and eight parachutists each carrying equipment not exceeding 75 lb. in weight. Equipment loads are also limited to the following maximum dimensions: —

    (a) Weapon stowage—52 in. long.

    (b) Kit stowage—24 in. long by 15 in. deep or 36 in. long by 10 in. deep.

Despatcher

2. The despatcher is to be a Parachute Jumping Instructor (*P.J.I.*), and is responsible for: —

(1) The pre-flight inspection of the aircraft (*in conjunction with the Captain of the aircraft*), for the parachutist dropping role.

(2) Supervising the preparation and emplaning of the stick for parachuting.

(3) Checking equipment.

(4) Despatching the stick and subsequently retrieving the parachute static lines and bags.

(5) Maintaining intercommunication with the Captain and informing him of the progress of the parachuting drills.

3. The P.J.I. Despatcher is to wear a back type parachute at all times whilst in flight. When he is working in the vicinity of the parachute exit doorway he is to wear a safety harness; the belt is to be fastened round his waist over his parachute pack and the anchorage strap is to be attached to the aft end of the parachutists' static line anchor cable.

BEFORE EMPLANING

Inspection of the aircraft

4. The P.J.I. Despatcher (*in conjunction with the Captain*) is to inspect the aircraft before each flight in accordance with the instructions given in Sect. 5, Chap. 2 and Appendix 6 thereto.

Inspection of the parachutists

5. The Chalk Commander is to form up the sticks in two ranks on the port side of the aircraft, forward of the door and facing the tailplane. The P.J.I. Despatcher is then to inspect the parachutists as detailed in Sect. 5, Chap. 3.

RESTRICTED

Load manifests

6. The Chalk Commander is to ensure that the load manifest forms are completed, signed and passed to the Airborne Forces Liaison Officer.

EMPLANING

7. The drill procedure for emplaning is as follows: —

(1) The P.J.I. Despatcher is to order STICK—NUMBER, and the stick is to number from right to left.

(2) The P.J.I. Despatcher is to enter the aircraft and, from the parachute exit doorway, give the order STICK—EMPLANE.

(3) The stick is to emplane in the reverse of numerical sequence, i.e. with the highest number of the stick leading; the parachutists are to stack their equipment, if carried, take up their seat positions (*fig. 1 or 4 as appropriate*) and fasten their safety belts.

(4) When the stick is seated and all safety belts are secured, the P.J.I. Despatcher is to close the canvas door curtain (*if necessary*), and inform the Captain of the aircraft STICK READY FOR TAKE-OFF.

Note...

The parachutists' equipment is to be lashed to the compartment floor if the flight to the Dropping Zone (D.Z.), is of long duration.

AIRCRAFT DRILL

Prepare for action

8. The action to be taken when the command PREPARE FOR ACTION is given depends on whether the parachutists are in clean fatigue dress only (*not carrying additional equipment*), or whether they are carrying equipment. The drill procedures are as follows: —

Clean fatigue: —

(1) The Captain of the aircraft is to give the order PREPARE FOR ACTION at a pre-arranged time.

(2) The P.J.I. Despatcher is to repeat the order to the parachutists.

(3) The parachutists are to hook up their static lines to their respective strops assisted by the P.J.I. Despatcher. No. 1 and 2 are to hook up over the aft end of their respective seats.

(4) The parachutists are then to unfasten their safety belts.

(5) No. 10 of the stick is to move forward and sit on the step to the flight deck; No. 4 to 9 are each to move forward one seat and No. 3 is to move across and occupy the seat vacated by No. 4 (*fig. 2*).

(6) No. 1 and 2 are to stand up and move aft of their seat so that the P.J.I. Despatcher can fold up and stow the two seat units on the starboard side.

(7) The remainder of the stick are then to stand up, fold up and stow all seat units on the port side.

(8) The parachutists will then stand in stick order along the centre of the compartment, facing aft; No. 1 is to be level with the aft end of the static line anchor cable and No. 5 to 10 are to be staggered alternately as shown in fig. 3.

Carrying equipment: —

(1) On the command PREPARE FOR ACTION the parachutists are to hook up their static lines to their respective strops assisted by the P.J.I. Despatcher. No. 1 is to hook up over the aft end of his seat unit.

(2) The parachutists are then to unfasten their safety belts.

(3) No. 8 of the stick is to move forward and sit on the step to the flight deck.

(4) No. 2 to 7 are each to move forward one seat and No. 1 is to move across and occupy the seat vacated by No. 2 (*fig. 5*).

(5) The P.J.I. Despatcher is to fold up and stow the seat unit on the starboard side and unlash the parachutists' equipment.

(6) The parachutists are to take off their reserve parachutes and fit their equipment, using the seats for support.

(7) The parachutists are then to re-fit their reserve parachutes, fold up and stow all seat units on the port side.

(8) They will then stand in stick order along the centre of the compartment facing aft as shown in fig. 6.

Equipment check

9. When all the parachutists in the stick have hooked up and fitted their equipment, the P.J.I. Despatcher is to inspect each man. He will then give the order CHECK EQUIPMENT and each man is to check the following: —

(1) The security of his own strop snap-hook and safety pin.

(2) The position of his own static line.

(3) The freedom of his strop on the static line anchor cable.

(4) The security of his harness quick-release box.

(5) The security of his reserve parachute.

(6) The correct attachment and security of the quick-release hooks, suspension rope attachments and leg strap of his equipment container.

(7) The attachment of the jettison device to the leg strap of his parachute harness.

(8) The security of all visible ties and the static line of the man in front of him in the stick. The visible ties and the static line of the last man in the stick are to be checked by the man in front of him.

RESTRICTED

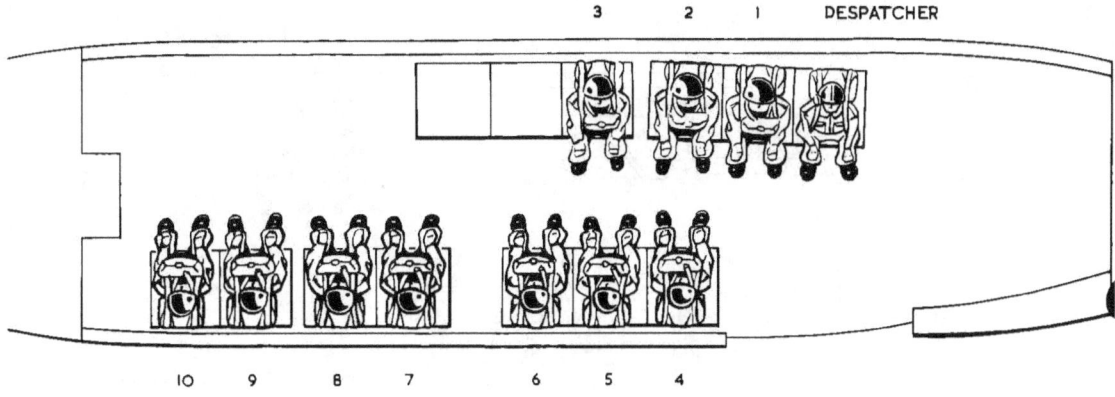

Fig.1. Ready for take-off — clean fatigue

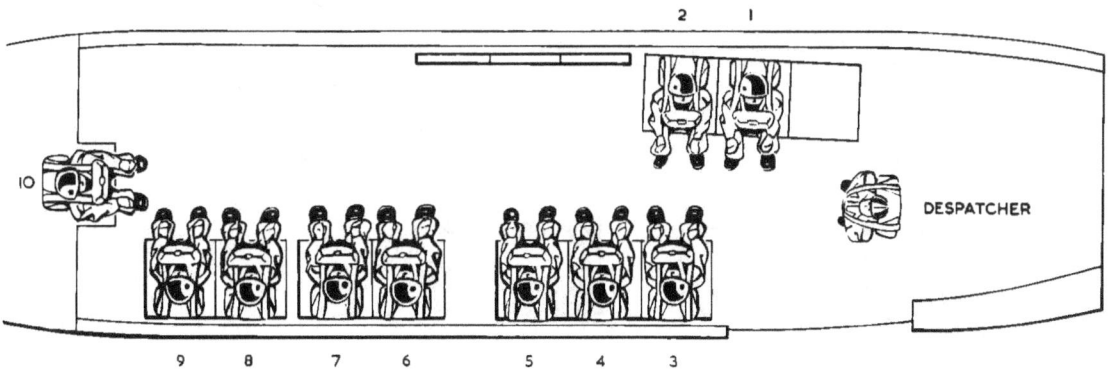

Fig.2. Preparing for action — clean fatigue

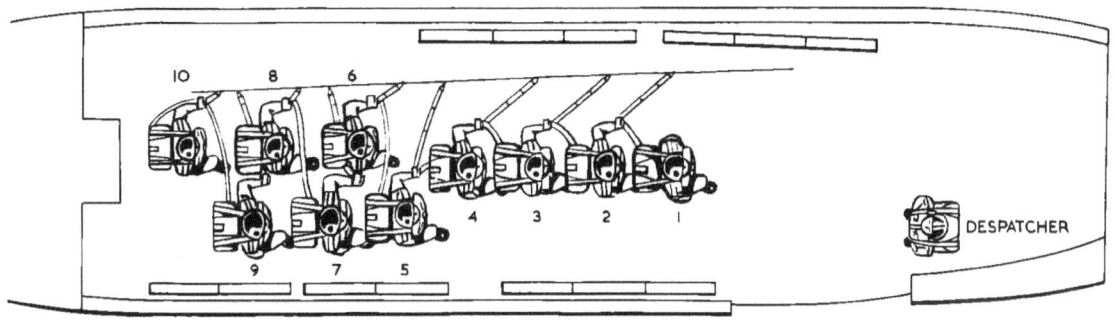

Fig.3. Prepared for action — clean fatigue

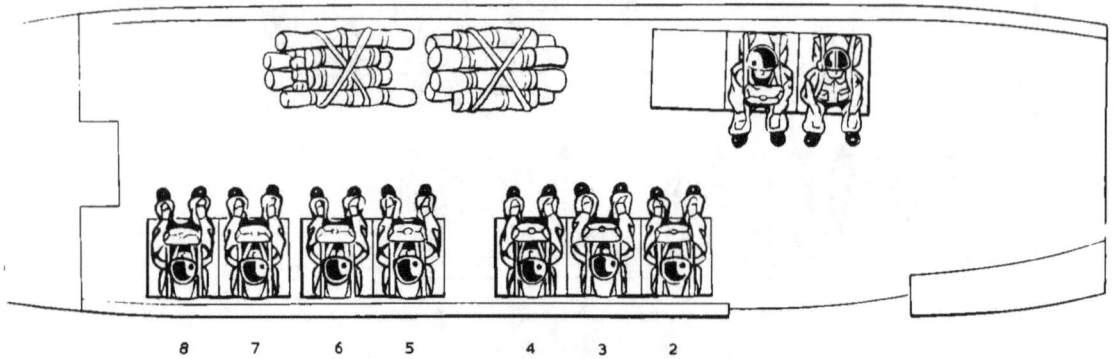
Fig.4. Ready for take-off – carrying equipment

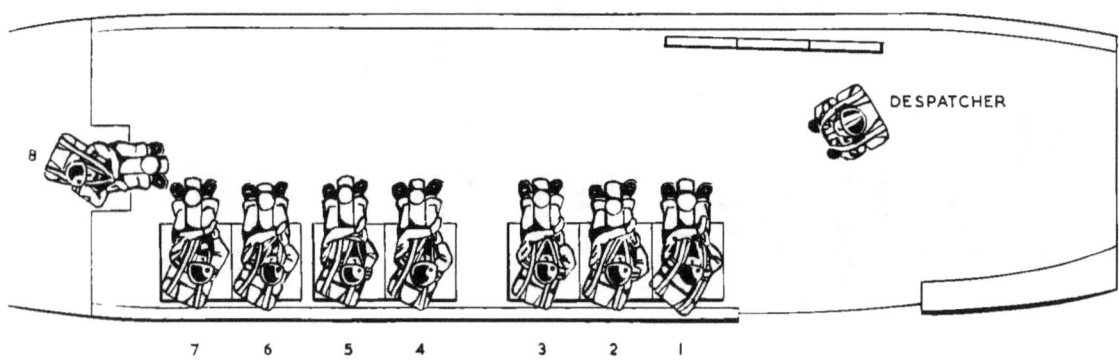
Fig.5. Preparing for action – carrying equipment

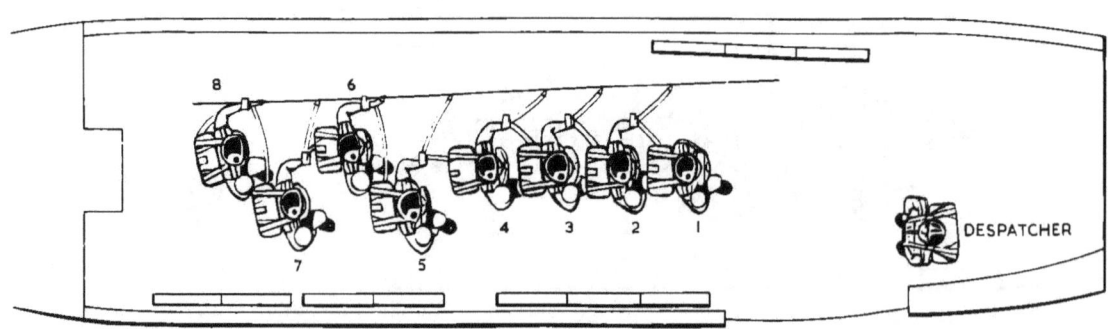
Fig.6. Prepared for action – carrying equipment

RESTRICTED

Tell off for equipment check

10. When all the parachutists have completed their checks satisfactorily the procedure is as follows:—

(1) The P.J.I. Despatcher is to give the order TELL OFF FOR EQUIPMENT CHECK.

(2) The parachutists are to call out in succession (*in the reverse of their numerical sequence in the stick*), NO. 10, O.K., NO. 9, O.K. and so on back to No. 1. As each man calls out his number he is to tap the shoulder of the man in front of him with his right hand.

(3) The No. 1 of the stick is to report to the P.J.I. Despatcher NO. 1, O.K.—STICK O.K.

(4) The P.J.I. Despatcher is then to report to the Captain STICK READY FOR ACTION, and, if necessary, ask permission to open the canvas curtain at the parachute exit doorway.

IMPORTANT...

If the operation is taking place at night, the parachutists' compartment lighting should be switched OFF at this stage of the drill.

Action stations

11. Five minutes before the time of the drop the Captain is to give the order ACTION STATIONS. The procedure is then as follows:—

(1) The Despatcher is to take up his position immediately aft of the parachute exit doorway and is to repeat the order to the parachutists.

(2) The No. 1 man of the stick is to stand one pace from the exit doorway with both hands (*clean fatigue*), or his free left hand (*carrying equipment*), on the top of the exit doorway.

(3) The remainder of the stick are to close up behind No. 1 in their action station positions.

Note...
The five minute interval between the command ACTION STATIONS *and the time of the drop may be reduced for training descents.*

Red light ON

12. Five seconds before reaching the Release Point the Captain is to switch ON the Red despatch signal light. The procedure is then as follows:—

(1) The Despatcher is to give the order STAND IN THE DOOR.

(2) The No. 1 man of the stick is to move one pace forward to the approved position, preparatory to exit, in the parachute exit doorway. He will bring his free left hand to his equipment (*if carried*), or to the top of his reserve parachute pack (*clean fatigue*).

(3) The remainder of the stick are to close up behind the No. 1 man and each man is to prepare for his exit.

Green light ON

13. The Captain is to switch ON the Green despatch signal light as soon as the Release Point is reached. The procedure is then as follows:—

(1) The Despatcher is to tap the No. 1 man on the shoulder and shout GO.

(2) The No. 1 man is to make an immediate exit, followed by the remainder of the stick in the correct sequence.

(3) The Despatcher is to despatch each man in turn by calling out his stick number and by tapping him on the shoulder.

Strop carrying

14. As the stick moves aft to the parachute exit doorway each man is to carry the strop of the man preceding him in the stick; he is to guide the strop along the anchor cable and release it as he comes to the No. 2 position. The last man of the stick is to carry his own strop in addition to that of the man in front of him.

Movement to the door

15. The parachutists are to be warned that they are not to stamp their feet as they move aft towards the parachute exit doorway as the floor of this aircraft is of comparatively light and flexible construction.

Exits

16. Port door exit technique is to be used by the parachutists in making their exits (*Sect. 3, Chap. 2*), but owing to the width of the parachute exit doorway the left hand is not to be used to assist in the making of an exit. The left hand is to be transferred to the equipment (*if carried*) or to the top of the reserve parachute pack (*clean fatigue*), after the static line strop has been released (*para. 14*). The exit is to be made through the forward part of the exit doorway where the head-room is greatest. The parachutists are to be briefed that they must stoop slightly before they reach the exit doorway and that they must avoid ducking their heads which will cause them to make a diving exit.

Dropping Zone limit

17. The Captain is to switch ON the Red despatch signal light when the aircraft reaches the limit of the Dropping Zone (D.Z.); the procedure is then as follows:—

(1) The Despatcher is to shout RED LIGHT ON and is to prevent the remainder of the stick, if any, from jumping.

(2) The Captain will then fly the aircraft as slowly as possible, while the Despatcher retrieves the trailing parachute bags and strops, until the Despatcher finally reports PARACHUTE BAGS IN.

RESTRICTED

EMERGENCY PROCEDURES

Refusals

18. During the flight to the D.Z., if a parachutist states that he will refuse to jump, he is to be unhooked by the Despatcher and is to be taken to the forward end of the parachutists' compartment. His strop is to be re-serviced, and is to be carried by the next man in the stick in addition to the strop he is already carrying.

19. If a parachutist refuses to jump on arrival at the exit doorway when the aircraft is over the D.Z., he is to be moved immediately by the Despatcher to a position aft of the exit doorway so that the remainder of the stick can jump without further delay.

Sickness

20. If a parachutist becomes too sick to jump, or is wounded, he is to be unhooked by the Despatcher and laid on the floor of the compartment in a position where he will not impede the movements of the remainder of the stick. Any essential equipment carried by the casualty may be distributed among the remaining parachutists. First-aid is to be given to the casualty as soon as jumping operations permit.

Retrieval of a suspended parachutist

21. If a parachutist becomes caught up outside the aircraft, e.g., by being entangled in the trailing strops or static lines, he is to be hauled back into the parachutists' compartment by means of the block and tackle. It is imperative that the series of operations which are detailed in sub-para. (1) to (6) are performed with the maximum speed and efficiency, particularly during the final stages of retrieval, as a suspended parachutist can suffer serious injury through being buffeted against the aircraft. The Despatcher is to wear his safety harness and have it connected to the anchor cable when assisting the parachutist back into the compartment. The procedure is as follows:—

(1) The Despatcher is to report to the Captain that a man is caught up.

(2) The Captain is to fly the aircraft as slowly as possible in a turn to port.

(3) The Second Pilot or Navigator is to move aft and assist the Despatcher to remove the retrieval gear from its stowage and pay out the tackle.

(4) The Despatcher, with his safety harness connected to the anchor cable, is to connect the retrieval gear to the trailing strops.

(5) The Second Pilot or Navigator is to assist the Despatcher on the block and tackle in hauling the parachutist to the doorway.

(6) The Despatcher is to move to the doorway and assist the parachutist over the door sill.

22. If a parachutist cannot be hauled back into the compartment the following action is to be taken:—

(1) The Captain is to maintain an altitude of at least 2,000 feet above ground level and avoid flying over water or built-up areas.

(2) The parachutist is to indicate that his reserve parachute is ready for use by placing one or both of his hands on the top of his helmet.

(3) When the parachutist has indicated that his reserve parachute is ready for use, the towing static line or strop is to be cut immediately, unless the aircraft is over deep water. The decision to cut the parachutist free is to be made by the Captain of the aircraft.

WARNING...

The parachutist must not activate his reserve parachute until his connection with the aircraft has been severed.

CHAPTER 10

HASTINGS AIRCRAFT DRILL—OPERATIONAL

Chapter 10

HASTINGS AIRCRAFT DRILL—OPERATIONAL

LIST OF CONTENTS

	Para.		Para.
Introduction	1	Prepare for action	12
Suspended loads	2	Equipment check	13
Supplies containers	3	Removal and replacement of doors	14
Air Despatchers	4	Action stations	17
Safety harness	5	Red despatch signal lights	18
Chalk/Stick commander	6	Green despatch signal lights	19
Aircraft drill—		Strop retrieval	20
Inspection of the aircraft	7	**Emergency procedures—**	
Inspection of the parachutists	8	Refusals	21
Emplaning	9	Sickness	22
Before take-off	10	Retrieval of a suspended parachutist	23
After take-off	11		

LIST OF ILLUSTRATIONS

	Fig.
Emplaning	1
Take-off positions	2
Prepare for action—STAND UP	3
Action stations—STAND IN THE DOOR	4

LIST OF APPENDICES

	App.
Hastings Aircraft — parachutists' role — inspection check list	1
Hastings Aircraft — parachutists' role — inspection sheet	2

INTRODUCTION

1. For the operational parachutists dropping role, the flying crew of the Hastings C, Mk. 1 or 2, Aircraft will normally consist of a Captain, Second Pilot, Navigator/Supply Aimer, Signaller Air and a Flight Engineer. In addition one Parachute Jumping Instructor (*P.J.I.*), and one Air Quartermaster (*A.Q.M.*), are carried as Air Despatchers. The operational complement consists of 30 parachutists carrying suspended loads, plus 20 C.L.E. containers. The latter are carried on externally fitted racks underneath the aircraft.

Suspended loads
2. The parachutists' suspended loads are carried in Containers, weapon and personal equipment (*P.W.C.*), which are subject to the following limitations.

(1) The first three parachutists in each stick may carry P.W.C. weighing up to, but not exceeding, 95 lb.

(2) The remaining parachutists in each stick may carry P.W.C. weighing up to, but not exceeding, 75 lb.

(3) The length of the weapons, stretchers or other similar loads carried must not exceed 52 inches.

(4) The suspended load is to be carried on the right side of the body by the port stick of parachutists, and on the left side by the starboard stick.

(5) The carriage of a three-inch mortar barrel, or similar bulky and heavy loads, is restricted to the No. 1, 2 and 3 of either stick.

RESTRICTED

Supplies containers

3. The supplies containers may be dropped with parachutists in any one of the following sequences:—

(1) Supplies containers followed by parachutists.

(2) Supplies containers and parachutists simultaneously; when this is intended the containers parachutes must be fitted with delay-opening devices, set to a delay of 3·0 seconds.

(3) Parachutists followed by supplies containers.

(4) Parachutists followed by supplies containers, followed by parachutists.

Notes . . .

(a) When mixed loads of containers and parachutists are being dropped the Captain of the aircraft is to ensure that the Aircrew, Despatchers and parachutists are carefully briefed as to the dropping sequence.

(b) Reference must be made to A.P.4203A, Vol. 1, Sect. 2 and 3, Chap. 1, 3, and 4 for detailed information concerning aircraft equipment, supply container carriers and their loading, and the jumping and dropping sequences for uniform or mixed loads.

Air despatchers

4. The duties of the P.J.I. and the A.Q.M. are as follows:—

(1) *Parachute Jumping Instructor:*—

(a) Pre-flight inspection of the aircraft.

(b) Preparing of personnel for parachuting.

(c) Inspection of parachutists' equipment.

(d) Despatch of parachutists from the starboard exit door.

(e) Retrieval of trailing parachute bags and strops.

(f) Emergency retrieval of a suspended parachutist.

(2) *Air Quartermaster:*—

(a) Ensuring that the correct complement of safety equipment is carried.

(b) Manning the intercom. system in the parachutists' compartment and relaying the Captain's orders and instructions to the P.J.I. Despatcher.

(c) Despatching the port stick of parachutists from the port exit door.

(d) Assisting the P.J.I. Despatcher to retrieve the trailing parachute bags and strops.

(e) Assisting the P.J.I. Despatcher in any emergency.

Safety harness

5. The P.J.I. and the A.Q.M., when carrying out their duties as Air Despatchers, are each to wear a back-type parachute and an Air Despatcher's safety harness (*Ref. No. 6F/282 which is described in A.P. 1182B, Vol. 1, Sect. 1, Chap. 4*).

The safety harness belt is to be worn over the parachute pack and the strap is to be so adjusted that while the Air Despatcher has complete freedom of movement, he is not in danger of falling out of a parachute exit door.

Chalk/Stick commander

6. The Chalk/Stick commander is appointed by the Army Formation or Unit. He is responsible for the preparation of the men in his stick for parachuting and their delivery to the P.J.I. Air Despatcher, at the aircraft of the appropriate Chalk No.

AIRCRAFT DRILL

Inspection of the aircraft

7. The P.J.I. Despatcher is to inspect the aircraft before flight as detailed in Appendix 1 and is to complete and sign the Aircraft Inspection Sheet, an example of which is given in Appendix 2.

Inspection of the parachutists

8. The Chalk/Stick Commander is to line up the sticks in two ranks on the port side of the aircraft, forward of the door and facing the tailplane. The P.J.I. Despatcher is then to inspect each parachutist's equipment for the serviceability and correct fitting of the following items:—

(1) The parachute harness.

(2) The quick-release box on the harness.

(3) The parachute pack and all visible ties.

(4) The parachute static line and 'D' ring.

(5) The steel helmet and helmet straps.

(6) The airborne life-jacket if worn, ensuring that the physical inflation valve is closed and that the CO_2 cylinder is inserted correctly.

(7) The weapons and equipment carried.

(8) The packing and security of all suspended loads paying particular attention to the security and attachments of the suspension rope and quick-release fitting.

(9) The efficient functioning of the jettison devices, which are to be checked physically.

(10) The authorised weight and bulk of the suspended loads.

Note . . .

When the checks are completed the A.Q.M. is to complete the Load Manifest Forms and pass them to the Airborne Forces Liaison Officer.

Emplaning

9. The P.J.I. Despatcher is to give the following orders for the parachutists to emplane:—

(1) STARBOARD STICK NUMBER
The starboard stick (*front rank*), is to number from left to right.

(2) PORT STICK NUMBER
The port stick (*rear rank*), is to number from right to left.

RESTRICTED

F.S./2

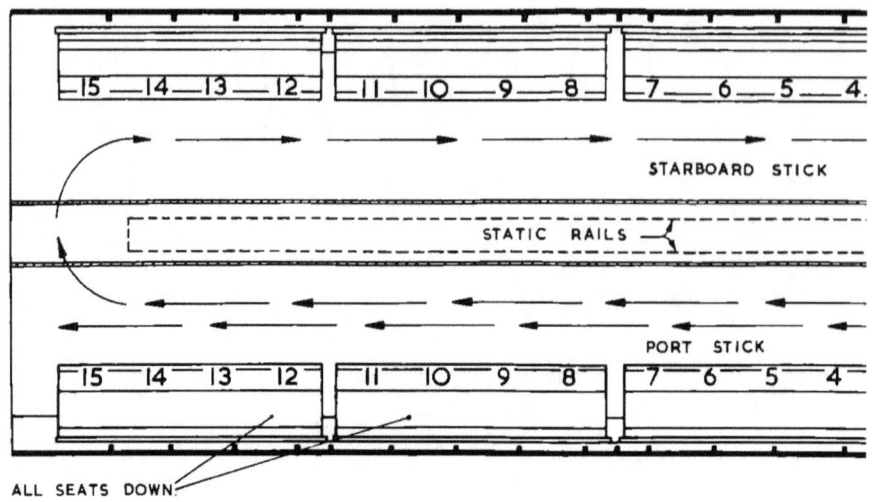

Fig. 1. - Emplaning

A.P.4215, Sect.5, Chap.10.
A.L.9, Feb.61.

STATIC CABLES

P.J.I.

STARBOARD STICK

RESTRICTED

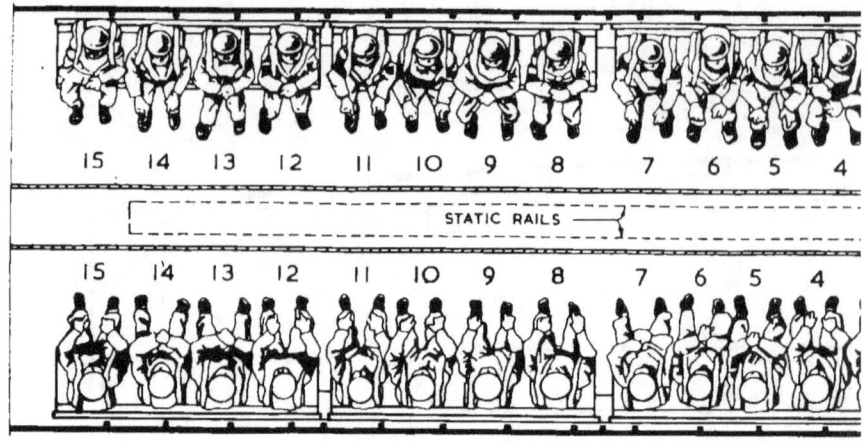

Fig. 2. - Take-

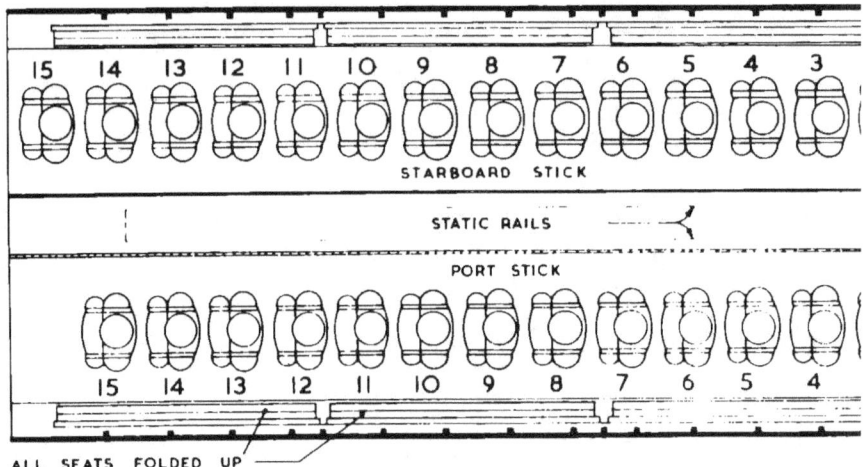

Fig. 3. - Prepare for Ac

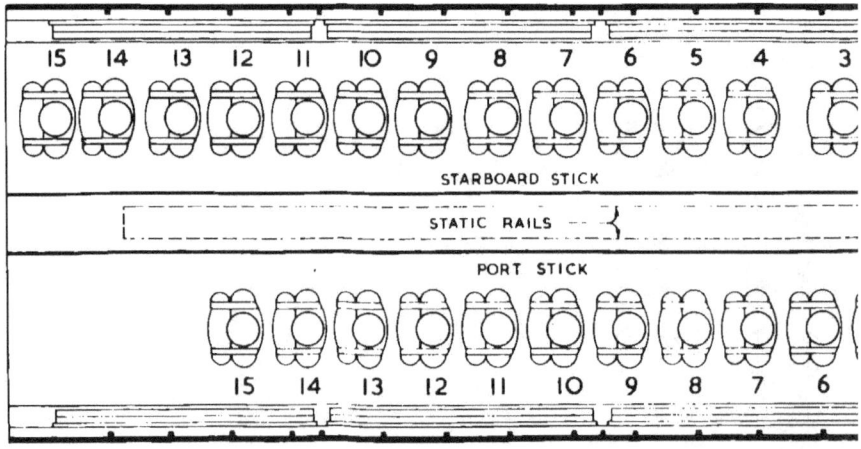

Fig. 4. - Action Stations -

RESTRI

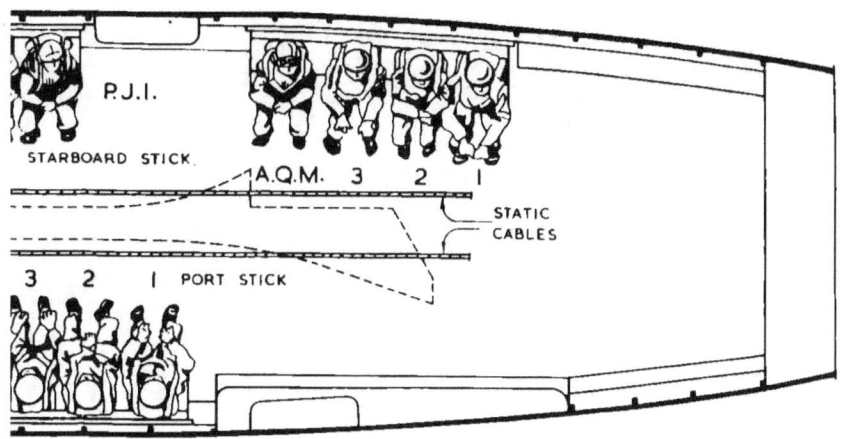

-off Positions

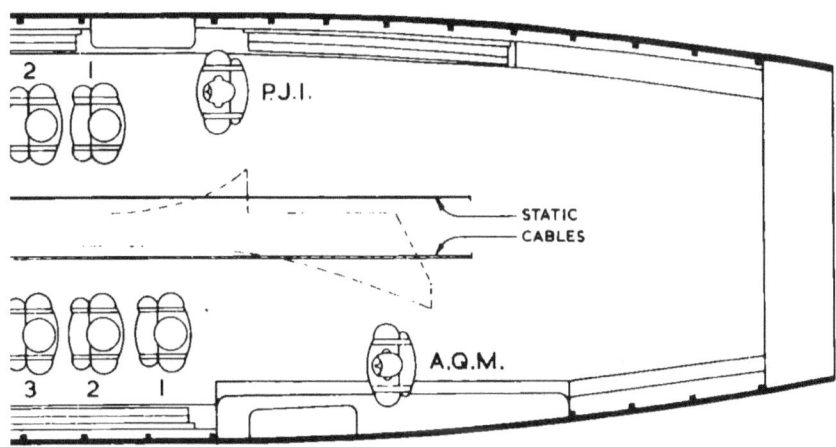

tion - STAND UP.

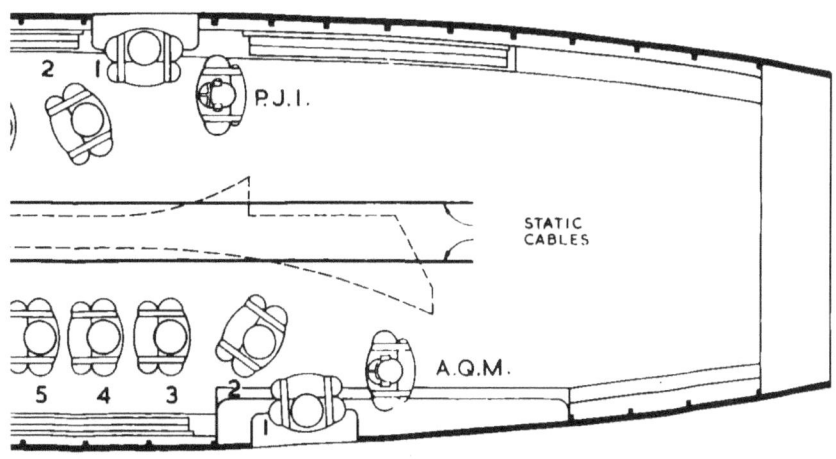

STAND IN THE DOOR.
CTED

(3) LEFT TURN
Both sticks are to turn to the left and face the port door of the aircraft.

(4) EMPLANE
This order is to be given from the door of the aircraft. The first parachutist of the starboard stick is to lead into the aircraft, his stick following him forward along the port side of the parachutists' compartment, under the forward end of the anchor cables and back along the starboard side of the compartment. The last man of the port stick is to follow the last man of the starboard stick, and all parachutists are to occupy the seats to which they have been detailed. Parachutists who are jumping with suspended loads are to carry them into the aircraft to their seating accommodation. Heavily laden personnel are to be assisted aboard by the A.Q.M. Suspended loads are to rest on the compartment floor between the parachutists' legs; on long flights to the D.Z. the suspended loads are to be secured to the tie-down fittings in the centre of the floor.

(5) When all parachutists are seated the steps are to be removed, and the A.Q.M. is to close the port door and ensure that both doors are secured.

(6) The P.J.I. Despatcher is to occupy the seat immediately forward of the starboard exit door; the A.Q.M. is to occupy the seat aft of the starboard exit door, with his intercom. plug engaged in the socket just aft of the starboard door frame. From this time onwards the A.Q.M. is to maintain communication with the Captain; if his duties necessitate movement away from his station the P.J.I. Despatcher is to take over on the intercom. system.

(7) The A.Q.M. is to report to the Captain over the intercom. system AIRCRAFT READY TO TAXY.

Before take-off

10. The drill procedure before take-off is as follows:—

(1) The Captain of the aircraft is to order SECURE SAFETY BELTS.

(2) The A.Q.M. is to repeat the order to the P.J.I. Despatcher and then fasten his own safety belt.

(3) The P.J.I. Despatcher is to order the parachutists to SECURE SAFETY BELTS.

(4) When all safety belts have been secured the A.Q.M. is to report to the Captain READY FOR TAKE-OFF.

After take-off

11. The Captain of the aircraft, after take-off, will normally order UNFASTEN SAFETY BELTS. In certain conditions, at the discretion of the Captain, safety belts may have to be worn continuously and be removed only on the receipt of a specific order, or on the order PREPARE FOR ACTION. The P.J.I. Despatcher is to prevent any unnecessary movements of the parachutists during flight.

Prepare for action

12. The drill procedure is as follows:—

(1) The Captain of the aircraft will give the order TWENTY MINUTES TO GO—PREPARE FOR ACTION to the A.Q.M. This order may be given twenty minutes before arrival at the D.Z., or at a pre-arranged time according to the loads carried by the parachutists

(2) The A.Q.M. is to repeat the order to the P.J.I. Despatcher.

(3) The P.J.I. Despatcher will give the order PREPARE FOR ACTION to the parachutists.

(4) The last parachutist of each stick is to release his safety belt, unfasten the strops at the forward end of the anchor cable nearest to him, retain the most forward strop and pass the remainder aft.

(5) Each parachutist in turn is to retain the most forward strop and pass the remainder aft until each man in his stick has a strop. No. 4 of the starboard stick is to pass the strops to the A.Q.M., who will pass them to the No. 3 of the starboard stick.

(6) Each man is to ensure that his static line is over his correct shoulder, i.e., on the port side, over the left shoulder and on the starboard side over the right shoulder.

(7) Each parachutist will then proceed as follows:—

(a) Hook up his static line, insert and secure his strop snap-hook safety pin.

(b) Unfasten his safety belt.

(c) Stand up, remove his reserve parachute and place it on the seat behind him with the Red handle down and to the rear.

(d) Sit down and transfer the quick-release hooks from his harness to the suspension plates on his load container or P.W.C.

(e) Fasten his jettison device to his right leg strap and then place the correct leg through the P.W.C. leg strap.

(f) Secure the P.W.C. or load container to the lower 'D' rings on his harness, replace his reserve parachute on the upper 'D' rings and tighten his leg strap.

(8) At the appropriate time the P.J.I. Despatcher will give the order STAND UP. The parachutists are to rise from their seats, release the sliding bolts securing the seats to the floor, fold up their seats and secure them with the

retaining straps. Each stick will then stand in single file facing aft.

Note ...

Before the seats are raised it must be ensured that the snap-hooks on the safety belts are not connected to the ' D ' rings at the back of the seats and that the belts are neatly folded and stowed.

Equipment check

13. The equipment check of the port and starboard sticks is to be carried out separately and as follows :—

(1) The P.J.I. Despatcher is to give the order PORT STICK—CHECK EQUIPMENT, followed by the order STARBOARD STICK—CHECK EQUIPMENT.

(2) Each parachutist is to make the following checks :—

(a) The security of his helmet.

(b) The hooking up of his static line to his strop and the security of his strop snap-hook safety pin.

(c) The position of his static line and the freedom of his strop on the anchor cable.

(d) The security of his quick-release box.

(e) The security of his reserve parachute.

(f) The security of his P.W.C. or suspended load quick-release snap hooks, the jettison device and the suspension rope attachments.

(g) The security of all visible ties on the parachute and static line of the parachutist in front of him; the last parachutist in each stick is to be checked by the man in front of him.

(3) The P.J.I. Despatcher is to check the hooking up and the fitting of each parachutist's equipment and suspended load. He is also to ensure that all strops move freely on the anchor cable and that all seats are folded and secured correctly.

(4) The P.J.I. Despatcher is then to give the order PORT STICK — TELL OFF FOR EQUIPMENT CHECK. After the check has been completely and correctly effected, the men in the port stick are to call out in succession NO. 15 O.K., NO. 14 O.K., and so on back to No. 1, who will then call out NO. 1 O.K., STICK O.K.

(5) After the port stick Tell Off, the P.J.I. Despatcher is to give the order STARBOARD STICK —TELL OFF FOR EQUIPMENT CHECK. The procedure for the starboard stick is similar to that for the port stick. On completion of the check the No. 1 parachutist of each stick is to report PORT (OR STARBOARD) STICK READY FOR ACTION.

(6) The P.J.I. Despatcher is then to inform the A.Q.M., TROOPS READY FOR ACTION.

Removal and replacement of doors

14. Seven minutes before arrival at the D.Z., the A.Q.M. is to assist the P.J.I. Despatcher to remove the parachutist exit doors and secure them in the stowages just forward of the toilet bulkhead. When the doors are stowed the A.Q.M. is to report to the Captain THE STICKS ARE READY FOR ACTION. The procedure for the removal and replacement of the doors is detailed in para. 15 and 16.

15. The procedure for the removal of a parachutist's starboard exit door in flight is as follows :—

(1) The P.J.I. Despatcher is to position himself forward of the door, grasp the bottom handle with both hands and hold it firmly in position.

(2) The A.Q.M. is to position himself aft of the door, and when the P.J.I. Despatcher is ready, is to push the door securing lever forward.

(3) The A.Q.M. is then to turn facing outboard, square with the door, grasp both upper door handles and pull the top of the door towards himself and into the compartment.

(4) The door is to be lowered in this way until it is at an angle of 30 degrees or less to the compartment floor, when it can be withdrawn completely into the compartment. The lugs on the bottom of the door are not to be disengaged from their recesses in the door sill until the door has been lowered sufficiently.

(5) The door is then to be stowed correctly on its own side of the fuselage aft of the doorway.

Note ...

The removal procedure for the port door is similar to that for the starboard door. If the operation takes place at night, the A.Q.M. is to dim the interior lighting before the doors are removed.

16. The procedure for the replacement of a parachutist's starboard exit door in flight is as follows: —

(1) The P.J.I. Despatcher is to position himself forward of the door, and with the A.Q.M., remove the door from its stowage and place it in position facing, and aligned with the exit aperture.

(2) From his forward position the P.J.I. Despatcher is to grasp the bottom door handle with both hands, while the A.Q.M. holds the door firmly by the upper handles.

(3) Together the P.J.I. Despatcher and the A.Q.M. are to carefully align and engage the lugs on the bottom of the door in their recesses in the door sill.

(4) When the P.J.I. Despatcher is satisfied that the lugs are correctly and securely located, the A.Q.M. is to raise the top of the door into the exit aperture and then lock the door by pulling the door securing lever aft.

Note ...

The replacement procedure for the port door is similar to that for the starboard door.

Action stations

17. The drill procedure for Action Stations is as follows:—

RESTRICTED

(1) The Captain is to give the order ACTION STATIONS to the A.Q.M. five minutes before arrival at the D.Z.

(2) The A.Q.M. is to repeat the order to the P.J.I. Despatcher, and is immediately to take up his own despatching station aft of the port exit door, with his intercom. plug engaged in the socket just aft of the doorway.

(3) The P.J.I. Despatcher is to give the order ACTION STATIONS to the parachutists and take up his despatching station aft of the starboard exit door with his intercom. plug engaged in the socket just aft of the doorway.

(4) The P.J.I. Despatcher will use the intercom. system to communicate with the Navigator/Supply Aimer if the despatch signal lights should fail.

(5) The P.J.I. Despatcher and the A.Q.M. are, if required, to pass four, three, two and one minute signals to the Chalk/Stick Commander.

Red despatch signal lights

18. The switching ON of the Red despatch signal lights is the signal for the No. 1 parachutist of each stick to STAND IN THE DOOR. The drill procedure is as follows: —

(1) The Navigator/Supply Aimer is to switch ON the Red despatch signal lights and call out RED–ON five seconds before reaching the Ground Dropping Signal or release point.

(2) As soon as the Red lights are switched ON the A.Q.M. is to report to the Captain RED–ON, and he and the P.J.I. Despatcher are to give the order STAND IN THE DOOR.

(3) The No. 1 parachutist is to take up the approved position in his respective doorway.

(4) The remainder of each stick are to take up the appropriate positions and prepare to make an immediate exit in turn.

Green despatch signal lights

19. The switching ON of the Green signal lights is the signal for the No. 1 parachutist of each stick to make an immediate exit followed by the remainder of his stick. The drill procedure is as follows: —

(1) The Navigator/Supply Aimer is to switch ON the Green despatch signal lights as soon as the aircraft is directly over the Ground Dropping Signal or the release point and call out GREEN–ON.

(2) As soon as the Green lights are switched ON the A.Q.M. is to report to the Captain GREEN–ON.

(3) Immediately GREEN–ON has been reported, the P.J.I. Despatcher and the A.Q.M. are to tap their respective No. 1 men on their shoulders and shout GO.

(4) The No. 1 men are to make immediate exits.

(5) The remainder of each stick is to follow its No. 1 man in the correct sequence while the Green lights are ON.

IMPORTANT . . .

(a) If the despatch signal lights fail the P.J.I. Despatcher and the A.Q.M. are to commence despatching immediately on hearing the Navigator/Supply Aimer call out GREEN—ON over intercom. system.

(b) As the sticks move towards the exits each man is to grasp the strop of the man preceding him and guide it along the anchor cable, releasing it as he himself comes to the No. 2 position in the doorway. The last man of each stick is to carry his own strop in addition to that of the man in front of him in the stick.

(c) If a parachutist finds that the strop of the man preceding him in his stick is jammed, he is to prevent him from jumping; the whole stick affected is to cease to jump until the strop is cleared.

(6) The Despatchers are to count off the parachutists as they make their exits, and if a Red light is switched ON while the aircraft is over the D.Z. they are to call out immediately RED–ON and prevent any further jumping.

(7) When all the parachutists have made their exits the A.Q.M. is to report to the Navigator/Supply Aimer ALL TROOPS GONE.

(8) The Navigator/Supply Aimer is to switch ON the Red despatch signal light and call out RED—ON as soon as the aircraft is over the D.Z. Ground Limit Signal.

(9) The P.J.I. Despatcher and the A.Q.M. are to repeat RED—ON and are to prevent any remaining parachutists from jumping. The A.Q.M. is to inform the Captain if, and why, any members of a stick have been prevented from jumping.

(10) When the jumping operation has been completed the P.J.I. Despatcher is to retrieve the trailing strops assisted by the A.Q.M.

Strop retrieval

20. The trailing strops and bags are to be retrieved, using the winch if required, as follows: —

(1) The A.Q.M. is to operate the winch to pay out the cable.

(2) The P.J.I. Despatcher is to take the cable and the retrieval strop aft.

(3) The P.J.I. Despatcher is then to attach the retrieval strop to the cable and secure it round the trailing strops.

(4) The A.Q.M. is to operate the winch until the cable is wound in fully.

(5) The anchor strop is then to be fitted round the retrieved strops and the procedure repeated until all strops have been retrieved.

EMERGENCY PROCEDURES

Refusals

21. *During flight:—*

If a parachutist states, during the flight to the D.Z., that he will refuse to jump, he is to be unhooked by the P.J.I. Despatcher and taken forward in the aircraft to the A.Q.M.'s compartment. The P.J.I. Despatcher is to re-service the vacated strop and hand it to the next parachutist in the stick who is to carry it in addition to the strop of the man in front of him in the stick.

During jumping:—

If a parachutist refuses to jump at the door, he is to be removed to a position aft of the exit door by the P.J.I. Despatcher so that the remainder of the stick can jump without further delay. The parachutist concerned is not to be unhooked until he has been moved forward of the exit doors to the forward end of the parachutists' compartment.

Sickness

22. If a parachutist is wounded or becomes too sick to jump, he is to be unhooked by the A.Q.M. or the P.J.I. Despatcher and laid on the floor of the compartment, in a position where he will not impede the movements of the remainder of the parachutists. First-aid is to be rendered as soon as possible and essential equipment that is carried by the casualty may, if time permits, be distributed among the other parachutists. The vacated strop is to be re-serviced by the P.J.I. Despatcher and handed to the next parachutist in the stick who is to carry it in addition to the strop of the man in front of him in the stick.

Retrieval of a suspended parachutist

23. A standard procedure for the retrieval of a suspended parachutist who is being towed behind an aircraft is defined in A.P. 4200, Vol. 1 (2nd Edn.), Sect. 3, Chap. 3 (*War Office Code No. 8297*) If a parachutist is suspended outside a Hastings Aircraft by being entangled in the trailing strops or static lines, he is to be hauled back into the parachutists' compartment by the strop retrieval winch. The retrieval procedure is detailed in sub-para (1) to (6).

Note . . .

An alternative course of action is detailed in para. 24.

IMPORTANT . . .

It is imperative that the series of operations which follows is performed with the maximum speed and efficiency, particularly during the final stages of retrieval, as a suspended parachutist can suffer serious injury through being buffeted against the aircraft. Despatchers who are assisting the parachutist over the door sill must have their safety harnesses fitted and secured to compartment tie-down rings or to the overhead anchor cable.

(1) The A.Q.M. is to inform the Captain of the aircraft that a parachutist is suspended from the aircraft, and is to state from which side he is caught up.

(2) The Captain will fly the aircraft, as slowly as possible, on a circuit towards that side.

(3) The A.Q.M is to man the retrieval winch and disengage the pawl and ratchet so that the P.J.I. Despatcher can pull out the cable.

(4) The P.J.I. Despatcher is to attach the single side retrieval strop to the snap-hook on the end of the cable and secure the strop round all the trailing strops at the door on the side from which the parachutist is suspended. He is then to give the A.Q.M. the order to WIND IN.

(5) The A.Q.M. is to re-engage the pawl, and ratchet-wind in the cable; if any member of the Aircrew is available he is to assist the A.Q.M. at the winch.

(6) The P.J.I. Despatcher is to remain near the door to assist the parachutist over the door sill and into the compartment.

24. If the parachutist cannot be hauled back into the compartment by the use of the retrieval winch, the following action is to be taken :—

(1) The Captain of the aircraft will maintain an altitude of at least 1,000 ft. above the ground, and will avoid flying over water or built-up areas.

(2) The parachutist is to indicate that his reserve parachute is ready for use by placing one or both of his hands on the top of his helmet.

(3) When the parachutist has indicated that his reserve parachute is ready for use, the towing static line or strop is to be cut immediately. The decision to cut the parachutist free will be made by the Captain of the aircraft.

(4) The parachutist must not activate his reserve parachute until his connection with the aircraft has been released or severed.

RESTRICTED

Appendix 1

HASTINGS AIRCRAFT

PARACHUTISTS' ROLE—INSPECTION CHECK LIST

1. Ensure that the intercom. system between the A.Q.M./P.J.I. Despatchers' positions, the downward observation position and the Captain's position is serviceable.

2. Ensure that the Red and Green despatch signal lights at both the port and starboard parachute exit doors function correctly by switching RED–ON, RED–OFF, GREEN–ON, GREEN–OFF ; check the lights with the Navigator/Supply Aimer from the downward observation position.

3. When the despatch signal lights and intercom. system checks have been completed correctly, the A.Q.M. is to confirm with the Navigator/Supply Aimer over the intercom. LIGHTS AND INTERCOM., O.K.

4. Ensure that the parachutists' anchor cables are serviceable, that both ends of each cable are secure and the tensioning turnbuckles are locked.

5. Ensure that the parachutists' anchor cables are tensioned correctly.

6. Ensure that the Despatchers' anchorage cables are serviceable, that both ends of each cable are secured to the aircraft structure and the tensioning turnbuckles are locked.

7. Ensure that there are sufficient strops on the anchor cables, of the correct number on each side, that the strops are serviceable, folded in the correct manner and attached to the anchor cables so that the tongues of the snaphooks face forward when the strops are extended fully.

8. Ensure that all snap-hooks, pins and ' D ' rings are serviceable, and that the strops are secured at the forward ends of the anchor cables when not in use.

9. Ensure that the strop retrieval winch and its mounting are serviceable and that the retrieval and anchor strops are available in the aircraft.

10. Ensure that the requisite number of parachutists' safety belts are installed and that their quick-releases face in the correct direction, i.e., so that the quick-releases pull aft on the port side and forward on the starboard side.

11. Ensure that the seats, their securing fittings and retaining straps are serviceable and that the seats can be folded up.

12. Ensure that the requisite number of crash belts (*seventeen double belts*), are stowed correctly and that their elastic cords are secure.

13. Ensure that the bar on the forward edge of the port cargo door is withdrawn fully and that the securing screw is tightened.

14. Ensure that the handle inside and aft of the port exit door is securely masked.

15. If the aircraft has been converted from the personnel carrying role ensure that the lashing point blanking plate adjacent to the starboard exit door has been removed.

16. Ensure that there are no sharp edges or obstructions inside the aircraft that might damage or interfere with the parachutes or their static lines. Any such obstructions are to be masked or made good.

17. Ensure that the floor surfaces and door sills are safe and that anti-skid matting is serviceable and secure.

18. Ensure that a supply of vomit bags is available in the aircraft.

19. Ensure that the toilets outlets under the fuselage are of soft rubber.

20. Ensure that the cargo door hinges are efficiently masked and that the lower hinge fairing is masked with fabric if necessary.

21. Ensure that there are no sharp edges or obstructions on the outside of the aircraft that might damage or interfere with the parachutes or their static lines. Any such obstructions are to be masked or made good.

22. Ensure that the Inspection Sheet is completed and signed.

RESTRICTED

A.P.4215, Sect. 5, Chap. 10, App. 2

A.L.9, Feb. 61

Appendix 2

HASTINGS AIRCRAFT

PARACHUTISTS' ROLE—INSPECTION SHEET

Aircraft No.:...............................

	Tick as Checked	Remarks
1. Intercom. system serviceable		
2. Despatch signal lights functioning		
3. LIGHTS AND INTERCOM., O.K. checked over the intercom. with Navigator/Supply Aimer		
4. Parachutists' anchor cables secure and turnbuckles locked		
5. Parachutists' anchor cables correct tension		
6. Despatchers' anchor cables secure and turnbuckles locked		
7. Strops		
8. Snap-hooks, pins and 'D' rings		
9. Winch		
10. Safety belts		
11. Seats		
12. Crash belts		
13. Cargo door bar		
14. Masking of exit door handle		
15. Blanking plate at starboard exit		
16. Interior surfaces		
17. Floor surfaces, door sills and anti-skid matting		
18. Vomit bags		
19. Toilet outlets		
20. Masking of cargo door hinges		
21. Exterior surfaces		

Date........................ P.J.I. Despatcher's Signature..................................

RESTRICTED

CHAPTER 11

HASTINGS AIRCRAFT—EMERGENCY DRILL

Chapter 11

HASTINGS AIRCRAFT—EMERGENCY DRILL

LIST OF CONTENTS

	Para.		Para.
Introduction	1	*Exits and order of leaving the aircraft—*	
Crash belts	3	*Parachutists*	8
Dinghies and emergency packs	4	*Flying crew*	9
Ditching drill—		*Modified drill for training flights*	10
Preparation for ditching	5	**Crash landing drill—**	
Action on ditching	6	*Preparation for crash landing*	11
Action after ditching—		*Action on crash landing*	12
Launching of dinghies	7	*Action after crash landing*	13
		Abandoning the aircraft in the air	14

LIST OF ILLUSTRATIONS

	Fig.
Ditching and crash landing stations	1

INTRODUCTION

1. All parachutists are to be fully conversant with the correct emergency drill, which when the occasion arises, is to be followed as quickly as possible in a cool and disciplined manner. Reference must be made to A.P.4203A, Vol. 1, for detailed information concerning the role equipment carried in the aircraft and the emergency drills for the Flying Crew.

2. If a Parachute Jumping Instructor (*P.J.I.*), is carried instead of an Air Quartermaster (*A.Q.M.*), he will perform the duties detailed in this chapter for the A.Q.M. It is the responsibility of the A.Q.M. to ensure that:—

(1) The dinghies and emergency packs carried are appropriate for the number of personnel carried.

(2) The parachutists are fully conversant with the emergency drills.

Crash belts

3. The aircraft is to be equipped with 17 crash belts, which are rolled up, stowed along the sides of the compartment beneath the seats and secured by looped elastic cords. Each belt is of reinforced canvas, rectangular in shape, with a flap sewn to each corner to which anchor cables are attached. A snap-hook fitting connects the free ends of the two cables on each end of the belt. When required for use, the belts are removed from their stowages and unrolled; the snap-hooks are then attached to the red-painted tie-down points in the floor of the compartment, with their shortest cables nearest to the floor.

Dinghies and emergency packs

4. Six dinghies are normally carried; one in each of four dinghy stowages in the main planes and two, which are packed in valises, stowed in the parachutists' compartment aft of the parachute exit doors. An emergency pack containing survival equipment is provided for each dinghy; a first-aid kit is also carried in the compartment and, if required, two Type 6 packs containing, and marked, WATER, may be carried and stowed in the aft end of the compartment.

DITCHING DRILL

Preparation for ditching

5. The drill procedure to prepare for ditching is as follows:—

(1) The Captain of the aircraft is to order DINGHY—DINGHY—PREPARE FOR DITCHING, and is to flash D–D–D (—·· —·· —··) on the call light.

(2) The A.Q.M. is to acknowledge the order and repeat it to the parachutists and the P.J.I. Despatcher.

(3) All parachutists are to unfasten their safety belts, or unhook their static lines ; the men nearest to the escape windows (*except the port aft escape window*), are to remove the windows and pass them aft for stowage in the toilet compartment.

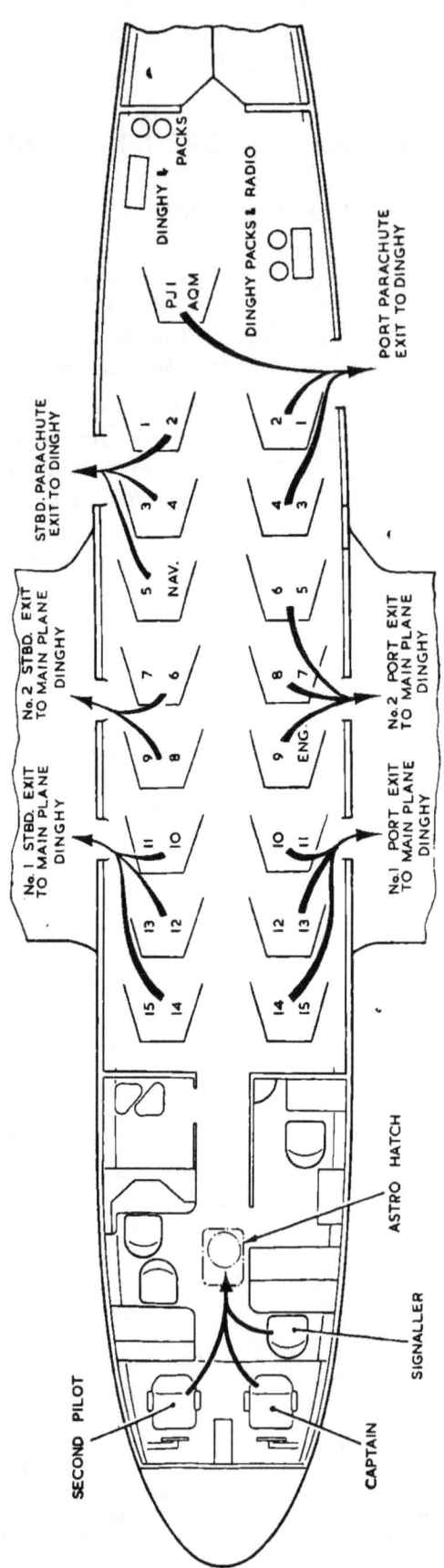

Fig. 1. Ditching and crash landing stations.

RESTRICTED

(4) The parachutists are to unfasten their seats, fold them up and secure them with the retaining straps.

(5) If time permits, the A.Q.M. and the P.J.I. Despatcher will remove the parachute exit doors; the A.Q.M. will supervise the quick and systematic jettisoning of parachutes and heavy equipment and then replace the doors. (*The equipment is to be passed aft to the men nearest to the doors but the parachutists who are of even numbers in their sticks are to retain their reserve parachutes, which they are to take aboard their dinghies as extra protection and cover*).

(6) The parachutists who are the odd numbers in both sticks are to remove the crash belts from their stowages and secure the belts to the floor (*para.* 3), assisted by the nearest even-numbered parachutists.

(7) As the crash belts are installed the parachutists are to take up their ditching stations as shown in fig. 1. Only the parachutists detailed to make their exits through the parachute exit doors are to inflate their life-jackets.

IMPORTANT ...

Personnel detailed to exit through escape windows must not inflate their life-jackets until they have made their exits.

(8) Each man is to be seated on the floor facing aft, with his knees bent and his feet flat on the floor; the hands are to be clasped behind the neck holding the head firmly down to the chest.

(9) At this stage those parachutists who are wearing parachutes are to turn and release their quick-release boxes, remove their leg straps and place their reserve parachutes beneath their knees.

(10) When all the parachutists (*and the Flying Crew members concerned*), are at their ditching stations, the A.Q.M. will take up his own station. His intercom. plug is to be engaged in its socket, he is to inform the Captain that all personnel in the compartment are ready for ditching and he is to remain on intercom.

(11) The Captain is to call out the decreasing altitude of the aircraft as it descends, and at 500 ft. he will press the call light button. At 100 ft. he will call out over the intercom., BRACE—BRACE and press the call light button as a signal to the parachutists to BRACE themselves.

(12) As soon as the A.Q.M. hears the Captain's order he is to shout BRACE—BRACE to all in the compartment.

Action on ditching

6. When the aircraft touches down there will normally be two phases of the impact; the first when the tail strikes the water and the second when the aircraft settles down. It is essential that the BRACE position is maintained until the aircraft has come to rest.

ACTION AFTER DITCHING

Launching of dinghies

7. When the aircraft has come to rest the dinghies are to be launched by the Flying Crew as follows:—

(1) The Signaller Air is to operate the dinghy release controls in the crew compartment which release the dinghies stowed in the main planes.

(2) The Flight Engineer is to operate the dinghy manual release controls in the parachutists' compartment.

(3) The Navigator/Supply Aimer is to open the starboard parachute exit door, assisted by the P.J.I. Despatcher and, by hand, launch the starboard valise stowed dinghy (*fig.* 1).

(4) The A.Q.M. is to open the port parachute exit door, assisted by the P.J.I. Despatcher and, by hand, launch the port valise stowed dinghy.

(5) The wing stowed dinghies are to be launched as detailed in para. 9.

Exits and order of leaving the aircraft

Parachutists

8. The parachutists are to lower their seats at the escape window positions; they are to take their rations and water bottles, and, where detailed, their reserve parachutes, and make their exits as follows: —

(1) No. 1 to 4 of the port stick and the P.J.I. Despatcher exit through the port parachute exit door and board the dinghy launched by the A.Q.M.

(2) No. 1 to 5 of the starboard stick exit through the starboard parachute exit door and board the dinghy launched by the Navigator/Supply Aimer.

(3) No. 5 to 9 of the port stick exit through the No. 2 port escape window on to the port inner main plane, then (*and not before*), inflate their life-jackets and board a wing stowed dinghy.

(4) No. 6 to 9 of the starboard stick exit through the No. 2 starboard escape window on to the starboard inner main plane, then (*and not before*), inflate their life-jackets and board a wing stowed dinghy.

(5) No. 10 to 15 of the port stick exit through the No. 1 port escape window on the port outer main plane, then (*and not before*), inflate their life-jackets and board a wing stowed dinghy.

(6) No. 10 to 15 of the starboard stick exit through the No. 1 starboard escape window on to the starboard outer main plane, then (*and not before*), inflate their life-jackets and board a wing stowed dinghy.

Note ...

The first men to make their exits through the No. 1 port and starboard escape windows respectively are to take the adjacent life-lines with them.

RESTRICTED

Flying crew

9. The Flying Crew are to make their exits, and proceed, as follows: —

(1) The Signaller Air is to be the first of the Flying Crew to leave the aircraft, having first operated the dinghy manual release controls in the crew compartment. He will make his exit through the astro-dome hatch on to the starboard main plane, then (*and not before*), inflate his life-jacket, remove the emergency pack from the starboard outboard dinghy stowage and manually assist the release and launching of the outboard dinghy. When all the parachutists detailed are aboard the outboard dinghy and the emergency pack has been transferred to it, he will board and take charge of this dinghy.

(2) The Co-pilot is to be the second of the Flying Crew to leave the aircraft, having first checked that the Signaller Air has operated the dinghy manual release controls. He will make his exit through the astro-dome hatch on to the starboard main plane, then (*and not before*), inflate his life-jacket, remove the emergency pack from the starboard inboard dinghy stowage and manually assist the release and launching of the inboard dinghy. When all the parachutists detailed are aboard the starboard dinghies he will transfer his emergency pack to, and board, the inboard dinghy. He will then take charge of all dinghies on the starboard side, endeavour to tie them together as a group and arrange an even distribution of men and equipment among them.

(3) The Navigator/Supply Aimer is to inflate his life-jacket and launch his dinghy (*para 7, sub-para.* (3)), supervise the parachutists boarding the dinghy and transfer to them his equipment, the emergency pack, the dinghy radio set and, if required, a WATER pack. He will then board and take charge of this dinghy.

(4) The Flight Engineer is to make his exit through the No. 2 port escape window on to the port main plane, having first operated the dinghy manual release controls in the parachutists' compartment. He will then (*and not before*), inflate his life-jacket, remove the emergency pack from the port outboard dinghy stowage and manually assist the release and launching of the outboard dinghy. When all the parachutists detailed are aboard the outboard dinghy and the emergency pack has been transferred to it he will board and take charge of this dinghy.

(5) The A.Q.M. is to inflate his life-jacket and launch his dinghy (*para. 7, sub-para* (4)), supervise the parachutists boarding the dinghy and transfer to them the emergency pack, the small first-aid kit, and, if required, a WATER pack. He will then board and take charge of this dinghy.

(6) The Captain is to be the last of the Flying Crew to leave the aircraft, having first satisfied himself that all drills have been completed and that all personnel have left the aircraft. He will make his exit through the astro-dome on to the port mainplane, then (*and not before*), inflate his life-jacket, remove the emergency pack from the port inboard dinghy stowage and manually assist the release and launching of the inboard dinghy. When all the parachutists detailed are aboard the port dinghies he will transfer his emergency pack to, and board, the inboard dinghy. He will then take charge of all dinghies on the port side, endeavour to tie them together as a group and arrange an even distribution of men and equipment among them. If it has not been necessary to do so before this time, the Captain will then order CUT PAINTERS—CAST OFF PORT SIDE.

(7) The Co-pilot is to give a similar order for the starboard side and both groups of dinghies are, if possible, to be tied together as one group. The drogues should be streamed, if necessary, to prevent the dinghies from drifting from the proximity of the aircraft, where they should be kept stationed for as long as possible to facilitate search and rescue.

Notes . . .

(*a*) *If only one valise stowed dinghy is carried in the parachutists' compartment, the Navigator/Supply Aimer will launch it and board it with the A.Q.M.*

(*b*) *If the foregoing procedures are changed to suit particular circumstances, the personnel affected are to follow their drills and make their exits in accordance with instructions which are to be given at the pre-flight briefing or as ordered at the time.*

Modified drill for training flights

10. On training flights the No. 1 P.J.I. Despatcher will perform the duties of the A.Q.M. Other Despatchers who cannot be accommodated in crash belts are to take up ditching positions with their backs against the forward bulkhead; they will make their exits through the No. 1 escape windows (*two via the port window, two via the starboard window*), and will board the outboard main plane dinghies.

CRASH LANDING DRILL

Preparation for crash landing

11. When it is known that an aircraft is to be crash landed the following is the drill procedure for the personnel concerned: —

(1) The Captain is to order PREPARE FOR CRASH LANDING and will flash C–C–C in morse (— — · — — · — · — — ·), on the call light.

(2) The A.Q.M. is to acknowledge the Captain's order and is to repeat the order to the parachutists and Despatcher(s) in the compartment.

(3) All parachutists are to unfasten their safety belts, or unhook their static lines; the men nearest to the escape windows are to remove the windows and pass them aft for stowage in the toilet compartment.

(4) The parachutists are to unfasten the bolts securing the seats, fold the seats up and secure them with their retaining straps.

(5) If time permits, the A.Q.M. and the P.J.I. Despatcher will remove the parachute exit doors; the A.Q.M. will supervise the quick and systematic jettisoning of parachutes and heavy equipment and then replace the doors. (*The equipment is to be passed aft to the exit doors and*

jettisoned by the No. 1 and 2 men of the port stick and No. 3 and 4 of the starboard stick.)

(6) The parachutists who are the odd numbers, in both sticks, are to remove the crash belts from their stowages and secure the belts to the floor (*para.* 3), assisted by the nearest even-numbered parachutists.

(7) As the crash belts are installed the parachutists are to take up their crash landing stations (*fig.* 1). Each man is to be seated on the floor facing aft, with his knees bent and his feet flat on the floor; the hands are to be clasped behind the neck, holding the head firmly down to the chest.

(8) At this stage those parachutists who may still be wearing parachutes are to turn and release the quick-release boxes, remove their leg straps and place their reserve parachutes beneath their knees.

(9) When all the parachutists (*and the Flying crew members concerned*), are at their stations, the A.Q.M. will take up his own crash landing station. He is to remain on intercom, and is to inform the Captain as soon as all personnel in the compartment are ready for crash landing.

(10) The Captain is to call out the decreasing altitude of the aircraft as it descends, and at 500 ft. he will press the call light button. At 100 ft. he will call out over the intercom. BRACE–BRACE and press the call light button as a signal to the parachutists to BRACE themselves.

(11) As soon as the A.Q.M. hears the Captain's order he is to shout BRACE–BRACE to all in the compartment.

Action on crash landing

12. When the aircraft touches down there may be more than one phase of the impact or a violent change of direction. It is essential that the BRACE position is maintained until the aircraft has come to rest.

Action after crash landing

13. When the aircraft has come to rest the drill procedure is as follows:—

(1) The A.Q.M. and the Navigator/Supply Aimer, assisted by the P.J.I. Despatcher, are to remove the port and starboard parachute exit doors respectively.

(2) The parachutists are to lower the seats at the escape window positions.

(3) The parachutists and the Flying Crew are to make their exits as quickly as possible in a cool and disciplined manner and in the order detailed in para. 8, 9, and 10.

ABANDONING THE AIRCRAFT IN THE AIR

14. If it is necessary to abandon the aircraft in the air the drill procedure is as follows: —

(1) The Captain is to order over the intercom. PUT ON PARACHUTES—PREPARE TO ABANDON AIRCRAFT. He will flash P–P–P on the call light in morse (·— —. ·— —. ·— —·), and switch ON the Amber despatch signal lights.

(2) The A.Q.M., P.J.I. Despatcher and the Flying crew will acknowledge the order in turn from aft to forward. If the operation takes place at night the compartment lights are to be switched ON.

(3) The Flying Crew are to follow the drill procedure detailed in A.P. 4203A, Vol. 1, Sect. 3, Chap. 5.

(4) The parachutists are to release their safety belts and attach their static lines to their respective strops; they will take up their normal STAND IN THE DOOR positions (*Chap.* 9 *and* 10), and will commence to jump on receiving the Captain's order JUMP—JUMP which he will give as he switches on the Green despatch signal lights.

(5) The A.Q.M. and the P.J.I. Despatcher are to despatch their respective sticks; the latter is to jump after the last man of the starboard stick.

(6) The A.Q.M. is to inform the Captain when all the parachutists and the P.J.I. Despatcher have jumped, disconnect his intercom. plug and then jump from the port parachute exit door.

(7) The Captain is to disconnect his intercom. plug after hearing that all personnel have left the aircraft and make his exit through the flying crew emergency hatch.

Note . . .

Survival on land or at sea is dealt with in Air Ministry Pamphlets No. 214, 224, 225 and 226, and in Air Diagrams No. 3992 to 3996.

August, 1961   Air Publication 4215

WAR OFFICE
AIR MINISTRY

MILITARY PARACHUTISTS MANUAL

ADVANCE INFORMATION LEAFLET NO. 1/61

Insert this leaflet in A.P.4215, Sect.5, Chap.15, to face fig.4.

Disposition of parachute troops' equipment

1. Insofar as it implies that the parachute troops' equipment may be loaded on the starboard side, forward of the starboard seats, Sect.1, Chap.4, fig.4 is to be disregarded, as with this arrangement the c.g. position of the aircraft is beyond the permissible forward limit.

2. The equipment containers must be laid on the floor in a single row of up to two layers along the centre of the cabin floor, the fore-and-aft position of the stacked equipment being such as to satisfy the c.g. limit requirements of the aircraft as defined in the aircraft Weight and Balance Data Handbook.

3. Where the flight to the dropping zone is of long duration the equipment must be secured to the floor with crossed tie-downs attached to tie-down fittings inserted in the floor seat rails.

Notes
(1) The information contained in this leaflet will be incorporated by normal amendment list action in due course.

(2) If, after receipt of this leaflet, an amendment list with a prior date and conflicting information is received, the information in the leaflet is to take precedence.

Z.1804X

RESTRICTED

A.P.4215, Sect. 6

SECTION 6

AIRCRAFT EQUIPMENT

RESTRICTED

Section 6

AIRBORNE EQUIPMENT

LIST OF CHAPTERS

1 Personal Equipment and Weapons Container

2 Parachutists' Life Jacket (*to be issued later*)

3 Supplies dropping containers (*to be issued later*)

A.P.4215, Sect. 6, Chap. 1
A.L. 12, June 61

CHAPTER 1

PERSONAL EQUIPMENT AND WEAPONS CONTAINER

Section 6

AIRBORNE EQUIPMENT

LIST OF CHAPTERS

1 Personal Equipment and Weapons Container

2 Parachutists' Life Jacket (*to be issued later*)

3 Supplies dropping containers (*to be issued later*)

RESTRICTED

A.P.4215, Sect. 6, Chap. 1
A.L. 12, June 61

Chapter 1

PERSONAL EQUIPMENT AND WEAPONS CONTAINER

LIST OF CONTENTS

	Para.
Introduction	1
Description	2
Dimensions and weight limitations	4
Typical items of equipment that can be carried in the P.W.C.	5
Inspection before packing	6
Packing the container	7
Packing a weapon	9
Methods of securing and releasing straps to and from buckles	10
Servicing a packed P.W.C.	11
Fitting the P.W.C. to a parachutist	12
Aircraft exit	13
Parachute flight with a P.W.C.	15
Emergencies during flight	17
Jettisoning a P.W.C.	18
Decision to jettison	19
Landing	20
Action after landing	21
Recovering the P.W.C. after landing	22

LIST OF ILLUSTRATIONS

	Fig.
Personal equipment and weapons container	1
Personal equipment and weapons container details	2
First stage of packing	3
Second stage of packing	4
Third stage of packing	5
First method of lacing	6
Fourth stage of packing	7
Fifth stage of packing	8
Sixth stage of packing	9
Seventh stage of packing	10
Eighth stage of packing	11
Second method of lacing	12
Weapon packed in caps	13
Method of making quick-release attachment	14
Suspension rope stowage and attachments	15
Jettison device and quick-release snap-hook fitting	16
Attachment of jettison device to parachute harness	17
Attachment of container to parachute harness	18
Method of releasing container (front view)	19
Method of releasing container (side view)	20

Fig. 1. Personal equipment and weapons container

	Fig.
P.W.C. carried pack fashion	21
Container supported by fittings behind the ammunition pouches	22
Container, less weapon carried pack fashion	23

RESTRICTED

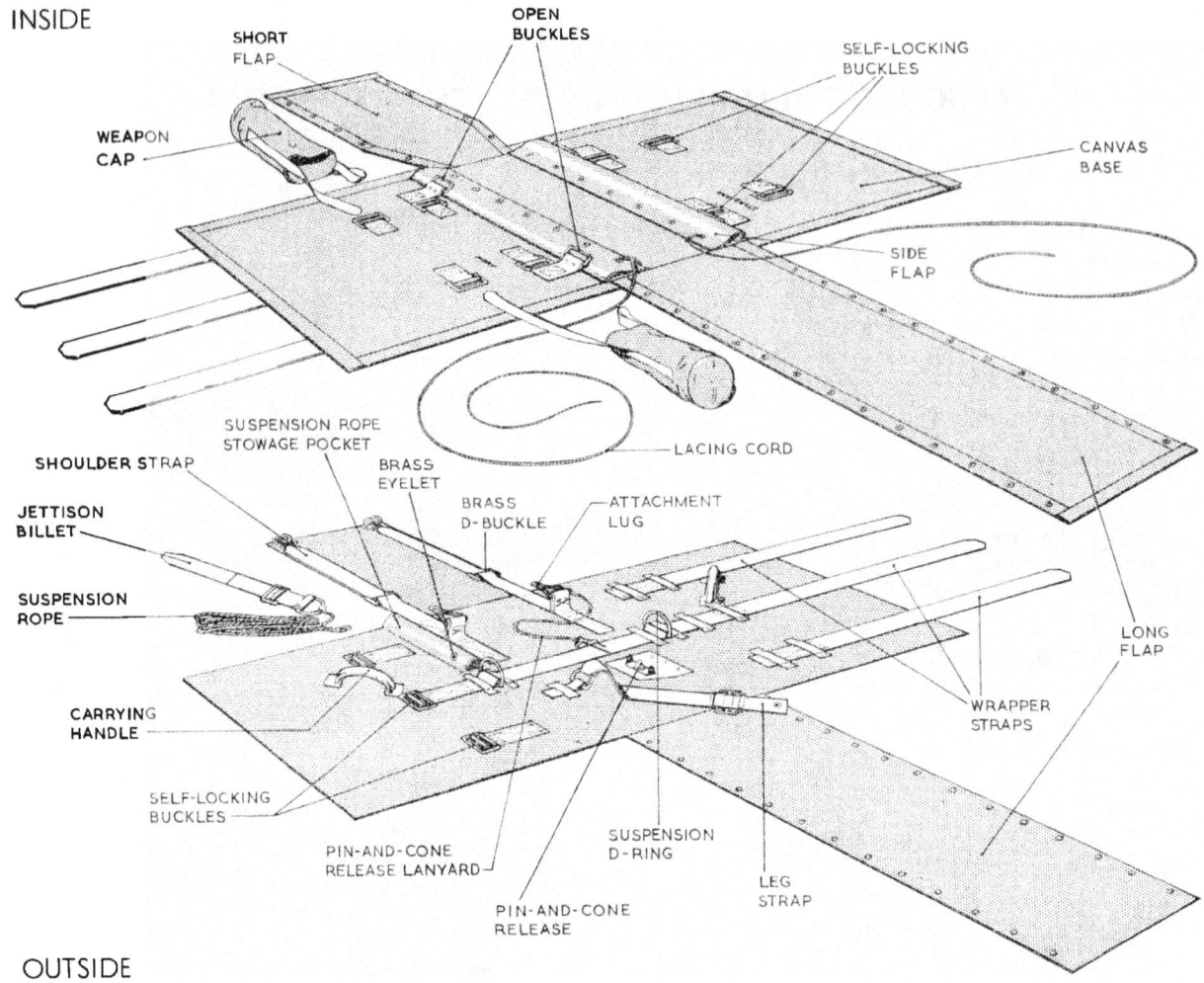

Fig. 2. Personal equipment and weapons container details

Introduction

1. The purpose of the personal equipment and weapons container (P.W.C.) is to enable a parachutist to carry personal equipment and a weapon (*fig.* 1) when making a descent by parachute and to be able to have them available immediately after landing. The P.W.C. can also serve as a pack which can be carried on the parachutist's back when he is on the ground.

Description

2. The P.W.C. (*fig.* 2) is manufactured in strong canvas, and is designed on the hold-all principle. The body of the P.W.C. is made so that it can be laid out flat for packing. It consists of a central panel which has six flaps. Four of these flaps, one at each side, one at the top and the other at the bottom are eyeletted, and when they are laced together over the packed equipment form the central part of the P.W.C. The remaining two flaps, one at each side are wrapper flaps which provide accommodation for a weapon or any other necessary piece of equipment such as a folding stretcher. On the inner face of each of the two side flaps are four buckles and two D-rings which are used to secure a weapon to the centre part of the P.W.C. Two canvas caps are provided to cover the ends of the weapon or piece of equipment carried. Details of the interior of the container are shown in fig. 2.

3. When the P.W.C. is made up, it is held together by three securing straps, the outer two of which are attached to the exterior of one side flap and fasten in two buckles on the exterior of the other flap. The third strap (*centre*) has a buckle at one end and is attached to both the side wrapper flaps and the centre section of the container so that the buckle lines up with the other two buckles that accommodate the top and bottom securing straps. A hand grip is provided on each of the side flaps. The following fittings are attached to the exterior of the central panel (*fig.* 2).

(1) Two metal suspension plates, to which the quick-release hooks are attached.

(2) A quick-release leg strap.

(3) A suspension rope stowage pocket.

(4) A quick-release pin and lanyard.

(5) Two suspension D-rings, a 15 ft. length of nylon rope is attached to one of these D-rings. The free end of the nylon rope is attached to a jettison device.

(6) Two shoulder straps.

RESTRICTED

Dimensions and weight limitations

4. (1) Maximum permissible dimensions of the centre section 36 in. × 12 in. × 12 in.

(2) Maximum permissible length of loaded weapon sleeves 52 in.

(3) Weight of empty container 16 lb.

(4) Normal loaded weight 75 lb.

(5) Maximum permissible loaded weight 95 lb.

Typical items of equipment that can be carried in the P.W.C.

5. (1) Personal equipment.
   (2) Rifle.
   (3) Sten gun.
   (4) Bren gun.
   (5) Vickers machine gun.
   (6) 3 in. Mortar
   (7) Mortar bombs.
   (8) 3·5 in. Rocket launcher.
   (9) 3·5 in. Rockets.
   (10) Anti-tank grenades.
   (11) Entrenching tools.
   (12) Shovels.
   (13) Picks.
   (14) Folding stretcher.

Inspection before packing

6. The canvas and all stitching is to be thoroughly checked for wear and tear and the following attachments checked for serviceability.

   (1) Buckles.
   (2) Webbing straps.
   (3) Quick-release lanyard, pin, buckle and cone and leaf spring.
   (4) Suspension plates and hooks.
   (5) Suspension rope and jettison device.
   (6) Handgrips.
   (7) Lacing cord and eyelets.
   (8) Suspension rope stowage pocket.
   (9) Weapon caps.
   (10) Suspension D-rings.

Packing the container

7. There are two methods of packing the centre section, both of which will be described. In the first method (*fig.* 3), the container is laid out flat, inside uppermost (*fig.* 3) and the equipment to be packed is placed on the centre section. Any extension of length which may be necessary must be made downwards along the long (*bottom*) flap. The bottom flap is folded over the equipment (*fig.* 4) and the short (*top*) flap is folded down over the bottom flap (*fig.* 5). The centre section and flaps are now secured by passing the lacing cord through the eyelets as shown in fig. 6. Starting from the bottom, the lacing cord is tightened ensuring that there are no gaps through which equipment could be lost. The ends of the lacing

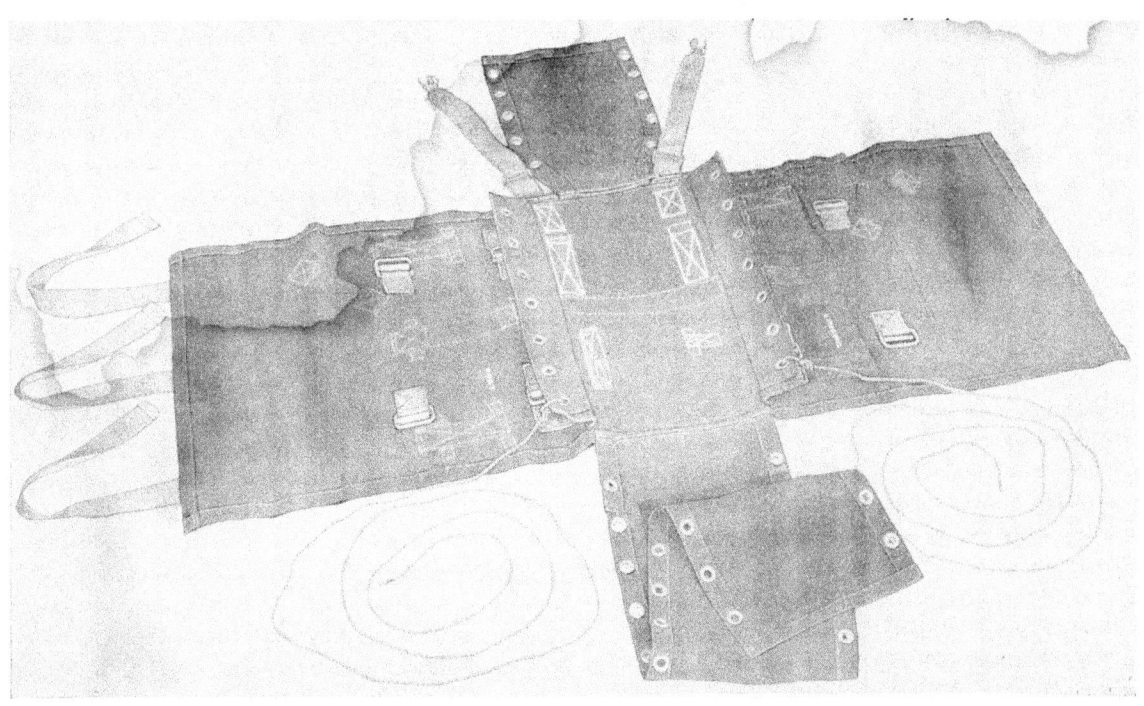

Fig. 3. First stage of packing

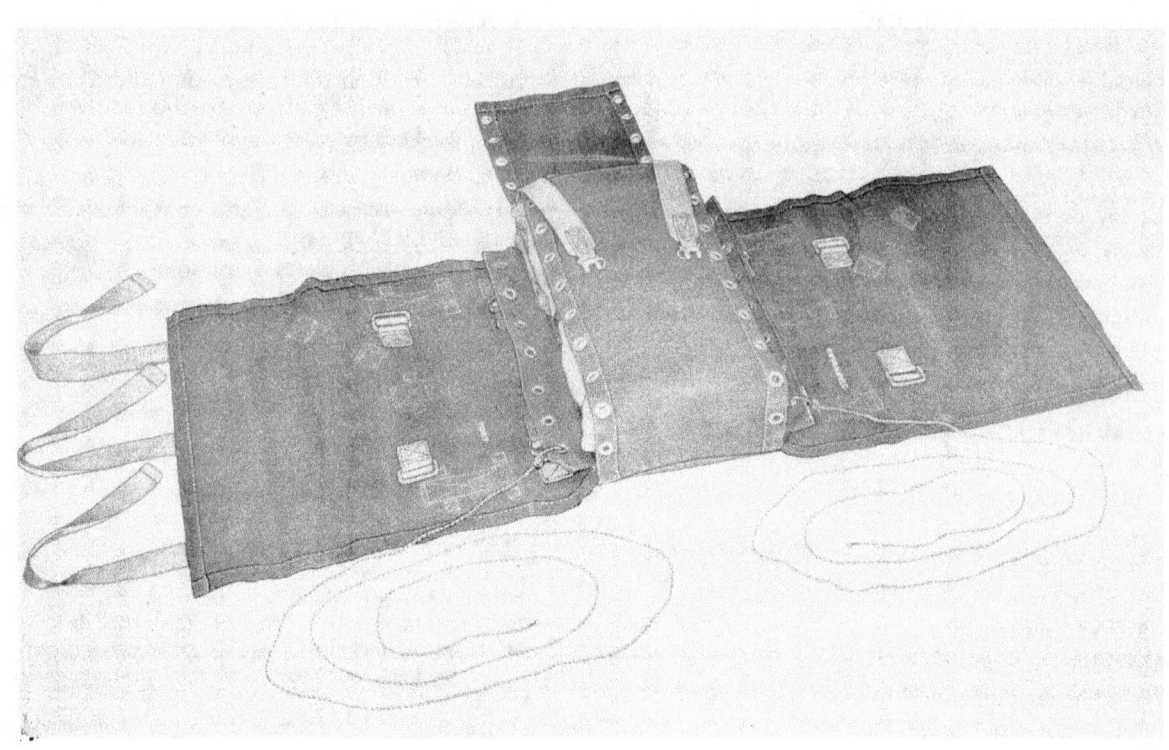

Fig. 4. Second stage of packing

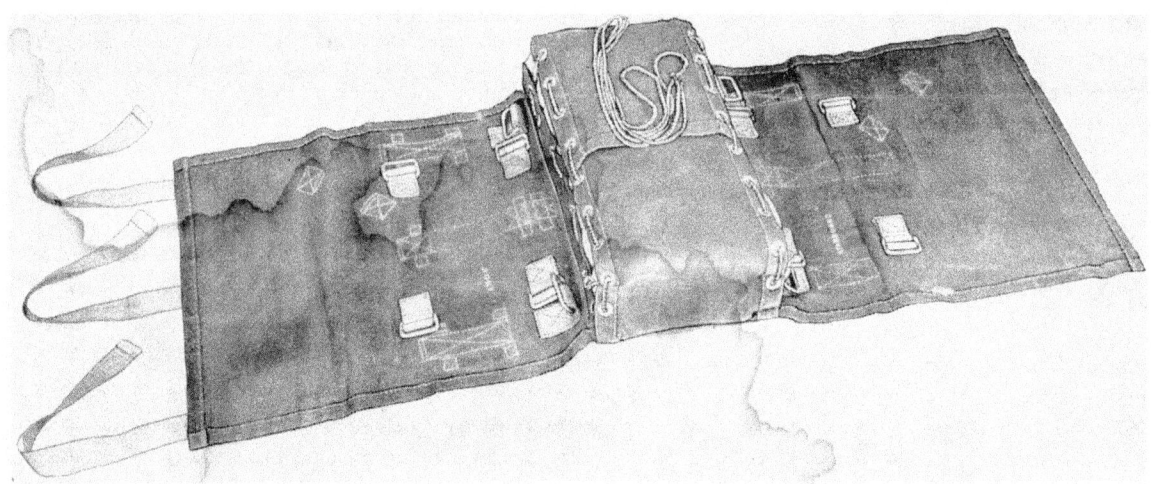

Fig. 5. Third stage of packing

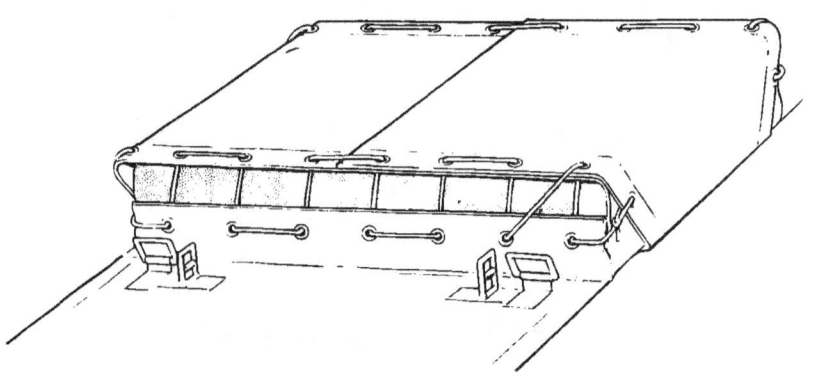

Fig. 6. First method of lacing

Fig. 7. Fourth stage of packing

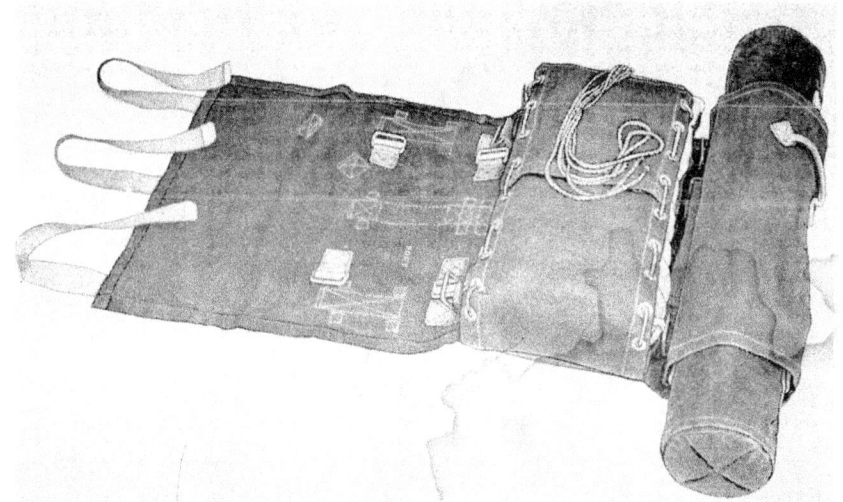

Fig. 8. Fifth stage of packing

Fig. 9. Sixth stage of packing

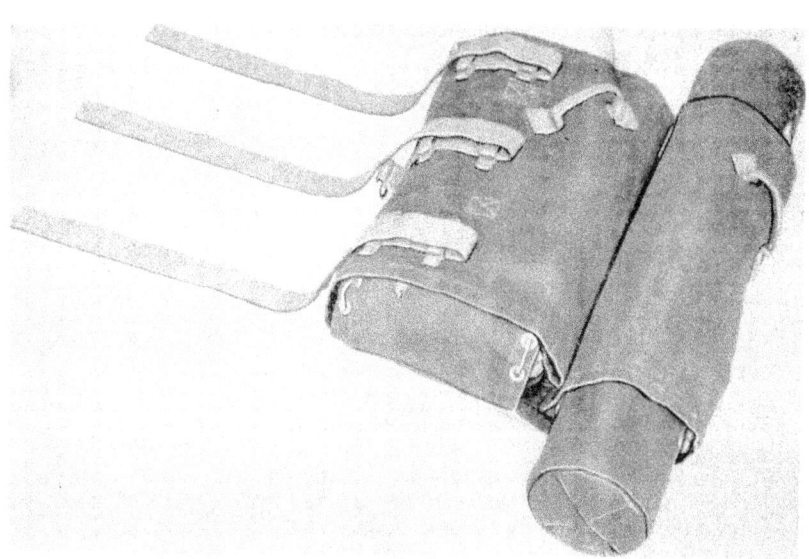

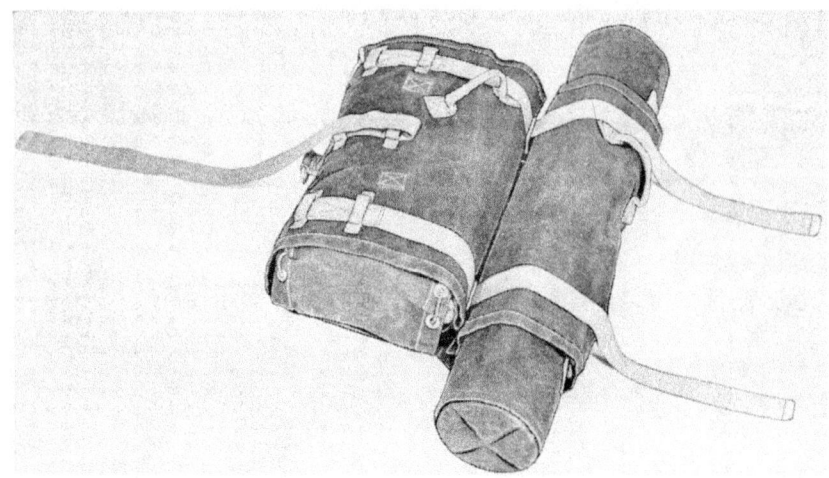

Fig. 10. Seventh stage of packing

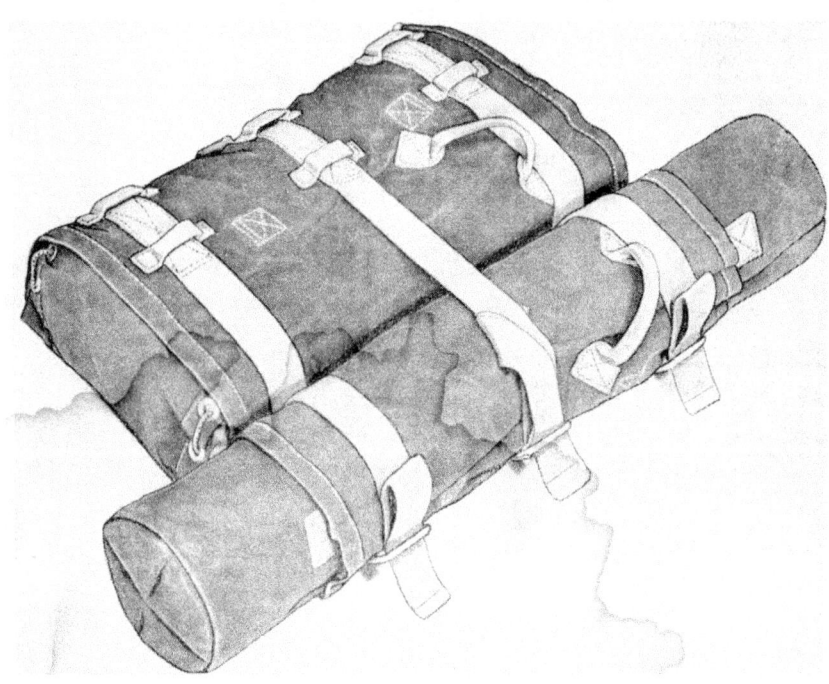

Fig. 11. Eighth stage of packing

cords are brought together and secured, next attach the weapon caps to the buckles on one side flap (*fig.* 7) and fold the flap inwards as shown in fig. 8. The two shoulder straps are folded double and placed down the sides of the centre section. The other side flap is folded over the centre section in such a manner as to leave one hand grip exposed (*fig.* 9). The outer two securing straps are threaded through the open D-rings between the packed weapon and the centre section. The three securing straps on one side flap are now secured to the corresponding buckles on the opposite flap. (*fig.* 10). When it is considered necessary with awkward loads, the top strap can be passed through the hand grip. A packed P.W.C. is shown in fig. 11.

8. The second method (*fig.* 12) incorporates a quick-release of the lacing in the form of a length of steel wire. The steel wire consists of a 27 in. length of $\frac{3}{16}$ in. Round steel bar (Ref. No. 30C/3223) bent so that the top 4 in. forms a handle or loop to which a cord can be tied. The centre section is

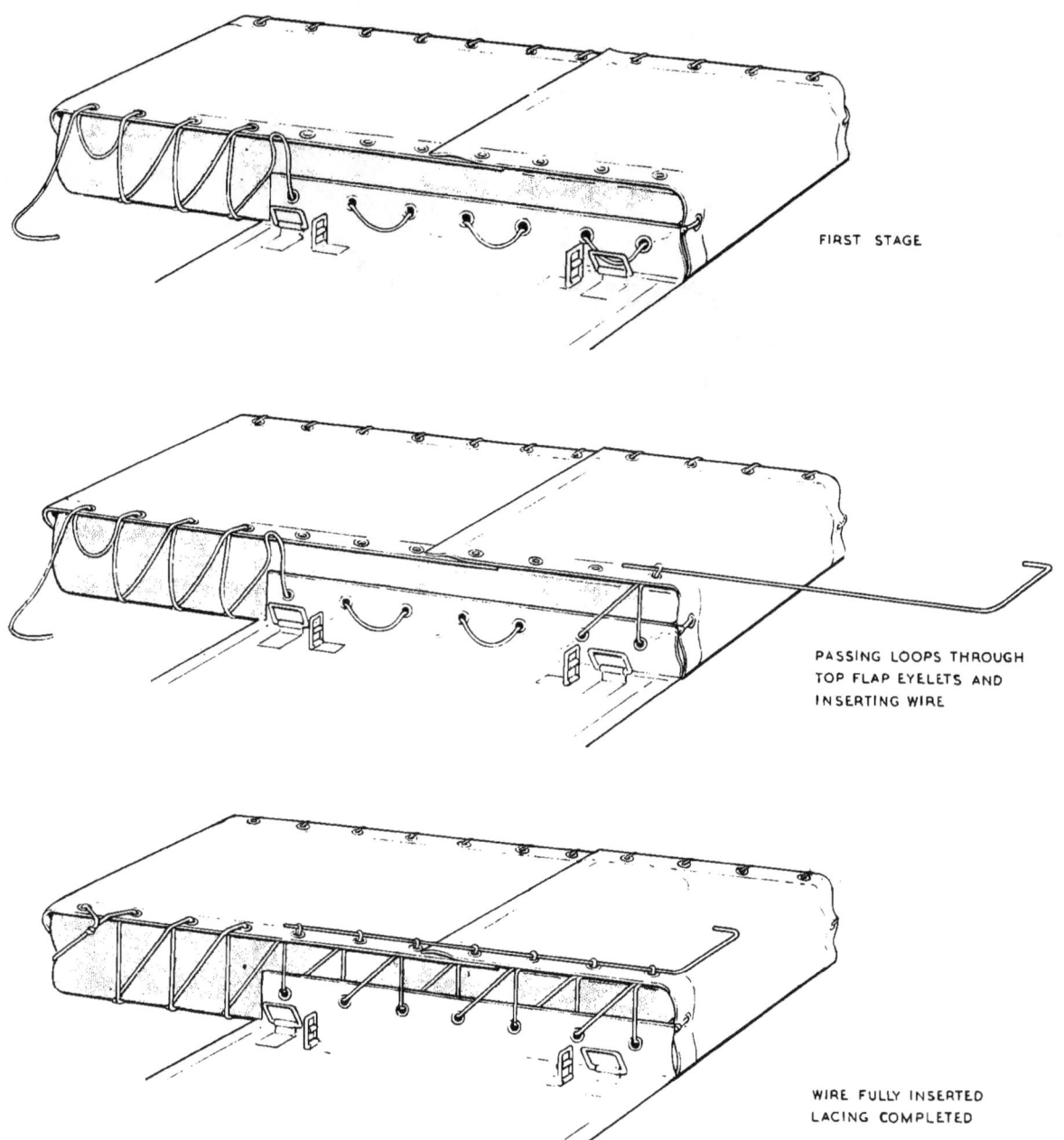

Fig. 12. Second method of lacing

packed in a similar manner to that described in para. 7. Then proceed as follows:—

(1) Lace one side (the fixed side) of the container by cross lacing the flap eyelets with one of the lacing cords, but do not secure the end of the lacing cord.
(2) Secure one end of the other lacing cord to the top eyelet of the top flat of the container and then pass the cord loosely through all the eyelets on the side flap.
(3) Starting at the top pass a loop of the lacing cord through each eyelet on the top flaps and secure the loops in turn by passing the steel wire through them.

(4) Tighten the lacing cords on each side of the centre section and secure the ends.

(5) Stow the ends of the lacing cords under the flaps.

(6) Ensure that the steel wire does not protrude from the laced centre section.

Notes . . .

1. *The length of centre section should not exceed 24 in. for this method of packing and lacing.*

2. *If the centre section is longer than 24 in. the quick-release lacing employing the steel wire must be confined to the top 24 in of the*

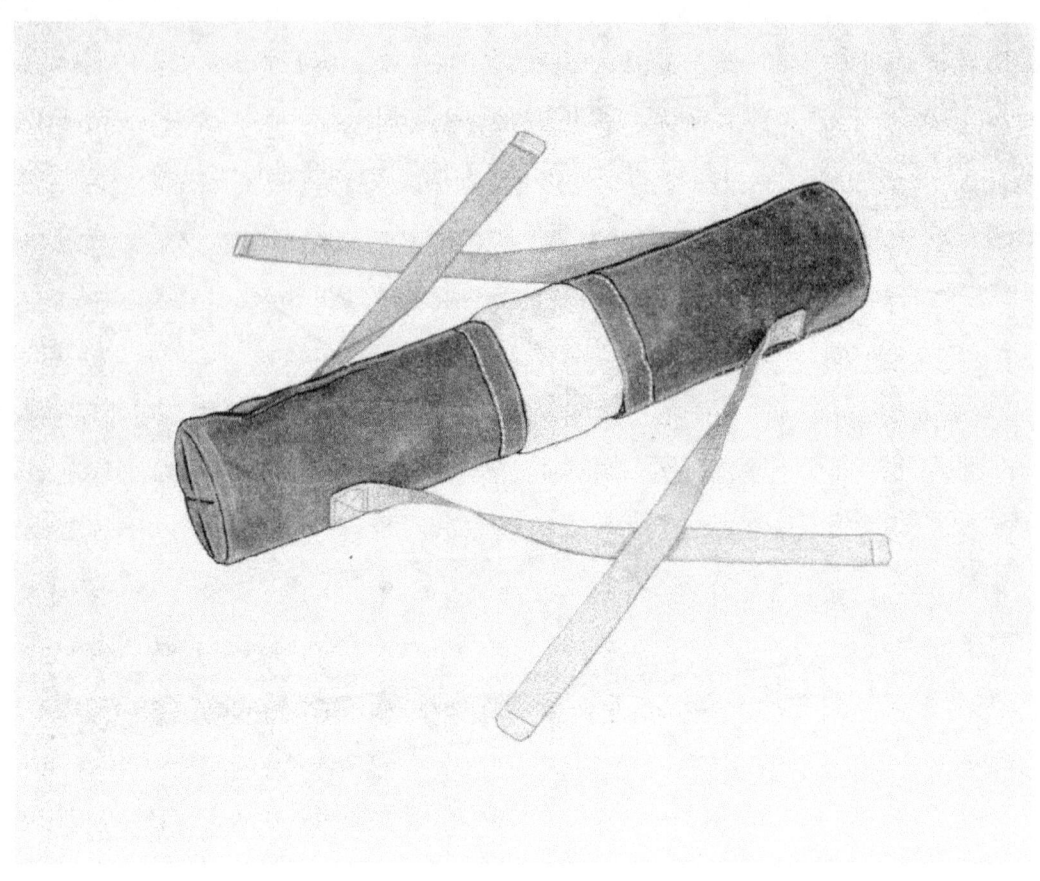

Fig. 13. Weapon packed in caps

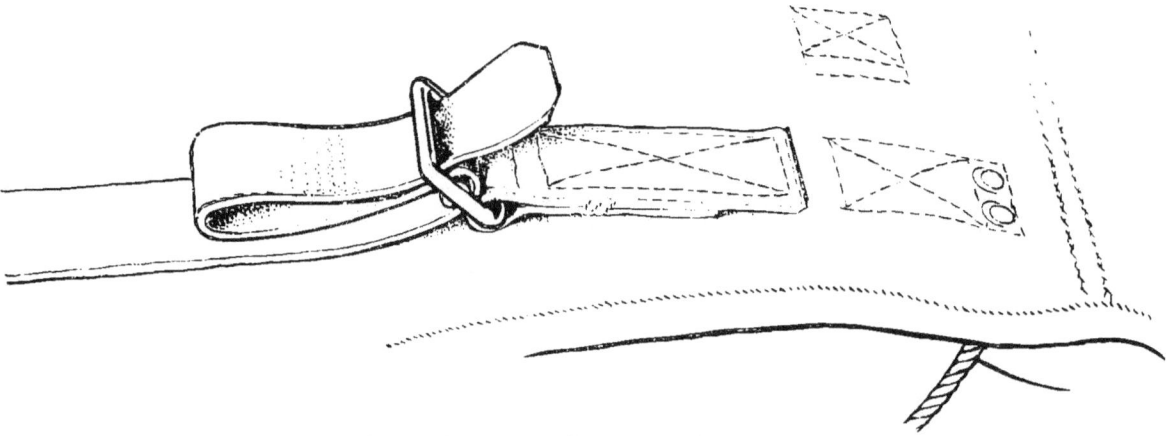

Fig. 14. Method of making quick-release attachment

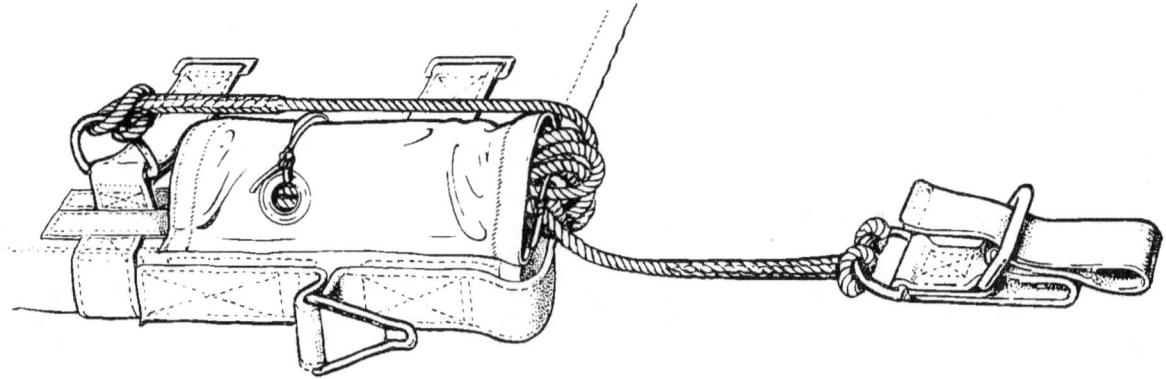

Fig. 15. Suspension rope stowage and attachments

RESTRICTED

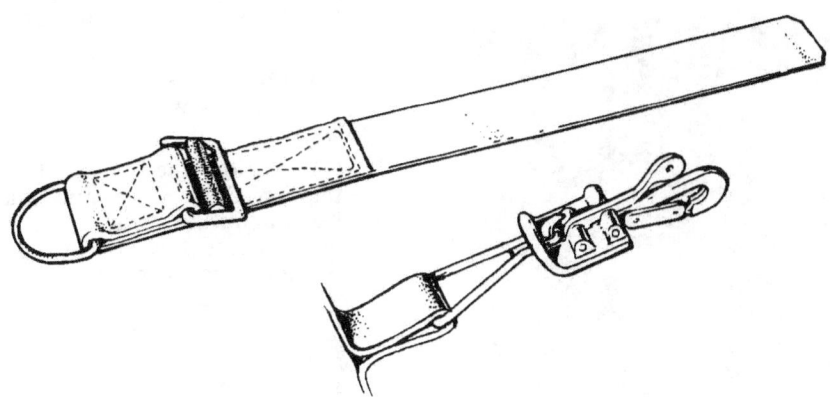

Fig. 16. Jettison device and quick-release snap-book fitting

centre section and the length exceeding 24 in. must be laced in a similar manner to that described in para. 7.

Packing a weapon

9. A weapon or any other piece of equipment that is to be carried between the weapon caps (*fig.* 13) must be packed for protection i.e. wrapped in a blanket. The weapon caps are then placed over the ends of the weapon and attached by their securing straps to the buckles on the appropriate side flap (*fig.* 7). (*The side flaps are marked—* PORT LEFT or STARBOARD RIGHT) indicating the side the weapon should be packed depending on which side of the aircraft the exit is to be made. The attachment of the weapon to the container is shown in fig. 8. The side flap to which the weapon caps have been attached is now folded round the weapon and the opposite side flap is then folded over the packed centre section. When possible the hand grips are to be left exposed. The top and bottom weapon securing straps are now passed through the appropriate D-rings on the side flap to which the weapon caps are attached. The container is now secured as detailed in para. 7.

Methods of securing and releasing straps to and from buckles

10. To secure a strap to a buckle, pass the strap through the buckle below the locking bar, back through the buckle over the locking bar and pull tight. Thread the free end of the strap back

Fig. 17. Attachment of jettison device to parachute harness

RESTRICTED

Fig. 18. Attachment of container to parachute harness

through the upper section of the buckle as shown in fig. 14. To release the strap from the buckle, pull the free end vigorously.

Servicing a packed P.W.C.

11. A packed P.W.C. (*fig.* 11) has to be serviced as follows before it is ready for use.

(1) The free end of the suspension rope, i.e., the end that is not attached to the jettison device, must be secured to the suspension D-ring on the side of the P.W.C. which contains the equipment requiring the most protection from shock when it contacts the ground.

(2) Coil the suspension rope and stow it in the stowage pocket on the P.W.C. (*fig.* 15). Ensure that the length of rope not stowed is the minimum required to allow the jettison device (*fig.* 15) to be secured to the parachute harness.

(3) Pass a single length of No. 18 thread through the eyelets in the stowage pocket so that it passes through the bottom coils of the suspension rope (*fig.* 15). Tie the ends of the thread so that the rope is secured in the stowage pocket.

(4) The exposed coils of the rope at the open end of the stowage pocket must be tied together by a length of No. 18 thread as shown in fig. 15.

(5) Secure the leg straps by placing the eyelet over the cone and insert the quick-release pin so that it faces downwards. The leg strap should be left fully extended.

(6) Attach the jettison device to the leg strap to ensure that the suspension rope is not inadvertently pulled from the stowage pocket.

(7) Attach the suspension snap-hooks to the P.W.C. suspension D-ring not in use.

Fitting the P.W.C. to a parachutist

12. To fit a P.W.C. to a parachutist proceed as follows:—

(1) Remove the jettison device (*fig.* 16) from the P.W.C. leg straps and attach it to the right leg strap of the parachute harness, between the quick-release box (Q.R.B.) and the main suspension strap as shown in fig. 17.

(2) The parachutist will place his appropriate leg through the P.W.C. leg straps (*right leg for a port side door exit or left leg for a starboard side door exit*).

(3) Remove the suspension snap-hooks (*fig.* 16) from the D-ring on the P.W.C. and secure them by their quick-release hooks to the suspension plates on the P.W.C.

(4) Attach the suspension snap-hooks to the lower pair of D-rings on the parachutist's harness (*fig.* 18). By turning the suspension hooks outwards on the suspension plates, bring the backs of the snap-hooks uppermost so that on attaching them to the parachute harness D-rings the quick-release levers are facing outwards. This method of attachment is shown in fig. 19.

(5) Tighten the P.W.C. leg strap.

Aircraft exit

13. When a parachutist carrying a P.W.C. makes an exit from an aircraft he supports the weight of

Fig. 19. Method of releasing container (front view)

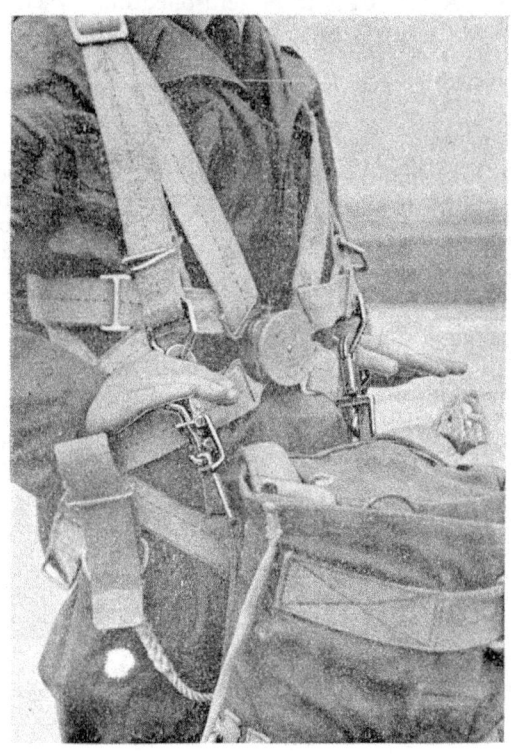

Fig. 20. Method of releasing container (side view)

the P.W.C. by grasping the hand grip with one hand and as he makes his exit, the other hand is brought across to grasp the hand grip on the P.W.C. or the wrist of the hand already holding the hand grip on the P.W.C. to give further support. When an exit is made from the port door of an aircraft, the right hand is used for the initial grip on the P.W.C. and the left hand is used when an exit is made from a starboard door.

14. Exit training for parachutists carrying P.W.C. can be taught by use of the following training devices.
   (1) Mock doors.
   (2) Mock fuselages.
   (3) Aircraft fuselages.
   (4) Outdoor exit trainer.

Parachute flight with a P.W.C.

15. The flight technique for parachute descents without suspended loads is to be carried out until clear of other descending parachutists. The P.W.C. is then to be lowered in the following manner:—
   (1) Pull the leg strap quick-release lanyard sharply upwards with the right hand to release the leg strap.
   (2) Check that there is no other parachutist directly below; then operate the two P.W.C. quick-release levers simultaneously by pushing then outwards with the thumbs (*fig.* 19 *and* 20),

and allow the P.W.C. to fall to the full extent of the suspension rope.
   (3) Continue to execute the normal parachute flight technique, i.e., from the 'Seat strap' operation onwards as described in Sect. 3, Chap. 4.

16. The following apparatus can be used for teaching flight technique when carrying a P.W.C.
   (1) Harness swing flight trainer.
   (2) Outdoor harness swing flight trainer.
   (3) Parachute jumping towers.

Emergencies during flight

17. In addition to the emergency actions detailed in Sect. 3, Chap 4 the following emergency actions are to be taken when a P.W.C. is carried:—
   (1) In the event of twists, a parachutist, after ensuring that he is clear of other parachutists, is to lower his P.W.C. immediately and then kick out of the twists.
   (2) In the event of an entanglement, the parachutists are to free themselves and then lower their P.W.C. If, however, they are unable

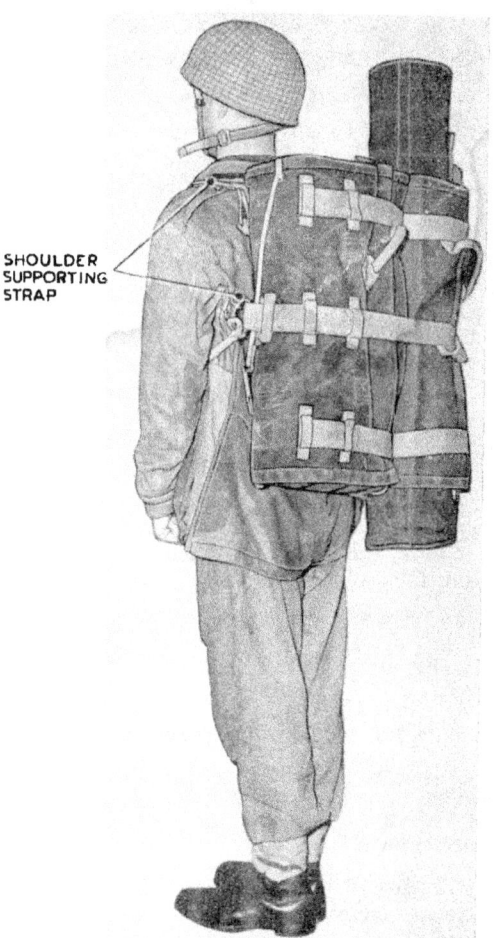

Fig. 21. P.W.C. carried pack fashion

Decision to jettison

19. A P.W.C. is to be jettisoned only when it is absolutely necessary and then only after ensuring that other parachutists would not be endangered by such an action.

Landing

20. Normal landing positions are to be adopted, ensuring that the suspension rope does not foul the legs during the actual landing operations. The Parachute Jumping Tower is the only apparatus suitable for landing training.

Action after landing

21. After landing a parachutist should collapse his parachute canopy pull his P.W.C. towards him and release his parachute harness after he has retrieved his P.W.C. If he is unable to deflate his parachute canopy, he is to release his P.W.C. and then release himself from his harness by the third method described in Sect. 3, Chap. 8. If this latter method of harness release is used, the parachutist must bear in mind that he will be separated from his P.W.C.

Recovering the P.W.C. after landing

22. When recovering his P.W.C. after landing

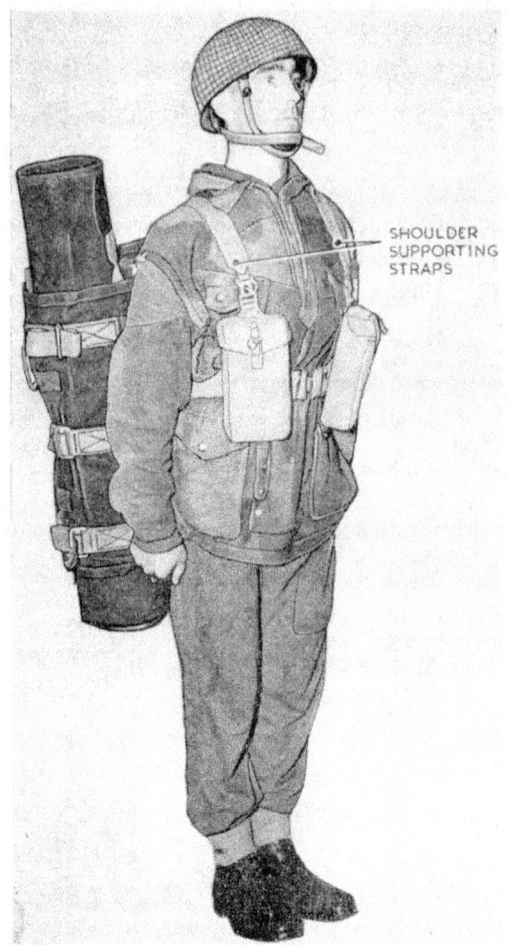

Fig. 22. Container supported by fittings behind the ammunition pouches

to disentangle themselves, they must lower their P.W.C. and prepare for landing.

(3) In the event of a descent into water or trees, the P.W.C. is to be jettisoned.

(4) In the event of the development of an abnormal main parachute canopy, a parachutist is to carry out the drill detailed in Sect. 3, Chap. 4 and then jettison his P.W.C.

Jettisoning a P.W.C.

18. If a P.W.C. has to be jettisoned a parachutist is to carry out the following procedure:—

(1) Release the P.W.C. jettison device.

(2) Release the P.W.C. leg strap by pulling the quick-release lanyard.

(3) Ensure that there are no other parachutists directly below; then operate the quick-release levers.

Note . . .

If the P.W.C. has already been lowered, the only action required is to pull and release the jettison device.

Fig. 23. Container, less weapon, carried pack fashion

(*fig.* 21, 22 *and* 23), a parachutist is to prepare it as follows:—

(1) Remove the quick-release hooks from the parachute harness and connect them to one of the suspension D-rings on the P.W.C.

(2) Service the leg straps as described in para. 11, sub-para. (5).

(3) Wrap the suspension rope neatly round the P.W.C. and secure the jettison device to one of the suspension D-rings on the P.W.C.

(4) Pull out the shoulder straps and attach each of them to the appropriate suspension D-ring on the P.W.C.

(5) After a training or practice parachute descent, a parachutist will, after having rolled up his parachute canopy, fit the P.W.C. on his back like a rucksack, place his rolled up main parachute on top of it with the reserve parachute attached and hanging forward over his shoulder and leave the D.Z.

Notes . . .

1. *After an active service or an operational exercise descent, the P.W.C. would be prepared as described in sub-para. (1) to (5) with the exception that the parachutes and parachute harness would be left on the D.Z.*

2. *It may be necessary to remove arms or other military-equipment for immediate use on the D.Z. before the P.W.C. is prepared to be carried away as a rucksack.*

SECTION 7

DROPPING ZONES

RESTRICTED

A.P.4215, Sect 7
A.L.15, Sept. 61

SECTION 7

DROPPING ZONES

LIST OF CHAPTERS

1 Selection of a dropping zone

2 Organisation on a dropping zone (*to be issued later*)

RESTRICTED

CHAPTER 1

SELECTION OF A DROPPING ZONE

Chapter 1

SELECTION OF A DROPPING ZONE

LIST OF CONTENTS

	Para.		Para.
Introduction	1	*Control point*	7
Basic Parachute Training	2	*Accommodation and storage facilities*	8
Size and shape	3	**Continuation parachute training**	9
Local geography and meteorological factors	4	*Balloon dropping zones*	10
Distance and air-route from take-off airfield	6	*Aircraft dropping zones*	11

LIST OF APPENDICES

	App.
Dropping zone reconnaissance report	1
Air reconnaissance report of a dropping zone	2

INTRODUCTION

1. The requirements of a dropping zone (D.Z.) will depend on the purpose for which it is to be used, i.e., basic parachute training or continuation parachute training.

BASIC PARACHUTE TRAINING

2. When selecting a D.Z. for basic parachute training, the following factors should be considered:—

   (1) Size and shape
   (2) Local geography and meteorological factors
   (3) Distance and air-route from the take-off airfield
   (4) Control point
   (5) Accommodation and storage facilities

Size and shape

3. A dropping zone should be large enough to accept parachutists jumping in simultaneous sticks of 20 from three aircraft flying in V-formation. The minimum size and shape for such an operation is 1,500 yd. × 1,000 yd. The ideal shape is a square 1,500 yd. × 1,500 yd., which would permit aircraft to run-in from any side, according to the direction of the wind, and may in certain circumstances permit parachute dropping from a balloon at the same time as parachutists are being dropped from aircraft. Surrounding the D.Z. should be safe undershoot/overshoot areas to allow for errors or miscalculations in dropping.

Local geography and meteorological factors

4. The surface of a proposed D.Z. and the geography of the surrounding countryside will effect the selection. The surface of a D.Z. should be level, preferably grass, with a reasonably soft surface, yet firm enough to allow balloon winch vehicles *(five tons)* to travel across it.

5. The contours of the surrounding countryside must be considered. When wind blows over undulating country there is a tendency for the streamlines of the airflow to follow the rise and fall of the ground. This means that a parachutist landing up a slope, down which the wind is blowing, will strike the ground with a greater vertical speed than one landing on a slope up which the wind is blowing. Considering these characteristics of airflow, the criteria for choosing a D.Z. are that the choice of flat open country is desirable, but if the surrounding country is undulating, flat ground at the top of ridges or hills is more suitable than ground at the bottom of hollows or valleys. If it is necessary to site a D.Z. on sloping ground, choose a slope up which the prevailing wind blows. A dropping zone must not be sited within one mile from the high

water mark around the coast or where there is any possibility of parachutes being contaminated by salt water.

Distance and air-route from the take-off airfield

6. The distance and air-route from the take-off airfield must be considered with the following factors in mind:—

(1) The time factor of returning personnel and equipment to the parachute training school after parachute dropping has taken place.

(2) The flying time of aircraft to and from the proposed D.Z.

(3) Efficient operational control is simplified when a D.Z. is sited close to the take-off airfield.

(4) The air approach should be clear of hills, high obstructions and established air-routes.

Control point

7. The control point should be sited so that the officer-in-charge of parachuting has a full view of the D.Z., yet in such a position that it is not a hazard to descending parachutists. The following facilities should be available at the control point:—

(1) Radio (R/T) link with the aircraft from which the parachutists will jump.

(2) Direct telephone communication with the take-off airfield.

(3) A telephone link with the centre of the D.Z.

(4) An anemometer for wind speed reading.

Accommodation and storage facilities

8. The following accommodation and storage facilities should be available:—

(1) Living accommodation for the balloon crews (*close to the balloon beds*).

(2) Living accommodation for the D.Z. staff.

(3) Sufficient space clear of the D.Z. for the laying of balloon beds.

(4) A lock-up store for the safe custody of parachutes.

(5) A lock-up store for the safe custody of pyrotechnics and ground markers.

(6) Garages for loud-hailers, balloon winch vehicles and other vehicles used at the D.Z.

CONTINUATION PARACHUTE TRAINING

9. Dropping Zones for continuation training, i.e., airborne exercises and demonstrations, will normally be selected initially by Army formations. Before they may be used they are to be inspected by responsible R.A.F. personnel as follows:—

Balloon dropping zones

10. A reconnaissance of the proposed area is to be carried out by a qualified R.A.F. Commissioned Officer Parachute Jumping Instructor and a qualified R.A.F. Commissioned Officer or a Senior N.C.O. Balloon Operator. After the reconnaissance has been completed, a report as shown in Appendix 1, which should include a sketch map of the area and its immediate surrounds, is to be compiled by the individuals that have carried out the reconnaissance. This report is to be submitted to the R.A.F. higher formation, the parachute training school and the Army user units or formations.

Aircraft dropping zones

11. A ground reconnaissance of the proposed area is to be carried out by a qualified R.A.F. Commissioned Officer Parachute Jumping Instructor and an air reconnaissance is to be carried out by a qualified Transport Support Trained Pilot. After the reconnaissance has been completed, a report as shown in Appendix 1 is to be compiled by the Parachute Jumping Instructor and a report as shown in Appendix 2 is to be compiled by the Transport Support Pilot. These reports are to be submitted to the R.A.F. higher formation, the parachute training school and the Army user units or formations.

Note . . .

An air photograph or alternatively a sketch map should be attached to the air reconnaissance report.

Appendix 1

DROPPING ZONE RECONNAISSANCE REPORT
(GROUND)

1. **Proposed name of D.Z.** (*including nearest town or village*) ....
2. **Survey Map Reference** ... .
   Sheet No. ... .
   Location ... .
   Latitude and longitude ... .
   Co-ordinates ... .
3. **D.Z. height above sea level** ... .
4. **Description of surface** ... .
5. **If suitable for a 'Heavy Drop'** ... .
6. **If suitable as a Parallel D.Z.** ... ...
7. **Area available for dropping**
   Length (yd.) ... .
   Width (yd.) ... .
8. **Lengths of sticks recommended** ... .
9. **Recommended 'Run-in'** (*Degrees, magnetic*) ... .
10. **Aircraft 'Turn-off'** ... .
11. **Civil or Military area** ... .
12. **If cleared with Civil Authorities** ... .
13. **Obstructions and hazards** ... .
14. **Danger areas (ranges, etc.)** ... .
15. **Prevailing wind** ... .
16. **Access road** ... .
17. **Communications available** ... .
18. **Meteorological facilities**
19. **Nearest Service/Civil airfield** ... .
20. **Location and distance of nearest Service/Civil Hospital** ... .
21. **Air reconnaissance required** ... .
22. **Area approved/ not approved for parachuting from aircraft** ....
23. **Area approved/ not approved for parachuting from balloon** ....

RESTRICTED

24. General remarks

To include remarks such as undershoot and overshoot area available; any safety precautions to be observed; if life-jackets should be worn by the parachutists; if rescue launches will be necessary.

25. Inspecting Officer

(Rank).. (Name)..

(Unit) ....

(Date).. (Signature)...

Notes ...

(1) *The latitude and longitude is to be quoted in Degrees, Minutes and Seconds, and is to indicate the centre of the D.Z.*

(2) *The map reference is to be taken from the National grid (Military system) one inch to one mile G.S.G.S. No. 4620.*

(3) *This form of report is in accordance with Transport Support Standard Operating Procedure and is obtainable as a pro-forma as PTS/Form/26.*

RESTRICTED

A.P.4215, Sect. 7, Chap. 1, App. 2
A.L.15, Sept. 61

Appendix 2

AIR RECONNAISSANCE REPORT OF A DROPPING ZONE

1. Name of D.Z. ....

2. Location (*nearest town or village*)

3. Latitude and longitude ....

4. Map reference ....

5. Recommended pinpoints and suitable alternative Target Approach points ....

6. Recommended alternative lines of run-in

Ordnance Survey 1 in. to 1 mile Map Ref.		
Course Magnetic		

7. Details of any high ground or other flying obstructions (*Tall masts, etc.*) within T.A.P. radius of D.Z. ....

8. Details of active airfields, danger and prohibited areas and T.A.P. radius of D.Z. ....

9. General remarks ....

10. D.Z. inspected and agreed/not agreed as suitable from the flying aspect ....

....(Rank)

(Date)..

.... (Unit)

Notes . . .

(1) *The latitude and longitude is to be quoted in Degrees, Minutes and Seconds, and is to indicate the centre of the D.Z.*

(2) *The map reference is to be taken from the National grid (Military system) one inch to one mile G.S.G.S. No. 4620.*

(3) *This form of report is in accordance with Transport Support Standard Operating Procedure.*

RESTRICTED

www.ingramcontent.com/pod-product-compliance
Lightning Source LLC
Chambersburg PA
CBHW082014220426
43670CB00015B/2622